내신 및 시·도 교육청 영어듣기평가 완벽 대비

Listening

올리고

Level 1

중학영어듣기 모의고사

DARAKWON

Listening

올리고 Level 1

중학영어듣기 모의고사

지은이 정수진, 한길연, 박선화
펴낸이 정규도
펴낸곳 (주)다락원

초판 1쇄 발행 2014년 2월 7일
초판 9쇄 발행 2023년 10월 20일

편집 최혜영, 서정아
일러스트 채원희
디자인 김나경

다락원 경기도 파주시 문발로 211
내용문의: (02)736-2031 내선 503
구입문의: (02)736-2031 내선 250~252
Fax: (02)732-2037
출판등록 1977년 9월 16일 제406-2008-000007호

Copyright © 2014, (주)플러스에듀

저자 및 출판사의 허락 없이 이 책의 일부 또는 전부를 무단 복제 · 전재 · 발췌할 수 없습니다. 구입 후 철회는 회사 내규에 부합하는 경우에 가능하므로 구입문의처에 문의하시기 바랍니다. 분실 · 파손 등에 따른 소비자 피해에 대해서는 공정거래위원회에서 고시한 소비자 분.쟁 해결 기준에 따라 보상 가능합니다. 잘못된 책은 바꿔 드립니다.

ISBN 978-89-277-0711-0 54740
      978-89-277-0710-3 54740 (set)

http://www.darakwon.co.kr

- 다락원 홈페이지를 방문하시면 상세한 출판정보와 함께 동영상강좌, MP3자료 등 다양한 어학 정보를 얻으실 수 있습니다.

내신 및 시·도 교육청 영어듣기평가 완벽 대비

Listening

올리고

Level **1**

중학영어듣기 모의고사

DARAKWON

Structure & Features | 구성과 특징

Listening Test

전국 16개 시·도 교육청 주관 영어듣기능력평가 및 내신 교과서 반영!

최신 기출 유형을 철저히 분석, 반영하여 실제 시험과 유사하게 구성한 모의고사로 실전 감각을 키울 수 있습니다. 또한 영어 교과서의 주요 표현 및 소재들을 활용하여 내신까지 효과적으로 대비할 수 있습니다.

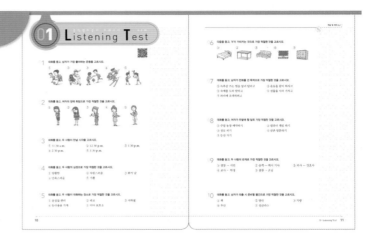

Further Study

주요 지문 심화학습으로 내신 서술형 완벽 대비!

Listening Test의 주요 지문만을 모아 서술형 문제로 다시 풀어볼 수 있도록 구성하였습니다. 보다 심화된 듣기 문제로 내신 서술형 평가에 철저히 대비하고, 듣기 실력을 강화할 수 있습니다.

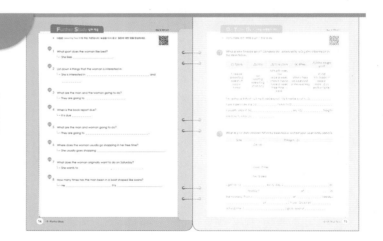

On Your Own

내신 말하기 수행평가 대비까지 한 번에!

Listening Test 및 기출 문제에서 출제된 주제와 소재를 응용한 다양한 연습 문제를 통해 별도로 준비하기 어려운 내신 말하기 수행평가까지 한 번에 대비할 수 있습니다.

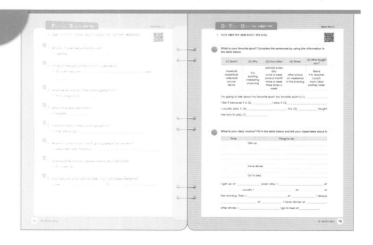

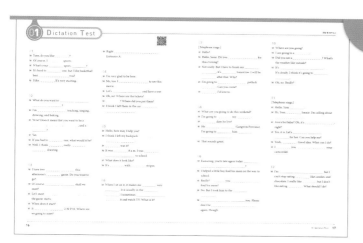

Dictation Test

전 지문 받아쓰기로 꼼꼼한 마무리 학습!

매회 전 지문 받아쓰기를 수록하여 놓친 부분을 빠짐없이 확인할 수 있습니다. 문제의 핵심이 되는 키워드, 중요 표현, 연음 등을 확인하며, 복습은 물론 자신의 취약점을 다시 한 번 확인할 수 있습니다.

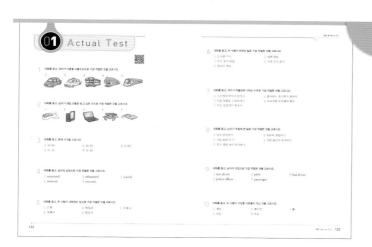

Actual Test

실전 모의고사로 최종 실력 점검!

실제 시험과 가장 유사한 모의고사로서 자신의 실력을 최종 점검해볼 수 있습니다. 시험에 자주 나오는 유형과 표현들을 100% 반영한 영어듣기능력평가 완벽 대비 모의고사입니다.

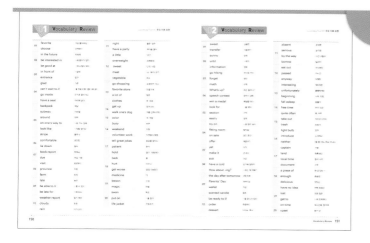

Vocabulary Review

중요 어휘 및 표현을 한눈에!

본문에 나오는 주요 어휘와 표현을 각 모의고사 회별로 한눈에 정리하여 단어 학습을 보다 효율적으로 할 수 있습니다.

Contents | 목차

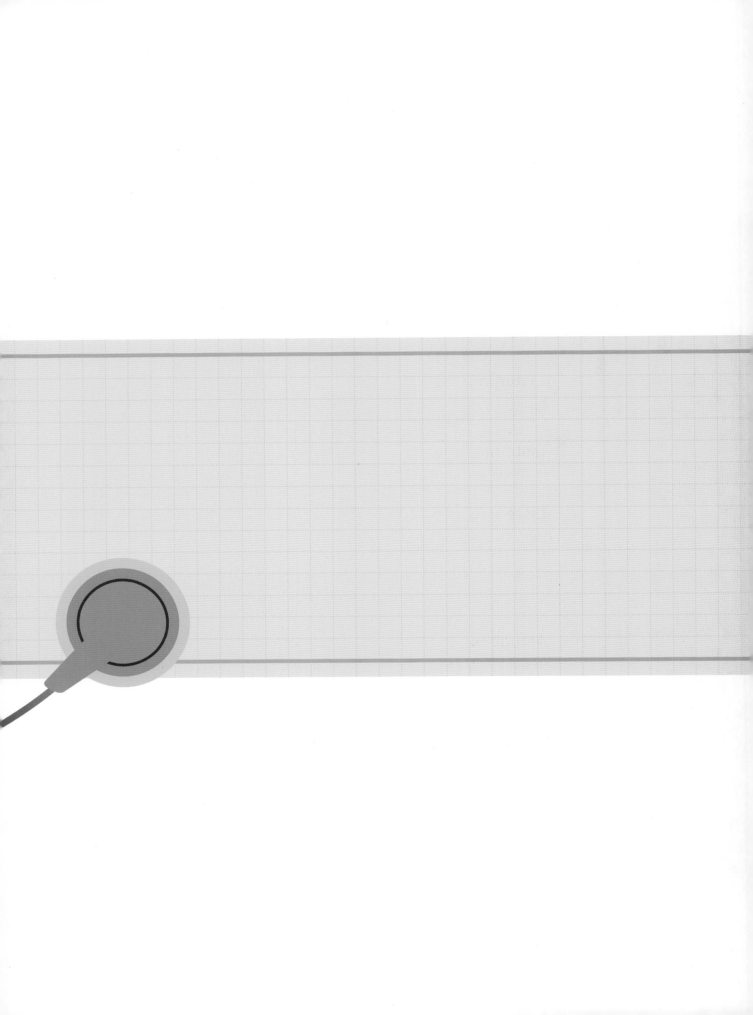

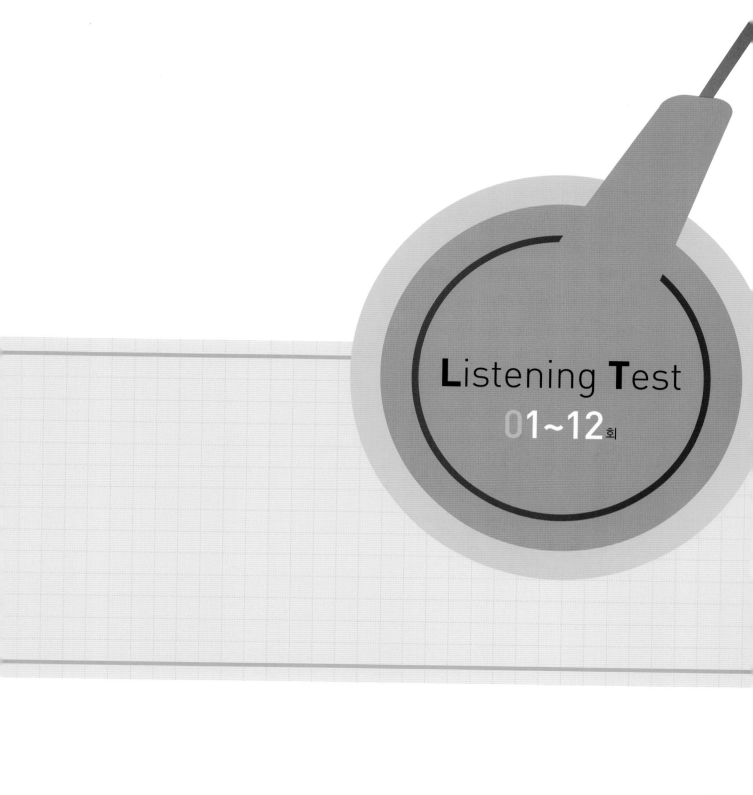

Listening Test
01~12회

01 대화를 듣고, 남자가 가장 좋아하는 운동을 고르시오.

①  ②  ③ ④  ⑤

02 대화를 듣고, 여자의 장래 희망으로 가장 적절한 것을 고르시오.

①  ②  ③  ④  ⑤

03 대화를 듣고, 두 사람이 만날 시각을 고르시오.

① 11:30 a.m.　　　　② 12:30 p.m.　　　　③ 1:30 p.m.
④ 2:30 p.m.　　　　⑤ 3:30 p.m.

04 대화를 듣고, 두 사람의 심정으로 가장 적절한 것을 고르시오.

① 당황함　　　　② 자랑스러움　　　　③ 화가 남
④ 만족스러움　　　　⑤ 기쁨

05 대화를 듣고, 두 사람이 대화하는 장소로 가장 적절한 것을 고르시오.

① 분실물 센터　　　　② 학교　　　　③ 지하철
④ 등산용품 가게　　　　⑤ 미아 보호소

06 다음을 듣고, 'it'이 가리키는 것으로 가장 적절한 것을 고르시오.

① ② ③ ④ ⑤

07 대화를 듣고, 남자가 전화를 건 목적으로 가장 적절한 것을 고르시오.

① 독후감 쓰는 법을 알려 달라고 ② 운동을 같이 하자고
③ 숙제를 도와 달라고 ④ 선물을 사러 가자고
⑤ 파티에 초대하려고

08 대화를 듣고, 여자가 주말에 할 일로 가장 적절한 것을 고르시오.

① 주말 농장 예약하기 ② 컴퓨터 게임 하기
③ 성묘 하기 ④ 삼촌 방문하기
⑤ 등산 가기

09 대화를 듣고, 두 사람의 관계로 가장 적절한 것을 고르시오.

① 경찰 ― 시민 ② 승객 ― 택시 기사 ③ 의사 ― 간호사
④ 교사 ― 학생 ⑤ 점원 ― 손님

10 대화를 듣고, 남자가 외출 시 준비할 물건으로 가장 적절한 것을 고르시오.

① 책 ② 양산 ③ 가방
④ 우산 ⑤ 선글라스

11 대화를 듣고, 여자가 남자에게 부탁한 일로 가장 적절한 것을 고르시오.

① 파티 장소 물색하기　　　　② 파티 장소 장식하기
③ 초대장 보내기　　　　　　④ 케이크 사오기
⑤ 비디오카메라 가져오기

12 다음을 듣고, 남자에게 해 줄 수 있는 조언으로 가장 적절한 것을 고르시오.

① You should go to bed early.
② You should not eat so much sugar.
③ You should brush your teeth every day.
④ You should go to gym to exercise regularly.
⑤ You should eat fewer sweets and have a more balanced diet.

13 대화를 듣고, 여자가 자신의 단골가게를 좋아하는 이유로 가장 적절한 것을 고르시오.

① 신상품이 많아서　　　　　② 가격이 저렴해서
③ 스타일이 다양해서　　　　④ 큰 치수 옷들이 많아서
⑤ 예쁜 액세서리가 많아서

14 다음을 듣고, 일과표의 내용과 일치하지 않는 것을 고르시오.

Tom's Daily Routine	
7:00 a.m.	Get up
7:30 a.m.	Walk my dog in the park
8:00 a.m.	Have breakfast
8:30 a.m.	Go to school
12:30 p.m.	Have lunch
3:00 p.m.	Play basketball
5:00 p.m.	Do homework
6:00 p.m.	Have dinner

①　　　　②　　　　③　　　　④　　　　⑤

15 다음을 듣고, 두 사람의 대화가 어색한 것을 고르시오.

①　　　　②　　　　③　　　　④　　　　⑤

16 대화를 듣고, 여자가 주말에 할 일로 가장 적절한 것을 고르시오.

① 숙제 하기　　　　② 영화 감상하기　　　　③ 독서하기
④ 자원봉사 하기　　⑤ 휴식 취하기

17 다음을 듣고, 내용과 일치하지 <u>않는</u> 것을 고르시오.

① 사진 속의 남자는 여자의 할아버지이다.
② 사진 속의 남자는 여전히 의사로 활동 중이다.
③ 사진 속의 남자는 바이올린을 잘 켜서 환자들이 좋아한다.
④ 사진 속의 남자는 매년 12월 자신의 병원에서 바이올린 연주회를 한다.
⑤ 여자는 사진 속의 남자처럼 되고 싶어 한다.

18 다음을 듣고, Jake가 Jennie에게 할 말로 가장 적절한 것을 고르시오.

① Not so good.
② How are you doing?
③ I'm getting worse and worse.
④ That's too bad. You'd better go to see a doctor.
⑤ I went to see a doctor and got some medicine.

[19-20] 대화를 듣고, 여자의 마지막 말에 이어질 남자의 응답으로 가장 적절한 것을 고르시오.

19 ① I don't think so.
② You're welcome.
③ That's a good idea.
④ I'm not busy right now.
⑤ It looks like an interesting lesson.

20 ① Oh, I see.
② I'll do it later.
③ What shall I do?
④ Let's swim across the river.
⑤ How about taking off your life jacket?

다음은 Listening Test 01의 주요 지문입니다. 녹음을 다시 듣고, 질문에 대한 답을 완성하세요.

Q1
1 What sport does the woman like best?

↳ She likes _____.

Q2
2 List down 4 things that the woman is interested in.

↳ She is interested in _____, _____, _____, and

_____.

Q4
3 What are the man and the woman going to do?

↳ They are going to _____.

Q7
4 When is the book report due?

↳ It is due _____.

Q11
5 What are the man and woman going to do?

↳ They are going to _____.

Q13
6 Where does the woman usually go shopping in her free time?

↳ She usually goes shopping _____.

Q16
7 What does the woman originally want to do on Saturday?

↳ She wants to _____.

Q20
8 How many times has the man been in a boat shaped like swans?

↳ He _____. It is _____.

● 자신의 상황에 맞게 내용을 완성하고 말해 보세요.

What is your favorite sport? Complete the sentences by using the information in the table below.

(1) Sports	(2) Why	(3) How often	(4) When	(5) Who taught you?
baseball basketball volleyball soccer tennis	fun exciting interesting charming	(almost) every day once a week once a month twice a week three times a week	after school on weekends in the evening	friend P.E. teacher coach mom / dad brother / sister

I'm going to talk about my favorite sport. My favorite sport is (1)_____.

I like it because it is (2)_____. I play it (3)_____.

I usually play it (4)_____. My (5)_____ taught

me how to play (1)_____.

What is your daily routine? Fill in the table below and tell your classmates about it.

Time	Things to do
	Get up
	Have dinner
	Go to bed

I get up at _____ every day. I _____ at

_____. Usually I _____ at _____ in

the morning. Then, I _____ at _____. I always

_____ at _____. I have dinner at _____.

After dinner, I _____. I go to bed at _____.

01

W Tony, do you like _____?

M Of course. I _____ sports.

W What's your _____ sport, _____?

M It's hard to _____ one, but I like basketball best. _____ _____ you?

W I like _____. It's very exciting.

02

M What do you want to _____ _____ _____ _____?

W I'm _____ _____ teaching, singing, drawing, and baking.

M Wow! Does it mean that you want to be a _____, _____, _____, and a _____?

W Yes.

M If you had to _____ one, what would it be?

W Well. I think _____ really _____ _____ drawing.

03

M I have two _____ _____ this afternoon's _____ game. Do you want to go?

W Of course. _____ _____ shall we meet?

M Let's meet _____ _____ _____ the game starts.

W When does it start?

M It _____ _____ 2:30 P.M. Where are we going to meet?

W Right _____ _____ _____ Entrance A.

04

W I'm very glad to be here.

M Me, too. I _____ _____ to see this movie.

W Let's _____ _____ and have a seat.

M Oh, no! Where are the tickets?

W _____? Where did you put them?

M I think I left them in the car. _____ _____ _____.

05

M Hello, how may I help you?

W I think I left my backpack _____ _____ _____.

M _____ was it?

W It was _____ 8 a.m. I was _____ _____ _____ to school.

M What does it look like?

W It's _____ with _____ stripes.

06

W When I sit on it, it makes me _____ very _____. It is usually in the _____. I sometimes _____ _____ _____ it and watch TV. What is it?

07

[Telephone rings.]

W Hello?

M Hello, Susie. Do you _____ _____ for this evening?

W Not really. But I have to finish my _____ _____, it's _____ tomorrow. I will be _____ after that. Why?

M I'm going to _____ _____ potluck _____. Can you come?

W _____. I'd love to.

08

M What are you going to do this weekend?

W I'm going to _____ my _____.

M _____ does he live?

W He _____ _____ Gangwon Province. I'm going to _____ him _____ _____ _____.

M That sounds great.

09

W Eunseong, you're late again today. _____ _____ _____ _____?

M I helped a little boy find his mom on the way to school.

W Really? _____ you _____ _____ find his mom?

M No. But I took him to the _____ _____.

W _____ _____ _____ you. Please don't be _____ _____ _____ again, though.

10

W Where are you going?

M I am going to a _____.

W Did you see a _____ _____? What's the weather like outside?

M It's _____ _____ _____. It's cloudy. I think it's going to _____ _____.

W Oh, no. Really?

11

[Telephone rings.]

M Hello, Tom _____.

W Hi, Tom. _____ Jennie. I'm calling about _____ _____.

M Ann's birthday? Oh, it's _____ _____, right?

W Yes, it is. Let's _____ _____ _____ for her. Can you help me?

M Yeah, _____. Good idea. What can I do?

W I _____ you _____ _____ your camcorder.

12

M I'm _____ _____ _____ but I can't stop eating _____ like candies and chocolate. I really like _____ but I don't like eating _____. What should I do?

13

M _____ do you usually _____

_____ ?

W I usually _____ _____ _____

Dongdaemun Market.

M Do you have a _____ _____ ?

W Yes. The name of my _____ _____ is

Full-Coordi.

M _____ do you like it?

W It has a lot of _____ _____

_____ .

14

① M Tom _____ _____ at 7:00 a.m.

② M _____ _____ Tom walks his dog in

the park.

③ M Tom _____ _____ _____ at

8:30 in the morning.

M Tom _____ _____ at 3:00 in the

afternoon.

⑤ M Tom does his homework _____

_____ _____ _____ .

15

① M _____ do they _____ ?

W They are in _____ _____

_____ .

② M What's your _____ _____ ?

W My favorite color is _____ .

③ M What're _____ in your hand?

W They're our _____ _____ .

④ M Let's _____ *Music Live* on Channel 9.

W Okay. I'm _____ in music.

⑤ M What's your favorite _____ of the week?

W I love _____ .

16

W Tom, let's go to the _____ this Saturday.

M Sorry, I can't. I'm busy _____ _____

_____ .

W What do you _____ _____

_____ _____ ?

M I do _____ _____ at Seoul

Metropolitan Library.

W Wow, that _____ _____ . Can I join

you?

M Sure.

17

W Hello, everyone. The man in this picture is

_____ _____ . He's _____

years old, but he _____ _____ . He's

_____ _____ . He tells _____

_____ so his patients like him. He

_____ _____ _____ very well.

Every December he holds a violin concert

_____ _____ _____ . I want to

grow up to be _____ _____ .

18

M _____ _____ _____ _____ ,

Jake met Jennie. She _____ look

_____ _____ . She said that

her _____ _____ a lot and was

_____ _____ . In this situation, what

would Jake say to Jennie?

19

W   Look, Mike! Here are the new _____

    _____.

M   What kind of _____ are there?

W   _____, hip-hop dancing, _____, and

    soccer lessons. What are you _____ in?

M   I'm interested in _____ _____. How

    about you?

W   Me, too. Then, let's take lessons _____.

M   That's a good idea.

20

M   Wow, this is _____ _____ _____

    I have been in _____ _____ shaped

    like a swan.

W   _____ a moment!

M   What's wrong?

W   Look at this _____. You have to put on

    _____ _____ _____ in this boat.

M   Oh, I see.

01 다음을 듣고, 'I'가 가리키는 것으로 가장 적절한 것을 고르시오.

①   ②   ③   ④   ⑤

02 대화를 듣고, 내일 오후의 날씨로 가장 적절한 것을 고르시오.

①   ②   ③   ④   ⑤

03 다음을 듣고, 여자가 전화를 건 목적으로 가장 적절한 것을 고르시오.

① 파티에 초대하려고   ② 시험 공부를 같이 하려고
③ 바뀐 전화번호를 알려 주려고   ④ 약속을 변경하려고
⑤ 수학 책을 빌리려고

04 대화를 듣고, 여자의 심정으로 가장 적절한 것을 고르시오.

① 부러움   ② 불안함   ③ 실망스러움
④ 걱정스러움   ⑤ 기쁨

05 대화를 듣고, 두 사람이 대화하는 장소로 가장 적절한 것을 고르시오.

① 박물관   ② 식당   ③ 서점
④ 분실물 센터   ⑤ 식료품점

06 대화를 듣고, 남자가 지불할 금액을 고르시오.

① $13   ② $24   ③ $27   ④ $30   ⑤ $60

07 대화를 듣고, 두 사람이 방과 후에 할 운동으로 가장 적절한 것을 고르시오.

①   ②   ③   ④   ⑤

08 대화를 듣고, 대화를 마친 후 두 사람이 할 일을 고르시오.

① 책 읽기   ② 집 청소하기   ③ 요리하기
④ 선물 사러 가기   ⑤ 공부하기

09 대화를 듣고, 두 사람의 관계로 가장 적절한 것을 고르시오.

① 누나 — 남동생   ② 교사 — 학생   ③ 의사 — 환자
④ 딸 — 아버지   ⑤ 점원 — 손님

10 대화를 듣고, 두 사람이 주문한 음식이 <u>아닌</u> 것을 고르시오.

① 스파게티   ② 콜라   ③ 햄버거
④ 오렌지 주스   ⑤ 감자튀김

11 대화를 듣고, 여자가 남자에게 부탁한 일로 가장 적절한 것을 고르시오.

① 결석계 제출하기　　　　② 할머니 문병 가기
③ 책 반납하기　　　　　　④ 과제물 도와주기
⑤ 수업 노트 빌려 주기

12 대화를 듣고, 남자가 여자에게 제안한 것으로 가장 적절한 것을 고르시오.

① 쇼핑하기　　　　　　　② 외식하기
③ 요리하기　　　　　　　④ 생일 파티 하기
⑤ 생일 파티 장소 찾기

13 대화를 듣고, 여자가 영화를 다시 보고 싶어 하는 이유로 가장 적절한 것을 고르시오.

① 남자 주인공을 좋아해서　　② 너무 감동적이어서
③ 너무 재미있어서　　　　　④ 놓친 부분을 보고 싶어서
⑤ 결말을 다시 보고 싶어서

14 다음을 듣고, 표의 내용과 일치하지 <u>않는</u> 것을 고르시오.

Free Time Activity

Tom:　　　Go in-line staking
Jennie:　　Play badminton
Jake:　　　Use the Internet or play computer games
Kate:　　　Play the piano
Frank:　　Go in-line staking or walk his dog in the park

①　　　　②　　　　③　　　　④　　　　⑤

15 대화를 듣고, 남자의 아빠가 엄마를 위해 하는 일로 언급된 것을 고르시오.

① 안마해 주기　　② 쓰레기 버리기　　③ 욕실 청소하기
④ 설거지하기　　⑤ 전구 교체하기

16 다음을 듣고, 두 사람의 대화가 <u>어색한</u> 것을 고르시오.

①   ②   ③   ④   ⑤

17 다음을 듣고, 내용과 일치하지 <u>않는</u> 것을 고르시오.

① 방송을 하는 사람은 기장이다.
② 비행기는 30분 후 로스앤젤레스 공항에서 이륙할 것이다.
③ 로스앤젤레스는 현재 비가 오고 있다.
④ 현지 시각은 오전 7시 30분이다.
⑤ 남자는 착륙 전 개인 소지품 확인 및 서류 준비를 당부한다.

18 다음을 듣고, Peter가 Susan에게 할 말로 가장 적절한 것을 고르시오.

① I hope you enjoy your cake.
② I will have some chocolate cake.
③ Can I get you some more cake?
④ Can I have some more cake, please?
⑤ Would you like to have some more cake?

[19-20] 대화를 듣고, 남자의 마지막 말에 이어질 여자의 응답으로 가장 적절한 것을 고르시오.

19
① I worried about the result.
② What does that sign mean?
③ I think it's too difficult to do.
④ I don't have to worry about the test.
⑤ Well, I'm sure we can make it on time now.

20
① Okay. No problem.
② I am so happy for you.
③ I'm so upset about you.
④ It will be a great concert.
⑤ Oh, that's not a good idea.

● 다음은 Listening Test 02의 주요 지문입니다. 녹음을 다시 듣고, 질문에 대한 답을 완성하세요.

Q5

1 What is the title of the book the man is looking for?

└→ It is _____.

Q7

2 What did the woman buy last week?

└→ She bought _____.

Q8

3 What's wrong with the boy's and girl's mom?

└→ She _____.

Q9

4 What did the boy and the girl buy their parents on Parents' Day last year?

└→ They bought them _____.

Q11

5 Why was the woman absent?

└→ The reason is that _____.

Q12

6 When is the woman's birthday?

└→ Her birthday is on _____.

Q13

7 When and with whom did the woman see the movie?

└→ She saw the movie _____.

Q20

8 How much money is the woman going to get as prize money?

└→ He is going to _____.

● 자신의 상황에 맞게 내용을 완성하고 말해 보세요.

A   What did you do last Parents' Day? Fill in the table below and tell your classmates about it.

What I Did Last Parents' Day	
(1) What did you do last Parents' Day?	① ②
(2) How did your parents feel?	
(3) What did your parents say to you?	
(4) How did you feel?	
(5) What will you do next Parents' Day?	
(5) What will you do next Parents' Day?	

Today, I am going to talk about what I did last Parents' Day. I ①_____

and ②_____. My parents were very (2)_____

and said to me, "(3)_____." I felt very (4)_____.

Next Parents' Day, I think I will (5)_____.

B   What do you like to do in your free time? Fill in the table below and tell your classmates about it.

My Free-Time Activities	
Activities	Reasons I enjoy doing it
①	③
②	④

I'm going to talk about what I like to do in my free time. In my free time, I like

to ①_____. I enjoy doing it because ③_____

_____. Besides ①_____, I also like to

②_____. The reason is that ④_____

_____.

01

M I am very _____ and brown. Bees _____ _____ one flower _____ another flower and make me. People _____ use me _____ _____ sugar when they _____. Some people drink me as a _____. What am I?

02

W Did you _____ _____ _____ _____ this morning?

M What news?

W I mean the _____ _____ for tomorrow.

M Yeah. I _____ that it's going to be _____ _____ tomorrow morning. It will be _____ in the afternoon, and will _____ in the evening, though.

W I see. Thank you for the _____.

03

[Beep]

W Hello, Tim. This is Kathy. I'm very sorry, but I can't _____ _____ on Thursday. I forgot that I have a math test _____. Are you _____ _____ Saturday? If you are, let's go on Saturday. Please _____ _____ _____. My number is 010-1234-5678.

04

M You look very happy today. _____ _____?

W I was _____ _____ the _____ _____, but…

M But what? Did you _____ _____ _____?

W Right! I won the gold medal.

M Wow, _____!

W Thank you.

05

W May I help you?

M I'm _____ _____ a _____.

W What is the _____ of the book?

M It is *Who Moved My Cheese?*

W Oh, it is in _____ 7. You will find it _____.

M Thanks.

06

M _____ _____. Can I _____ this shirt _____?

W Sure. The _____ _____ is over there.

M Thanks. Is it _____ _____?

W Yes. We're offering a 20% discount. The _____ _____ of this shirt was $30.

M Okay. I will take it.

07

W David, what are you going to do _____

_____ ?

M I have _____ _____ yet. Why?

W I bought a _____ _____ last week, so I'd like to play tennis. Can you play with me?

M Nice. _____ _____ _____. When do you want to meet?

W _____ make it at 5 p.m.

08

W Mom doesn't _____ _____ today. Is she _____ ?

M She _____ _____ _____. How about doing some _____ _____ for her?

W Great. What can we do?

M Let's _____ _____ _____.

W That's a good idea. She will really like that.

09

W _____ _____ _____ _____ is Parents' Day.

M I know. What should we buy for Mom and Dad?

W _____ _____, we bought them _____.

M Then, how about buying scented _____ this year?

W That's a great idea.

10

W Are you _____ _____ _____ ?

M Yes. I'd like _____ and a _____. What about you?

W I'll have a _____ with an _____.

_____.

M What do you want _____ _____ ?

W I will have an ice cream.

11

M Hi, Jennie. What _____? Why were you _____ today?

W Hi, Tom. I had to _____ _____ _____ in the hospital.

M It must be _____. Is she okay now?

W Not yet. Thanks for _____. By the way, I need _____ _____.

M _____ can I do for you?

W Can I _____ _____ _____ for today's lessons if it is okay?

12

M Sue, do you want to _____ _____ ? I know a nice _____ _____. I'll _____ you _____.

W Sure, but why?

M Today is your birthday. It's _____ _____.

W Hahaha, Tony. My birthday is _____ _____. It's already _____, but thank you anyway.

13

M _____ _____ do you want to see?

W _____ _____ this movie?

M _____ _____ _____ this movie last week with Ann?

W Yes, I did, but I want to see it _____

_____ _____.

M Was it _____ _____?

W Yes, it was. Unfortunately, I _____ _____ _____ when I saw it with Ann because I _____ _____.

14

① M Bill likes to _____ _____ _____ in his free time.

② M Jennie _____ _____ in her free time.

③ M Jake _____ _____ _____ in his free time but he _____ _____ computer games.

④ M Kate _____ _____ _____ in her free time.

⑤ M Frank goes in-line skating or _____ _____ _____ in the park in his free time.

15

W Does your _____ _____ your mom _____ the house?

M Yes, _____ _____.

W What does he _____ _____ for her?

M He _____ _____ _____ _____ and cleans the bathroom. What about your dad?

W The only thing he does for my mom is to _____ _____ _____.

16

① M Let me _____ _____.

W Me _____.

② M Hi, Jennie. _____ are you _____?

W I'm _____ my room.

③ M _____ have you been?

W Not bad.

④ M I'd like you _____ _____ my brother, Tom.

W Hi, Tom. Nice to meet you.

⑤ M _____ do you _____ it is?

W It _____ _____ a cat.

17

M Good morning, everyone. This is your _____ _____. We will be _____ at Los Angeles Airport in about _____ _____. The weather in Los Angeles is _____ and the _____ _____ is 7:30 a.m. Before we _____ at the airport, please _____ that you have all of your _____ _____ and have all of your travel _____ ready. Thank you.

18

M On Halloween, Peter had a great _____ at Susan's house. After having the _____ _____, Susan gave him _____ _____ _____ chocolate cake and a cup of coffee _____ _____. He had had _____ but the cake was so _____ that he wanted to have some _____. In this situation, what would Peter say to Susan?

19

M   _____ are we?

W I have _____ _____. I think we're

    _____.

M Can we get to the station _____ _____?

W I'm not sure. Oh, look at _____ _____.

M It says the station is _____ _____.

W Well, I'm sure we can make it on time now.

20

M I _____ _____ this!

W _____ can't you believe?

M I _____ the piano contest!

W Wow, _____! I told you so.

M I'm going to _____ $100.

W I am so happy for you.

01 다음을 듣고, 오늘 밤의 날씨로 가장 적절한 것을 고르시오.

①   ②   ③   ④   ⑤

02 대화를 듣고, 여자의 모습으로 가장 적절한 것을 고르시오.

①   ②   ③   ④   ⑤

03 대화를 듣고, 남자가 지불할 금액을 고르시오.

① $7   ② $10   ③ $14   ④ $17   ⑤ $20

04 대화를 듣고, 여자의 심정으로 가장 적절한 것을 고르시오.

① 우울함   ② 지루함   ③ 화가 남
④ 짜증 남   ⑤ 자랑스러움

05 대화를 듣고, 여자가 가려고 하는 장소를 고르시오.

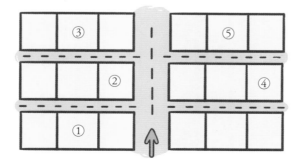

06 대화를 듣고, 남자가 구입할 물건으로 가장 적절한 것을 고르시오.

①   ②   ③   ④   ⑤

07 대화를 듣고, 남자가 전화를 건 목적으로 가장 적절한 것을 고르시오.

① 줄넘기를 같이 하려고 　　　② 줄넘기를 사러 가려고
③ 집들이에 초대하려고 　　　④ 안부를 물으려고
⑤ 여자의 엄마를 도우려고

08 대화를 듣고, 남자가 일요일에 할 일로 가장 적절한 것을 고르시오.

① 등산하기 　　　② TV 보기 　　　③ 집에서 쉬기
④ 축구 하기 　　　⑤ 공원 산책하기

09 대화를 듣고, 두 사람의 관계로 가장 적절한 것을 고르시오.

① 점원 — 손님 　　　② 은행원 — 고객 　　　③ 승무원 — 승객
④ 교사 — 학생 　　　⑤ 의사 — 환자

10 대화를 듣고, 두 사람이 주말에 할 일로 가장 적절한 것을 고르시오.

① 서점 가기 　　　② 영화 보기 　　　③ 도서관 가기
④ 보고서 쓰기 　　　⑤ 인터넷 검색하기

11 대화를 듣고, 여자가 남자에게 부탁한 일로 가장 적절한 것을 고르시오.

① 택배 찾아 오기   ② 소포 보내기

③ 소포 포장 도와주기   ④ 소포 들어 주기

⑤ 우체국까지 태워 주기

12 대화를 듣고, 여자가 남자에게 제안한 것으로 가장 적절한 것을 고르시오.

① 수리하기   ② 교환하기   ③ 반품하기

④ 환불 받기   ⑤ 새로 구입하기

13 대화를 듣고, 여자가 남자를 만나지 못한 이유로 가장 적절한 것을 고르시오.

① 약속을 잊어서   ② 약속 시간을 잘못 알아서

③ 다른 급한 약속이 생겨서   ④ 약속 장소를 잘못 알아서

⑤ 차가 막혀 너무 늦게 도착해서

14 다음을 듣고, 그래프의 내용과 일치하지 않는 것을 고르시오.

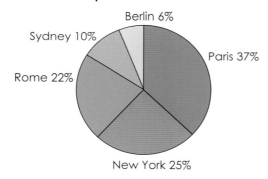

Popular Cities to Visit

Berlin 6%
Sydney 10%
Rome 22%
Paris 37%
New York 25%

①   ②   ③   ④   ⑤

15 대화를 듣고, Ann이 도착했을 때 세 사람이 할 일로 가장 적절한 것을 고르시오.

① 발표 주제 투표 하기   ② 발표 순서 정하기

③ 역할 분담 하기   ④ 발표 자료 만들기

⑤ 발표 연습하기

16 다음을 듣고, 두 사람의 대화가 <u>어색한</u> 것을 고르시오.

①   ②   ③   ④   ⑤

17 다음을 듣고, 내용과 일치하지 <u>않는</u> 것을 고르시오.

① 여자아이를 찾는 안내 방송이다.
② 여자아이의 이름은 Cathy Johns이다.
③ 여자아이의 나이는 6살이다.
④ 여자아이는 빨간색 셔츠에 흰색 바지를 입고 있다.
⑤ 안내 데스크는 1층에 있다.

18 다음을 듣고, Smith 선생님이 Jennie에게 할 말로 가장 적절한 것을 고르시오.

① It sounds great!
② You did a good job!
③ I'm sorry to hear that.
④ I'm sorry. I won't do it again.
⑤ I'm so upset that I made a mistake.

[19-20] 대화를 듣고, 남자의 마지막 말에 이어질 여자의 응답으로 가장 적절한 것을 고르시오.

19
① Here you are.
② To go, please.
③ Enjoy your meal.
④ Here's your change.
⑤ Okay. That's $10.50.

20
① Long time no see.
② How do you feel?
③ I'd like to introduce you to my friend.
④ I'm from Korea. Where are you from?
⑤ How do you do? Pleased to meet you, Mr. Brown.

● 다음은 **Listening Test 03**의 주요 지문입니다. 녹음을 다시 듣고, 질문에 대한 답을 완성하세요.

Q1 **1** What's the weather going to be like this afternoon?

↳ It is going to be _____.

Q6 **2** Why does the woman want to buy a gift for her mom?

↳ The reason is that her _____.

Q7 **3** What did the boy buy?

↳ He bought _____.

Q9 **4** Why did the man say "Congratulations!" to Minji?

↳ The reason is that her _____ was _____.

Q12 **5** Why did the man bring his broken MP3 player to the woman?

↳ He wanted _____.

Q15 **6** How did Tom know Ann was on her way?

↳ The reason is that _____.

Q19 **7** What did the man want to eat? List all the things he mentioned.

↳ He wanted to eat _____, _____, and _____.

Q20 **8** How many times have Jane and Mr. Brown met each other?

↳ They _____.

● 자신의 상황에 맞게 내용을 완성하고 말해 보세요.

 Give directions to different buildings marked on the map. Use the expressions in the table below.

Giving Directions	
(1) church / library / bookstore / pharmacy / school / hair shop	(2) go straight for one/two block(s)
(3) turn right/left at the corner	(4) on your right/left

I am going to show you how you can get to the (1)_____.

First, (2)_____.

Then, (3)_____. It is

(4)_____.

 What city do you want to visit most? What do you want to do there? Fill in the blanks and tell your classmates about it.

The City I Want to Visit	
(1) City name	
(2) Reason I want to visit the city	
Things to do	① ② ③ ④ ⑤

(1)_____ is the city I want to visit most. I really want to visit there

because I think (2)_____. I have many things to do

when I visit there. First, I'll ①_____. Second, I'll

②_____. Third, I'll ③_____. Then, I'll

④_____. Finally, I'll ⑤_____.

01

W _____ _____. This is the _____ _____ for today and tomorrow. It will be _____ and _____ this afternoon, and the rain will continue _____. Tomorrow, the rain will stop, and we'll have a _____ _____. Thank you.

02

M What a cute _____ _____!

W Thank you for saying so. I got this flower painting at the _____ _____.

M _____? Did you buy your _____ there, too?

W Yes. I wanted to buy a _____, but I didn't.

M You _____ _____ _____.

03

W How may I help you?

M I'd like to buy _____ for *Champion*. _____ _____ are the tickets?

W They are $7 for _____ and $3 for _____. How many do you _____?

M _____ adults and _____ child, please.

W Okay.

04

W Look at the children _____ _____ _____. They _____ so _____.

M Yes. Look at that boy _____.

W You mean the boy with the _____

_____ on?

M Yes. He's running very _____.

W Oh, that is my _____.

M Wow! Your son is a _____ _____.

05

W Excuse me, _____ _____ _____ _____ _____ a pharmacy?

M Go two blocks and turn left.

W Go _____ _____ and _____ _____?

M Yes. It's the second building _____ _____ _____.

W Okay. Thank you.

06

W Oh! Mom's birthday is _____ _____.

M You're right. What are you going to buy for her?

W Well. I'm _____ _____ a _____.

M Then, I will buy her a _____. It will be good if she wears it with the scarf.

W That's a _____ _____.

07

[Telephone rings.]

W Hello?

M Hello, Gloria. Are you free _____ _____?

W Well, I have to help my mom, but it won't _____ _____ _____.

M Nice. I bought a new _____ _____ so

I want to _____ it _____. Can you do with me?

W Sure. I'll go to your house at 5.

M Okay. _____ _____.

08

M What are you going to do on _____?

W _____ _____ _____. I may stay home and _____ _____. How about you?

M I'm going to _____ _____ in the park.

W Sounds great. _____ _____!

M Thank you.

09

M _____, Minji. Your English _____ _____ was the best in our school.

W Really? I _____ _____ it. I'm so happy now.

M I'm very _____ _____ you. I hope you will _____ _____ the good effort.

W Thank you. I will _____ _____ _____, Mr. Hanks.

M Good girl.

10

M What are you going to do this _____?

W _____ _____ _____. I may go to the bookstore.

M _____ _____?

W I want to buy some books to read. _____ _____ _____?

M I'm going to the _____ to _____ some

_____ for my _____.

W Then, _____ _____ we go together?

M Sounds good.

11

W Tom, are you _____ now?

M Not really. Why?

W Can I ask you _____ _____?

M _____ is it?

W I have to send these _____ _____. Would you mind _____ _____ of these _____ _____ _____ _____ for me?

M _____ _____. I'll take the _____ one.

12

M Would you take a look at this _____ _____?

W Yes, of course. Hmm... _____ _____ have you had it?

M About _____ _____. Can you tell me _____ _____ it'll cost _____ _____ it?

W It'll be _____ _____ $100. I suggest you _____ _____ _____ _____ instead of getting it _____.

13

W Hi, Sam. It's Kate. I _____ _____. _____ are you arriving?

M Hi, Kate. I'm _____ there. I've been waiting for you.

W I _____ _____ you. _____ are
   you now?

M I'm _____ _____ _____ exit 1 at
   Gangnam Station.

W Oh, I'm sorry. I thought we _____
   _____ _____ _____ at exit 1 at
   Shinchon Station.

14

① W This pie chart shows popular cities
      _____ _____ _____.

② W Paris is _____ _____ _____
      city to visit.

③ W Rome is _____ popular _____
      Berlin.

④ W New York is 12% _____ popular
      _____ Paris.

⑤ W Berlin is _____ _____ _____
      among five cities.

15

M Hi, Jennie. Come on in.

W Hi, Tom. Ann is _____ _____
   _____.

M Yeah, I know. She _____ _____ just
   _____ you arrived.

W _____ would you like to talk about for our
   _____ _____?

M I'd like to talk about _____ _____.

W Oh, I like _____ _____ better than
   mine. Let's _____ _____ _____
   when Ann gets here.

16

① M _____ _____ _____ come to
      my house?

   W _____ I'm sick.

② W _____ do you do _____ _____
      _____?

   M I work out and then have breakfast.

③ M _____ _____ is it?

   W It's 2 dollars.

④ M What's _____ _____ today?

   W It's October 27th.

⑤ M Help yourself.

   W No, thanks. I have had _____.

17

W Ladies and gentlemen, can I have your
   _____, please? A girl _____ Cathy
   Johns is looking for _____ _____.
   She is six years old. She is wearing _____
   _____ _____ with white _____.
   Will Cathy's _____ please come to the
   _____ _____ on the _____
   _____ right now?

18

M Jennie has _____ _____ tomorrow.
   Last night, she _____ _____ her
   computer for more than _____ _____
   to make _____ _____. She saved the
   file _____ _____ _____. This
   morning when she turned on her computer, it
   _____ _____. She told her teacher,
   Mr. Smith, about this _____. In this
   situation, what would Mr. Smith say to her?

19

M   _____ I help you?

W   Yes, please. _____ _____ a hamburger
with fries.

M   Anything _____ _____?

W   A large coke, please.

M   _____ _____ or _____
_____?

W   To go, please.

20

W   _____ _____ you _____, Billy?

M   Great. How about you, Jane?

W   Good. By the way, _____ is the man
_____ _____ you?

M   Oh, _____ _____ my English teacher,
Mr. Brown. Mr. Brown, _____ _____
my friend, Jane.

W   How do you do? Pleased to meet you, Mr.
Brown.

04 Listening Test

01 대화를 듣고, 뉴욕의 이번 주말 날씨로 가장 적절한 것을 고르시오.

① ② ③ ④ ⑤

02 다음을 듣고, 'it'이 가리키는 것으로 가장 적절한 것을 고르시오.

① ② ③ ④ ⑤

03 대화를 듣고, 남자가 전화를 건 목적으로 가장 적절한 것을 고르시오.

① 위치를 알려고　　　　② 책을 대출하려고
③ 이용 시간을 문의하려고　　　　④ 잃어버린 물건을 찾으려고
⑤ 예약을 취소하려고

04 대화를 듣고, 남자가 느꼈을 심정으로 가장 적절한 것을 고르시오.

① happy　　　　② bored　　　　③ worried
④ thankful　　　　⑤ angry

05 대화를 듣고, 남자가 가려고 하는 장소를 고르시오.

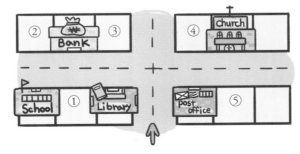

06 대화를 듣고, 두 사람이 지불할 금액을 고르시오.

MENU

Cake		Drinks	
Cheese cake	$5.50	Milk	$1.50
Chocolate cake	$4.00	Apple juice	$1.50
Strawberry cake	$3.00	Cola	$1.00

① $4.50   ② $6.50   ③ $9.50   ④ $11.00   ⑤ $13.00

07 다음을 듣고, 그림에 대한 설명으로 알맞은 것을 고르시오.

①   ②   ③   ④   ⑤

08 대화를 듣고, 대화를 마친 후 여자가 할 일을 고르시오.

① 병원 가기   ② 운동하기   ③ 책 읽기
④ 약 먹기   ⑤ 숙제 하기

09 대화를 듣고, 두 사람의 관계로 가장 적절한 것을 고르시오.

① 이웃 주민   ② 직장 동료   ③ 사촌
④ 친구   ⑤ 가족

10 대화를 듣고, 대화를 마친 후 두 사람이 갈 곳을 고르시오.

① 집   ② 학교   ③ 도서관
④ 서점   ⑤ 박물관

11 대화를 듣고, 여자가 남자에게 부탁한 일로 가장 적절한 것을 고르시오.

① 저녁 식사 준비하기　　　　② 음식 재료 다듬기
③ 냉장고 속 음식 재료 확인하기　　④ 주방 청소하기
⑤ 식료품 사오기

12 대화를 듣고, 여자가 남자에게 조언한 것으로 가장 적절한 것을 고르시오.

① 이를 잘 닦아라.　　　　② 초콜릿 섭취를 줄여라.
③ 진통제를 먹어라.　　　　④ 마음 편히 쉬어라.
⑤ 치과에 가라.

13 대화를 듣고, 남자가 도서관에 가는 이유로 가장 적절한 것을 고르시오.

① 책을 빌리려고　　　　② 책을 반납하려고
③ 시험 공부를 하려고　　　④ 친구를 만나려고
⑤ 발표 자료를 구하려고

14 대화를 듣고, 대화의 내용과 일치하지 <u>않는</u> 것을 고르시오.

```
                 Telephone Message
     To:      ① Ann
     From:    ② David
     Memo:    ③ Practice the play
              ④ Classroom 303 at school
              ⑤ 3 p.m. on Tuesday
```

15 대화를 듣고, 남자가 여자에게 부탁한 일로 가장 적절한 것을 고르시오.

① 세탁물 맡기기　　　　② 세탁물 찾기
③ 세탁기 돌리기　　　　④ 세탁소 전화번호 알려 주기
⑤ 세탁소 전화하기

16 다음을 듣고, 두 사람의 대화가 <u>어색한</u> 것을 고르시오.

① ② ③ ④ ⑤

17 다음을 듣고, 뉴스에서 언급되지 <u>않은</u> 것을 고르시오.

① 런던 동계 올림픽 5일째 되는 날이다.
② 뉴스 속보를 방송하는 중이다.
③ 한국 스케이트 팀이 결승전에 진출했다.
④ 스케이트 결승전은 토요일에 열린다.
⑤ 한국 스케이트 팀은 금메달을 한 개 땄다.

18 다음을 듣고, Bill이 Kate에게 할 말로 가장 적절한 것을 고르시오.

① Sounds perfect!
② Don't mention it.
③ Don't forget about that.
④ Why are you so happy?
⑤ Cheer up! You will do better next time.

[19-20] 대화를 듣고, 남자의 마지막 말에 이어질 여자의 응답으로 가장 적절한 것을 고르시오.

19
① I hope you like it.
② I don't think you can do it.
③ That's a good idea. I'll think about that.
④ I think you will be a great photographer.
⑤ I want to have a picture taken with K-pop stars.

20
① I'm happy to hear that.
② I'm interested in skiing, too.
③ I don't think I can make it then.
④ It doesn't matter. I can teach you.
⑤ Let's meet in front of the ticket office then.

● 다음은 **Listening Test 04**의 주요 지문입니다. 녹음을 다시 듣고, 질문에 대한 답을 완성하세요.

Q2

1 What is the animal famous for?

⌐→ It is _____.

Q4

2 Write down 3 reasons why the man didn't enjoy the party.

⌐→ (1) The party _____.

(2) The food _____.

(3) The people _____.

Q6

3 What did the woman order?

⌐→ She ordered _____ and _____.

Q8

4 What's wrong with the woman?

⌐→ She has _____.

Q11

5 Why does the woman want the man to drop by a grocery store?

⌐→ The reason is that she needs _____.

Q12

6 What did the man ask the woman to do?

⌐→ He asked the woman _____.

Q13

7 What is the man going to talk about in his presentation?

⌐→ He is going to _____.

Q17

8 What is the breaking news?

⌐→ It is that _____.

● 자신의 상황에 맞게 내용을 완성하고 말해 보세요.

 A   Talk about your birthday. Fill in the table below and tell your classmates about it.

My Birthday	
(1) When is your birthday?	
(2) Where do you usually have your birthday party?	
(3) Who do you usually celebrate your birthday with?	
(4) What do you like to do on your birthday?	
(5) What do you want to get for your birthday?	

I'm going to talk about my birthday. My birthday is on (1)_____.

I usually have my birthday party (2)_____. I also usually celebrate

my birthday with (3)_____. On my birthday, I like to

(4)_____. If I could get anything for my birthday, I would

like to get (5) _____. I wish every day was my birthday.

B   What do you want to be in the future? Fill in the table below and tell your classmates about it.

My Future Job	
(1) What do you want to be?	
(2) Why do you want to be a(n) _____?	① ②
(3) To be a(n) _____, what do you need to do?	③ ④

I want to be a(n) (1)_____ when I grow up. There are two reasons why

I want to be a(n) (1)_____. First, I want to ①_____ .

Second, I want to ②_____. To be a(n) (1)_____,

I need to ③_____. I also have to ④_____.

I believe I will be able to be a great (1)_____ someday.

01

W When are you going to New York?

M _____ _____.

W Did you check the _____ _____?

M Yes. It said it's going to snow _____

_____ _____.

W I see. You'd better pack a _____

_____.

02

W This is the _____ _____ you can see

in the _____. This animal _____

_____ _____ its long neck. It eats

leaves _____ _____ _____

trees. Its color is yellow and has _____

_____ all over its body. What is it?

03

[Telephone rings.]

W San Francisco Public Library. _____

_____ _____ you?

M Hi. I think I left my _____ _____

there. Have you seen it?

W What does it _____ _____? I will

_____ it _____.

M It is a _____ one with _____ stripes.

M Oh, it is here in the _____ basket.

W Thanks. I'll be there soon.

04

W Did you _____ _____ _____ last

night?

M It was _____ fun _____ _____. I

don't want to _____ _____ it.

W Come on! _____ _____?

M It was _____. The party place was

_____, the food was _____, and the

people came _____.

W Oh, I'm sorry to hear that.

05

M Excuse me, how can I get to a _____

_____?

W _____ one _____ and _____

_____.

M And then?

W It's on your right, _____ _____ the

_____ _____.

M Okay. Thank you very much.

06

M What do you want to _____?

W I'll have _____ _____ _____

cheese cake and a cola. How about you?

M I will have a piece of _____ cake.

W _____ _____ a drink?

M I will have _____ _____ _____

milk.

07

① W There is a _____ in the _____.

② W There is a _____ by the _____.

③ W A boy is _____ _____ the desk and _____ a computer.

④ W There is a _____ next to the _____.

⑤ W A boy is sitting at the _____ and _____ something.

08

M Are you okay, Sumi? You _____ _____.

W I _____ _____ _____. I have a _____ _____.

M I'm sorry to hear that. Did you take some _____?

W Not yet. But I think I should. Thanks.

M _____ _____.

09

[Doorbell rings.]

M Who is it?

W I'm your _____ from _____ _____.

M Hello. _____ _____ _____ _____?

W I can't _____ because it's too _____. What's going on in there?

M Oh, I'm very sorry. I _____ _____ last week so I'm having a _____ _____.

W Please _____ _____. It's 1 a.m.

10

W How was the class?

M It was fun. But the teacher gave _____ _____ _____ _____.

W That's her _____. You have to stay in the

library _____ _____ _____ _____ _____.

M I think so. That's where I am going now.

W _____ _____! I will go with you.

11

W Can you help me _____ _____, Tom?

M Of course, Mom. _____ can I do for you?

W On the way home, could you drop by _____ _____ _____?

M Okay, _____ do we need?

W We need some _____, cucumbers, and _____.

12

W Try some _____. It's so _____.

M No, thanks. I'll try some _____.

W Why? You love _____.

M Yeah, I'm _____ _____ it but my tooth really _____ now. I need a _____.

W Oh, you need to go _____ _____ _____.

M Well, if you are okay, would you _____ me _____ _____ _____?

13

W Hey, Tom. _____ are you _____?

M I'm going _____ _____ _____.

W Do you want to _____ _____ _____?

M No. I need _____ _____ for my presentation.

W _____ the presentation _____?

M It's about _____.

14

[Telephone rings.]

M Hello. _____ _____ David.

_____ I _____ to Ann?

W Sorry, she's _____. Can I _____

_____ _____?

M Yes. Please tell her that we will _____

the play in _____ 303 at school at 3 p.m.

_____ _____.

W Okay, I _____.

M Thank you very much.

15

W Honey, _____ are you doing?

M I'm looking for my _____ _____.

W Which _____?

M My _____ windbreaker _____.

W Oh, it is at the cleaners for _____

_____.

M Then, let me know the _____ _____.

I'll _____ and _____ when it will be

_____.

16

① M _____ _____ help you?

W No. I'm just _____ _____.

② M Thank you _____ _____.

W Thank you _____ _____ _____ me.

③ M _____ are you doing?

W I go to school _____ _____.

④ M _____ do you think it is?

W It _____ _____ a cat.

⑤ M I have _____ _____ _____.

W That's too bad.

17

M Hello. Welcome to _____ _____

_____. It is _____ _____

_____ of the London _____ Olympic

Games. We have _____ _____ now.

The Korean Skating team has _____

_____ _____ the final round. The

_____ _____ is going to be at 10

a.m. _____ _____ _____. We

hope the team will win _____ _____

_____ _____ in these Olympic

Games.

18

M Kate is Bill's _____ _____. She studies

very well. She always _____ _____

_____. She got _____ _____

_____ on her _____ _____

today. But she _____ _____

_____ on her _____ _____.

She was _____ _____ that she made

_____ _____ _____. In this

situation, what would Bill say to Kate?

19

M _____ do you want _____ _____,

Jenny?

W Well, I don't know _____ _____

_____ _____ _____.

M Well, _____ are you interested in?

W I'm interested in _____ _____.

M Then, _____ _____ becoming a
   professional _____?

W That's a good idea. I'll think about that.

20

W Do you have _____ _____ for this
   winter vacation?

M No, _____ _____. How about you?

W I'm planning to _____ _____. Do you
   want to join me?

M I'd like to, but unfortunately I _____
   _____.

W It doesn't matter. I can teach you.

중학영어듣기 모의고사 05회

Listening Test

01 대화를 듣고, 오늘 오후 서울의 날씨로 가장 적절한 것을 고르시오.

① ② ③ ④ ⑤

02 다음을 듣고, 'I'가 가리키는 것으로 가장 적절한 것을 고르시오.

① ② ③ ④ ⑤

03 대화를 듣고, 지하철이 도착할 시간으로 가장 적절한 것을 고르시오.

① 4:15　　② 4:17　　③ 4:52　　④ 4:55　　⑤ 4:57

04 대화를 듣고, 두 사람의 심정으로 가장 적절한 것을 고르시오.

① 외로움　　② 행복함　　③ 걱정스러움
④ 지루함　　⑤ 부러움

05 대화를 듣고, 두 사람이 대화하는 장소로 가장 적절한 것을 고르시오.

① pet shop　　② party place　　③ museum
④ toy shop　　⑤ parking lot

06 대화를 듣고, 남자가 보려고 하는 물건으로 가장 적절한 것을 고르시오.

① ② ③ ④ ⑤

07 다음을 듣고, 여자가 메시지를 남긴 목적으로 가장 적절한 것을 고르시오.

① 파티 참석 여부를 알리려고　　② 파티에 초대하려고
③ 병원을 예약하려고　　④ 약속 시간을 확인하려고
⑤ 안부를 물으려고

08 대화를 듣고, 대화를 마친 후 두 사람이 할 일을 고르시오.

① 스파게티 만들기　　② 외식하기
③ 장보러 가기　　④ 음식 주문 전화하기
⑤ 쇼핑 목록 작성하기

09 대화를 듣고, 두 사람의 관계로 가장 적절한 것을 고르시오.

① 교사 — 학생　　② 수리 기사 — 고객　　③ 사장 — 직원
④ 승무원 — 승객　　⑤ 엄마 — 아들

10 대화를 듣고, Jessica가 봄 방학 동안 한 일이 <u>아닌</u> 것을 고르시오.

① 영화 보기　　② 책 읽기　　③ 운동하기
④ 게임 하기　　⑤ 할머니 댁 방문하기

11 대화를 듣고, 여자가 남자에게 부탁한 일로 가장 적절한 것을 고르시오.

① 노래 불러 주기　　　　　　② 노래 내려받아 주기
③ 노래 내려받는 법 알려 주기　④ 노래 가사 알려 주기
⑤ 노래 녹음해 주기

12 대화를 듣고, 여자가 남자에게 해 준 충고로 가장 적절한 것을 고르시오.

① 쉬운 책을 골라라.　　　　　② 사전 없이 책의 첫 장을 읽어 봐라.
③ 모르는 단어는 사전을 이용해라.　④ 오디오북을 이용해라.
⑤ 반복해서 읽어라.

13 대화를 듣고, 여자가 쇼핑하러 가지 <u>않은</u> 이유로 가장 적절한 것을 고르시오.

① 피곤해서　　　　　　　　　② 숙제가 많아서
③ 집에서 게임하려고　　　　　④ 쇼핑을 좋아하지 않아서
⑤ 특별히 사고 싶은 것이 없어서

14 대화를 듣고, 대화의 내용과 일치하지 <u>않는</u> 것을 고르시오.

LOST DOG

Name:	① Ahji
Age:	② 3 months old
Appearance:	③ a small, white body
	④ a big black spot on its left ear
Contact No.:	⑤ 010-5432-9876

15 대화를 듣고, 여자가 할 일로 가장 적절한 것을 고르시오.

① 강아지 목욕시키기　　　　　② 강아지 먹이 주기
③ 공원 가기　　　　　　　　　④ 생일 선물 사기
⑤ 동물 병원 가기

16 다음을 듣고, 두 사람의 대화가 <u>어색한</u> 것을 고르시오.

①   ②   ③   ④   ⑤

17 다음을 듣고, 내용과 일치하지 <u>않는</u> 것을 고르시오.

① 방송 중인 때는 저녁이다.
② 바나나 할인 안내 방송이다.
③ 할인은 10분간만 진행된다.
④ 바나나 한 송이에 3달러이다.
⑤ 바나나 한 송이를 사면 한 송이를 무료로 준다.

18 다음을 듣고, Sue에게 할 말로 가장 적절한 것을 고르시오.

① Don't talk to me.
② I'm so envious of you.
③ I'll never do it again.
④ Don't worry. She'll be okay.
⑤ Cheer up! There's always next time.

[19-20] 대화를 듣고, 남자의 마지막 말에 이어질 여자의 응답으로 가장 적절한 것을 고르시오.

19
① That's too bad.
② You must be angry.
③ Of course. It's okay.
④ Sure. You can do that.
⑤ Yes, I do. I did my best.

20
① That's a good idea.
② Wow, it's beautiful!
③ I'm sure you'll like it.
④ I think I am a good painter.
⑤ I think he is one of the greatest artists ever.

● 다음은 Listening Test 05의 주요 지문입니다. 녹음을 다시 듣고, 질문에 대한 답을 완성하세요.

Q1

1 Where is the man going this afternoon?

↳ He is going to _____.

Q4

2 Who had a car accident?

↳ One of the boy's _____.

Q8

3 Why is the man starving?

↳ The reason is that _____.

Q9

4 When can the boy play computer games again?

↳ He can play computer games again when _____.

Q11

5 What does the man think of how to download songs?

↳ He thinks _____.

Q13

6 What did the woman do last night?

↳ She _____.

Q15

7 Where does the man want to meet the woman?

↳ The man wants to meet her _____.

Q19

8 Why didn't the man run fast enough in the relay?

↳ The reason is that _____.

● 자신의 상황에 맞게 내용을 완성하고 말해 보세요.

A What is your favorite food? Complete the sentences by referring to the examples.

My Favorite Food				
(1) Country	(2) Dishes	(3) Where	(4) When	(5) Why
Korean Japanese Chinese Italian American	*bulgogi* sushi/sashimi *jajangmyeon* pizza/spaghetti hamburger	home a restaurant	holidays my birthday special days ordinary days	delicious healthy cheap easy to cook

I am going to talk about my favorite food. My favorite food is (1)_____

food. I especially like (2)_____. I usually eat it at (3)_____. I also

eat it on (4)_____. I like it because it is (5)_____.

B Do you have a pet? If so, describe it. If not, imagine you have one. Fill in the table below and tell your classmates about it.

My Pet	
(1) Kind	
(2) Name	
(3) Age (month/year)	
(4) Appearance	
(5) What it likes to do	
(6) What you do for your pet	

I am going to introduce my pet. I have a(n) (1)_____ named

(2)_____. (He/She) is (3)_____ old. (He/She)

(4)_____. (He/She) likes to (5)_____

_____. What I do for my pet is (6)_____.

I love my pet very much. (He/She) is one of my best friends.

01

[Telephone rings.]

M Hello, can I _____ _____ Susie,
please?

W _____. Who's this?

M Hi, Susie. It's Adam. I'm _____ _____
_____ this afternoon for a _____.
How's the _____ there?

W It's a little cloudy right now, but the sun will be
_____ this _____.

M Oh, thanks.

02

M I _____ _____ China. I am very big. I
have _____ and _____ _____.
I have big black _____ around my eyes.
People think I am very _____. I was in a
movie called *Kung Fu*. What am I?

03

M _____ _____ is it now?

W It's 4:50.

M That's _____. The _____ is late.

W I don't think so. _____ _____ the
timetable, it runs every 7 minutes.
It arrives in _____ _____.

M Oh, I see. I thought it ran _____ 5
_____. Thank you.

04

W Hey, Jaemin, _____ _____?

M I just got some _____ _____.

W Bad news? What is it?

M One of my classmates was in a _____
_____.

W Oh, really? I'm so sorry.

M I think I have to go to the _____ right now.

05

M May I help you?

W I'd like to buy a gift for my _____
_____ _____.

M How about this toy car? This toy car is the
_____ _____ _____ in our shop.

W Really? What about this dinosaur _____
_____?

M Kids like that _____ _____, too.

W Okay. I'll take _____ of them.

06

W May I help you?

M Yes. I'm _____ _____ a present for
my _____. Can you _____ me one?

W Okay. Girls like to have _____, _____,
_____, or face lotion.

M Well, can you show me a ring?

W Sure. Which one do you like? The _____
shaped or the _____ shaped one?

M The heart _____ one, please.

07

[Beep]

W Hi, Jerry. This is Alice. I'm so sorry to

_____ _____ _____. I'm afraid

I _____ _____ to your _____

_____ tonight. My mom is _____.

I think I have to be with her. I hope you

_____. See you tomorrow _____

_____.

08

M Do we have _____ _____ _____

in the refrigerator?

W I don't think so. Why? Are you _____?

M Yes, I'm _____ because I didn't have

_____.

W Hmm… Let's _____ _____ to eat.

What do you want to eat?

M I want some Italian food. _____

_____ some _____?

W That sounds good.

09

W Did you _____ your _____, sweetie?

M No, not yet.

W Please _____ _____ computer games

and do your _____ now.

M If I _____ it by eight _____, can I play

computer games again?

W Yes, you can.

10

M Hi, Jessica. How was your _____

_____?

W It was great. I watched _____ _____,

read some _____ books, and also

_____ at the _____.

M Didn't you _____ your _____?

W Yes, I did. I _____ _____ with her. I

will _____ her _____ next month.

M I'm happy to hear that.

11

W Sam, do you know _____ _____

_____ a song?

M Yes, that's easy.

W Then, can you show me _____ _____

_____ it?

M Sure. _____ _____ do you want to

download?

W I want *Heal the World* by Michael Jackson.

12

W Did you _____ a book?

M Not yet. I don't know _____ book

_____ _____.

W It's not easy to select suitable _____

_____ _____.

M I want to try *the Harry Potter* series.

W Okay then, read the first chapter without

_____ a _____ and see if it is okay.

M Good idea. Thanks for your _____.

13

M Do you want to _____ _____ with

me?

W _____, what do you want to buy?

M _____ _____. I just want to look

around.

W Then, _____ _____ go home and _____ some _____ .

M Why? Didn't you sleep well _____ _____?

W No, I didn't. I stayed up _____ _____ playing online games.

14

W Tom, I lost my _____ . What should I do?

M Oh, I'm sorry to hear that. How about making a _____? I'll help you.

M [Pause] What's its _____?

W It's Ahji.

M _____ _____ is it?

W Just _____ _____ old.

M _____ does it _____ _____?

W It has a _____, _____ _____ and a big _____ _____ on its left ear.

M Good. What's your _____ _____?

W My number is _____ .

15

[Telephone rings.]

M Hi, Liz. It's me, Peter. I'm _____ _____ _____ near your house. Would you like to come out?

W Hi, Peter. Sure.

M Why don't you come here _____ _____ _____? I'm here with mine.

W Oh, that's one of your _____ _____, right? I can't wait to see him.

M I think they could be _____ _____ like us.

W They will. I'll be there _____ five _____ .

16

① M _____ me the salt, _____ .

W _____ you are.

② M _____ I take your coat?

W My _____ .

③ M _____ I speak to Jennie?

W This is _____ .

④ M What's _____?

W Not much.

⑤ M _____ bag is this?

W I guess it's Tom's.

17

W Good evening, shoppers! Thank you for shopping at CYJ Mart. For the _____ ten _____, bananas are on sale at 50% _____ . A bunch of bananas is _____ dollars. For _____ minutes, buy _____ _____ _____ bananas, and _____ another _____ . Hurry! Get your _____ now! Enjoy _____ .

18

W Sue is not very good at _____ . She had a singing _____ today. She _____ a lot for the test. She was so _____ that she made a _____ . One of her classmates, Wendy _____ _____ of her about the mistake. Sue felt very _____ . In this situation, what would you say to Sue?

19

M　My team _____ the _____ because of me.

W　_____ do you think so?

M　I sprained my _____ yesterday, so I couldn't _____ _____ enough.

W　Don't worry. It's not _____ _____ you. I know you did _____ _____.

M　Do you really think _____?

W　Of course. It's okay.

20

M　Susan, _____ do you think of this _____?

W　I think it is really _____. _____ painted it?

M　Van Gogh _____ it.

W　Oh, did he? I didn't know that.

M　_____ do you think of Van Gogh?

W　I think he is one the greatest artists ever.

Listening **T**est

01 다음을 듣고, 각 그림의 상황과 일치하지 <u>않는</u> 것을 고르시오.

① 　② 　③ 　④ 　⑤

02 대화를 듣고, 남자가 사려는 강아지를 고르시오.

① 　② 　③ 　④ 　⑤

03 다음을 듣고, 남자가 메시지를 남긴 목적으로 가장 적절한 것을 고르시오.

① 약속 시간을 정하려고　　　② 도서관에 함께 가려고
③ 약속을 미루려고　　　　　④ 학교에 같이 가려고
⑤ 약속 장소를 변경하려고

04 대화를 듣고, 두 사람의 심정으로 가장 적절한 것을 고르시오.

① worried　　　② satisfied　　　③ bored
④ lonely　　　⑤ proud

05 대화를 듣고, 두 사람이 대화하는 장소로 가장 적절한 것을 고르시오.

① bank　　　② department store　　　③ toy shop
④ library　　　⑤ church

06 대화를 듣고, 여자가 일주일에 몇 번 헬스클럽에 가는지를 고르시오.

① 1번   ② 2번   ③ 3번   ④ 5번   ⑤ 7번

07 대화를 듣고, 여자가 구입할 치마로 가장 적절한 것을 고르시오.

①    ②   ③   ④   ⑤

08 대화를 듣고, 남자가 겨울 방학 동안 한 일이 <u>아닌</u> 것을 고르시오.

① 봉사 활동 하기   ② 이모 댁 방문   ③ 스키 타기
④ 눈사람 만들기   ⑤ 눈싸움하기

09 대화를 듣고, 두 사람의 관계로 가장 적절한 것을 고르시오.

① 은행원 — 고객   ② 의사 — 환자   ③ 점원 — 손님
④ 사장 — 직원   ⑤ 교사 — 학생

10 대화를 듣고, 여자가 주말에 한 일로 가장 적절한 것을 고르시오.

① TV 보기   ② 방 청소하기   ③ 쇼핑하기
④ 시험공부하기   ⑤ 가방 수리하기

11 대화를 듣고, 여자가 남자에게 부탁한 일로 가장 적절한 것을 고르시오.

① 돈 빌려 주기 ② 엄마에게 전화해 주기
③ 휴대 전화 찾아 주기 ④ 휴대 전화 빌려 주기
⑤ 휴대 전화 충전하기

12 대화를 듣고, 여자가 남자에게 해 준 충고로 가장 적절한 것을 고르시오.

① 경찰서에 신고해라. ② 분실물 센터에 가 봐라.
③ 새것으로 구입해라. ④ 중고로 하나 구입해라.
⑤ 종이 책으로 읽어라.

13 대화를 듣고, 남자가 화가 난 이유로 가장 적절한 것을 고르시오.

① 주문한 수량보다 적게 배송되어서 ② 배송이 지연되어서
③ 주문한 물건과 배송된 물건이 달라서 ④ 결재된 금액이 달라서
⑤ 파손된 물건이 배송되어서

14 다음을 듣고, 그래프의 내용과 일치하지 <u>않는</u> 것을 고르시오.

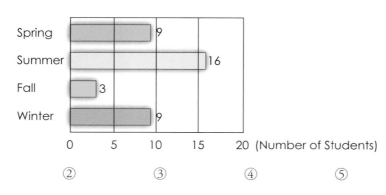

Favorite Season

① ② ③ ④ ⑤

15 대화를 듣고, 남자가 할 일로 가장 적절한 것을 고르시오.

① 재료 점검하기 ② 재료 다듬기 ③ 미트볼 만들기
④ 스파게티면 삶기 ⑤ 식료품 가게 가기

16 다음을 듣고, 두 사람의 대화가 <u>어색한</u> 것을 고르시오.

①   ②   ③   ④   ⑤

17 다음을 듣고, 내용과 일치하지 <u>않는</u> 것을 고르시오.

① 비행기 탑승 요청 방송이다.
② 탑승해야 할 승객은 2명이다.
③ 탑승해야 할 비행기는 런던행 OZ821편이다.
④ 탑승구는 6번 게이트이다.
⑤ 5분 내로 항공기 문이 닫힐 것이다.

18 다음을 듣고, Tom이 Jane에게 할 말로 가장 적절한 것을 고르시오.

① Stop asking me.
② You're welcome.
③ I don't think I can.
④ I need to practice more.
⑤ Remember, practice makes perfect.

[19-20] 대화를 듣고, 남자의 마지막 말에 이어질 여자의 응답으로 가장 적절한 것을 고르시오.

19 ① Don't be late.
② Sounds wonderful.
③ How about at 3:30 p.m.?
④ Let's meet in front of school.
⑤ Where do you want to meet?

20 ① I don't like a puppy.
② He likes to catch a ball.
③ Don't be afraid. It won't bite you.
④ Let's take him to the animal doctor.
⑤ I walked my dog in the park this morning.

● 다음은 **Listening Test 06**의 주요 지문입니다. 녹음을 다시 듣고, 질문에 대한 답을 완성하세요.

Q2

1 What is the man doing?

↳ He is _____ .

Q4

2 What does the man's and woman's son do these days?

↳ He _____ .

Q6

3 When does the woman go to the health club?

↳ She goes there every _____, _____, and _____ .

Q8

4 Where did the man go during his winter vacation?

↳ He went to _____ .

Q11

5 Why does the woman want to borrow the man's mobile phone?

↳ The reason is that _____ .

Q12

6 Where did the man think he lost his e-book reader?

↳ He thought _____ .

Q15

7 What does the man have to buy at the grocery store?

↳ He will buy _____ and _____ .

Q20

8 Why is the man worried about his puppy, Snoopy?

↳ The reason is that _____ .

자신의 상황에 맞게 내용을 완성하고 말해 보세요.

 A What did you do last weekend? Complete the sentences by referring to the examples in the table below.

(1) When	(2) What	(3) With whom	(4) Where	(5) Feelings
Saturday Sunday	watched a movie read a book rode my bike took a rest studied (subject) did my homework went shopping	with my friend(s) with my parents/ family with my brother/ sister alone	at a movie theater at home at my friend's house at the mall in the park in the library	great fun enjoyable exciting tiring boring relaxing

I am going to talk about what I did over the weekend. On (1)_____,

I (2)_____ (3)_____ (4)_____.

It was very (5)_____. On (1)_____, I (2)_____

(3)_____ (4)_____. It was very (5)_____.

Overall, I had a(n) (5)_____ weekend.

B Which season do you like the most? Fill in the table below and tell your classmates about it.

(1) My favorite season	(2) Reasons
	①
	②

My favorite season is (1)_____. The main reason I like (1)_____

is that I ①_____. Another reason is that I ②_____

_____. Every other season, I hope I (1)_____ comes again

soon.

01

① W A boy is playing a _____ _____.

② W A girl is _____ in the park.

③ W A boy is _____ his _____.

④ W A girl is _____ the _____.

⑤ W A girl is listening to music _____

_____.

02

W What are you doing?

M I'm _____ _____ the puppies. I'd like to buy one.

W I see. Which one do you like, the _____ one or the _____ one? Some of them are _____ _____ _____ while others are wearing a _____.

M Well. I will take the brown one with the _____ and the ribbon.

W Okay. Let's go in.

03

[Beep]

M Hello, Mary. This is Mark. Do you _____ that we _____ _____ meet tomorrow? We _____ _____ _____ meet at the public library but I'd like to _____ the _____ _____. I think it is too _____ _____ _____ both of us. Why don't we meet _____ _____ ? Please call me back _____ _____ _____ _____.

04

W Honey, I want to _____ _____ our son, Jake.

M Sure. Is there _____ _____?

W As you know, he used to study well and _____ _____.

M You _____ he's changed?

W Yes. _____ he plays _____ _____ all the time. He doesn't do what he _____ _____ _____.

M I will talk to him.

05

M Can I help you?

W Yes, please. I'm _____ _____ a present for my _____ _____.

M How about this _____? Your dad might _____ it.

W Well. I _____ this shirt. _____ _____ is it?

M It's $5 _____ _____ _____ the tie.

W Okay. I'll take it.

06

M You look really good, Amy.

W I started _____ _____ at the _____ _____.

M That sounds good.

W Why don't you go with me? It will help you to _____ _____.

M I will _____ _____ it. _____

_____ do you go?

W I go only _____ _____. I mean every
Monday, Wednesday, and _____.

07

M May I help you?

W Yes. I'm _____ _____ a skirt.

M Would you _____ a _____, a
_____ length or a _____ skirt?

W I want a short skirt.

M Then, how about this one with _____ and
_____ _____?

W I like the solid one. Oh, the white one with the
_____ _____ is _____. I will
_____ it.

08

W How was your _____ _____?

M It was _____. I visited my aunt's house
_____ _____ _____.

W Wow! What did you do there?

M I _____ _____. I also made a
_____ and had a _____ _____.

W It sounds like you really had a _____
_____.

09

W How may I help you?

M I heard you have a _____ _____ every
Wednesday.

W You mean our _____ Combo? We offer
_____ _____ of fried chicken and a
_____ for 3 dollars.

M Great. I'll _____ one.

W Okay.

10

M How was your _____?

W It was not bad. It was _____ _____.

M What did you do?

W I went to the _____ _____. I bought a
_____ and a _____. How about you?

M I _____ _____ and _____
_____ our test.

W Poor you!

11

W Tom, can you _____ me a _____?

M Sure. _____ can I do for you?

W Can I _____ your mobile phone, please?
I need to _____ my mom _____
_____.

M What's the _____ with your mobile?

W Its _____ is _____.

M Here you are.

12

W Hey, Tom. _____ _____?

M I can't find my _____ _____. I think I
_____ it.

W Oh, no. _____ did you _____ it?

M I think I _____ it on the _____.

W Then, why don't you _____ the Lost and
Found at the _____ _____?

M Okay, I will.

13

W ABC Mall _____ _____. How may I help you?

M I'm so upset that the item you sent me is not _____ _____ _____.

W Let me check. You _____ a 32 gigabyte USB _____ _____. What have you _____?

M I got a _____ gigabyte USB memory stick.

14

① M 6 more students like _____ more than _____.

② M Students' most favorite season is _____.

③ M The number of students who like _____ and _____ is the _____.

④ M More students like _____ more than _____.

⑤ M There are _____ students who like _____.

15

M Mom, what's for _____ today?

W Well, do you have anything special _____ _____?

M I'd like to have _____ _____ with meat balls.

W Okay. I'll make it for you. Let me check _____ _____ _____ first.

M [Pause] What do we need to buy? I'll go to the _____ store to get it.

W We need _____ _____ and _____.

16

① M I have a _____, Dr. Smith.

W Let me see.

② M Shall we _____ _____ after school?

W Sounds great.

③ M Where is the _____?

W It's _____ _____.

④ M Can you make it _____ _____?

W Yes, I can make _____ very well.

⑤ M Will you go to the _____ _____ with me?

W Sure, I'd love to.

17

W This is the _____ _____ _____ for passengers Tom and Jennie Smith booked on _____ OZ821 to _____. Please proceed to _____ _____ immediately. The _____ _____ are being completed and the _____ will _____ the _____ of the aircraft to be _____ _____ _____ five minutes. I repeat. This is the _____ _____ _____ for Tom and Jennie Smith. Thank you.

18

M Mid-term _____ will start next week. Jane is worried about her _____ _____ because she is not good at math. She asks Tom to give her some _____. Tom was in the _____ _____ as her last year but he is not worried about his grade _____. He tells her to _____ _____ _____ every day. However, she is _____ _____

about his advice. In this situation, what would
Tom to say to Jane?

19

M What are you going to do after school

    _____ _____?

W I'm going to the _____. Why?

M I have _____ _____ for the

    _____. I'd like to go with you.

W Sounds great.

M _____ _____ shall we meet?

W How about at 3: 30 p.m.?

20

M Jennie, I'm really _____ about _____

    _____, Snoopy.

W What's the _____ with him?

M I don't know. He's not _____ or _____.

W From _____?

M I don't think he's _____ anything since

    _____ _____.

W Let's take him to the animal doctor.

01 다음을 듣고, 그림의 상황과 일치하는 것을 고르시오.

①   ②   ③   ④   ⑤

02 대화를 듣고, 내용과 관련 있는 표지판으로 가장 적절한 것을 고르시오.

①   ②   ③   ④   ⑤

03 대화를 듣고, 두 사람이 만나기로 한 시각을 고르시오.

① 3:30 p.m.   ② 4:00 p.m.   ③ 4:30 p.m.
④ 5:00 p.m.   ⑤ 5:30 p.m.

04 대화를 듣고, 두 사람의 심정으로 가장 적절한 것을 고르시오.

① excited   ② scared   ③ proud
④ worried   ⑤ disappointed

05 대화를 듣고, 두 사람이 대화하는 장소로 가장 적절한 것을 고르시오.

① drugstore   ② hospital   ③ library
④ school   ⑤ bank

06 대화를 듣고, 서점의 위치로 가장 적절한 것을 고르시오.

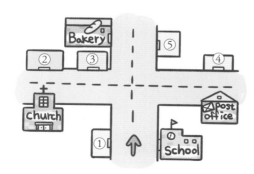

07 다음을 듣고, 남자가 전화를 건 목적으로 가장 적절한 것을 고르시오.

① 생일 파티 시간을 물어보려고
② 숙제를 도와 달라고 부탁하려고
③ 생일 파티에 대해 이야기하려고
④ 약속 장소를 변경하려고
⑤ 선물을 같이 사러 가자고 말하려고

08 대화를 듣고, 여자가 주말에 할 일로 가장 적절한 것을 고르시오.

① 영화 보기
② 등산 가기
③ 양로원 방문하기
④ 컴퓨터 게임하기
⑤ 조부모님 댁 가기

09 대화를 듣고, 두 사람의 관계로 가장 적절한 것을 고르시오.

① 요리사 — 손님
② 사장 — 종업원
③ 교사 — 학생
④ 남편 — 아내
⑤ 아빠 — 딸

10 대화를 듣고, 대화를 마친 후 두 사람이 할 일을 고르시오.

① 음악 감상
② 온라인 게임
③ 온라인 쇼핑
④ 콘서트 표 예매
⑤ 콘서트 관람

11 대화를 듣고, 남자가 여자에게 부탁한 일로 가장 적절한 것을 고르시오.

① 아침 일찍 깨워 주기　　　　② 비행기 표 예매하기
③ 공항까지 태워 주기　　　　④ 자명종 시계 맞추기
⑤ 공항 마중 나가기

12 대화를 듣고, 여자가 남자에게 해 준 충고로 가장 적절한 것을 고르시오.

① 일찍 출발해라.　　　　② 일기 예보를 확인해라.
③ 옷을 두껍게 입어라.　　　　④ 봉사 활동에 빠지지 마라.
⑤ 우비와 장화를 착용해라.

13 대화를 듣고, 대화의 내용과 일치하지 <u>않는</u> 것을 고르시오.

① 남자는 새 여행용 가방이 필요하다.
② 남자의 가방은 지퍼가 고장 났다.
③ 두 사람은 가방 가게에 있다.
④ 남자는 가볍고 튼튼한 가방을 좋아한다.
⑤ 여자는 남자가 사려는 가방이 비싸다고 생각한다.

14 다음을 듣고, 표의 내용과 일치하지 <u>않는</u> 것을 고르시오.

Tom's Weekly Activity Plan						
Sun	Mon	Tue	Wed	Thu	Fri	Sat
—	soccer	soccer	basketball	soccer	basketball	baseball
①	②	③	④		⑤	

15 대화를 듣고, 두 사람이 저녁 식사 후 할 일로 가장 적절한 것을 고르시오.

① 설거지하기　　　　② 쇼핑하기　　　　③ 공원 산책하기
④ 영화 보기　　　　⑤ 불꽃놀이 보기

16 다음을 듣고, 두 사람의 대화가 <u>어색한</u> 것을 고르시오.

①   ②   ③   ④   ⑤

17 다음을 듣고, 내용과 일치하지 <u>않는</u> 것을 고르시오.

① 바나나를 여러 조각으로 자른다.
② 바나나 조각과 블루베리를 얼린다.
③ 얼린 바나나와 블루베리를 믹서기에 넣는다.
④ 찬물을 넣는다.
⑤ 부드러워질 때까지 섞는다.

18 다음을 듣고, Tom이 점원에게 할 말로 가장 적절한 것을 고르시오.

① What's up?
② This is for you.
③ May I help you?
④ What did you do to me?
⑤ Would you recommend something for me?

[19-20] 대화를 듣고, 남자의 마지막 말에 이어질 여자의 응답으로 가장 적절한 것을 고르시오.

19
① Will you join us?
② Let's go look together.
③ Wow, you have a great idea.
④ I can't believe it. I envy you.
⑤ Don't worry. It's my pleasure.

20
① Okay. I'll give it a try.
② I'll leave Hawaii in three days.
③ How long did you stay there?
④ You should bring your passport.
⑤ Please send me some pictures of yourself.

● 다음은 **Listening Test 07**의 주요 지문입니다. 녹음을 다시 듣고, 질문에 대한 답을 완성하세요.

Q2

1 What happens to the roads when it rains or snows?

↳ They become _____ and _____.

Q5

2 Where did the boy go before going to the class?

↳ He went to _____.

Q7

3 What time will the party start?

↳ It will start at _____.

Q9

4 What is Rosa doing?

↳ She is _____.

Q11

5 Why does the boy want to get up so early tomorrow?

↳ The reason is that _____.

Q12

6 Why does the man have to go out now?

↳ The reason is that _____.

Q13

7 Why does the man like the bag?

↳ The reason is that _____.

Q15

8 What are the woman and the man supposed to do tonight?

↳ They are supposed to _____.

자신의 상황에 맞게 내용을 완성하고 말해 보세요.

What kinds of movies do you like and dislike? Complete the sentences by using the information in the table below.

(1) What	(2) Why	(3) How often	(4) Where / With whom
romance / horror / action / animation / science fiction / fantasy / comedy	fun / exciting / thrilling / touching / scary / boring / cruel / violent	every week once/twice/three times a month rarely (almost) never	at the movie theater at home with my friend(s) with my family alone

My favorite kind of movie is (1)_____. The reason why I like

(1)_____ movies is that they are (2)_____.

I usually watch them (3)_____. On the other hand, I don't like

(1)_____ movies. I don't like (1)_____ movies because they

are (2)_____. I (3)_____ watch them.

I like to watch movies (4)_____ (4)_____.

I hope I can watch one soon.

What food can you make? Fill in the table below and tell your classmates how to make it.

How to Make _____	
(1) Name of the food	
(2) Ingredients	
(3) How to make it	① ② ③ ④

I'd like to tell you how to make (1)_____. To make (1)_____,

you need (2)_____. First, ①_____

_____. Next, ②_____

_____. Then, ③_____. Finally,

④_____. Enjoy it! It is easy to make but very tasty.

01

① W A girl is _____ _____ in front of a _____ _____ to buy a ticket.

② W The man _____ the ticket booth is _____ _____.

③ W People are standing in _____ _____.

④ W The woman with a _____ has long _____ hair.

⑤ W A man and a woman are _____ hands.

02

M _____ _____ _____?

W Yes, I am.

M You have to _____ _____ _____ when it rains or _____. The roads become _____ and _____.

W You're right. That's why there is a _____ _____ of the danger.

M Let's _____ _____.

03

W Do you remember our _____ planned _____ _____?

M Of course. We are going to _____ _____ _____.

W Right. The play _____ at 4:30 p.m. _____ shall we meet?

M How about _____ _____ _____ the play starts?

W That sounds good. _____ _____ _____.

04

W The movie is _____ _____. Shall we _____ _____?

M Sure. _____ _____ our seats.

W They are C1 and C2.

M Good! I can't wait to see the _____.

W Me too. I heard this movie is _____ _____ 1 in _____ _____.

05

W You are late again. _____ _____ _____ you?

M I had a _____ _____, so I went to a _____ before _____ _____ class.

W Why didn't you call me?

M I thought I would be able to _____ _____ _____. I'm so sorry.

W Okay. _____ and _____ _____ _____.

06

W Can you tell me how I can get to the _____?

M Sure. _____ _____ for one block. It is _____ _____ _____ _____ the next block.

W You mean just go straight?

M Yes. It's on your _____, _____ _____ the _____.

W Thank you very much.

07

[Beep]

M Hey, Kate. This is Michael. Tomorrow is
Peter's _____, so we are _____ to
have a birthday party for him. If you want to
_____ us, please _____ _____
_____. You can come to Peter's house
_____ _____ _____. It's a
surprise party, so _____ _____ him.
Bye.

08

M What are you going to do _____
_____?

W I'm planning to _____ my _____.

M _____ do they _____?

W They live in New Jersey.

M I see. _____ _____ _____
_____ with them.

09

M I'm home. _____ Rosa?

W She's in her room _____ _____
_____.

M I'm hungry. Is _____ _____?

W Yes. It's on the _____.

M I will call Rosa. Let's have dinner all _____.

10

M I'm going to _____ _____ _____
on Saturday. _____ _____ _____
_____ come with me?

W Wow! I'd love to, but I don't have a ticket.

M _____ _____. I think tickets are
_____ _____. We can buy one
_____.

W Then, _____ _____ _____
right now. I will _____ _____ my
computer.

M Good.

11

M Mom, I need to ask you to do me a _____.

W Sure, what is it?

M Would you mind _____ me _____ at
5 a.m. tomorrow?

W No problem. Why do you want to _____
_____ so early? It's _____ tomorrow.

M I have to go to the _____ to _____ my
friend _____.

W Oh, I see.

12

M What's it _____ _____?

W It's _____ pretty hard and it's _____
today.

M I think _____ makes me _____. Oh, I
should leave now.

W Why don't you stay _____ today?

M Sorry, Mom. I don't want to miss my _____
_____.

W Then, you'd better wear your _____ and
_____ _____.

13

M I need a new _____ _____.

W   Why?

M   The _____ on my old one is _____.

W   Oh, there are a lot of _____ over there.

M   [Pause] I like this one. It's _____ and it looks _____.

W   I think the price is _____, too.

14

① M   Tom doesn't do any activities on _____.

② M   Tom _____ plays basketball on _____.

③ M   Tom plays baseball _____ a week.

④ M   Tom plays basketball _____ a week.

⑤ M   Tom plays soccer _____ _____ a week.

15

M   Oh, it was a _____ _____, wasn't it?

W   Yes, it was. I _____ because all the dishes were so _____.

M   _____ _____ I.

W   Let's watch a movie.

M   Did you forget? We are supposed to go to _____ _____ at Yeouido tonight.

W   Oh, I forgot. We'd better _____ _____. Shall we take the _____?

16

① M   Do you _____ _____ the _____?

W   Yes, of course. Go ahead.

② M   _____ _____ do you meet her?

W   _____ _____ a week.

③ M   _____ do you _____ that express train?

W   We _____ it the _____.

④ M   I'm really _____.

W   What's about?

⑤ M   Do you want some more _____ _____?

W   Yes, please.

17

W   I'd like to show you _____ _____ _____ a blueberry-banana smoothie. First, _____ a banana into pieces. Then, _____ the pieces and 3 tablespoons of blueberries for about 2 hours. After that _____ the _____ banana _____ and blueberries into a _____ and _____ a small pack of cold milk. _____ until smooth. That's really _____, isn't it? It's _____ for a _____.

18

M   _____ _____ is coming. Tom wants to buy _____ for his mom and dad. He _____ _____ a department store. He _____ _____ for an hour but he has _____ _____. A _____ is coming _____ him. In this situation, what would Tom say to the clerk?

19

M   You know _____? I had an _____ day

yesterday!

W What _____ ?

M Do you know the _____, PSY?

W Of course, I know him. He is a _____

_____ now.

M Last night, he was _____ _____ the

next table at a cafe. I took a _____ with

him. He _____ me his _____. Look!

W I can't believe it. I envy you.

20

M What are you planning to do _____ the

_____ ?

W I am planning to _____ _____.

M _____ are you going?

W I _____ decided yet. What do you

_____ _____ Hawaii?

M I _____ that Hawaii is very beautiful.

W Okay. I'll give it a try.

01 대화를 듣고, 두 사람이 이야기하고 있는 소년을 고르시오.

①  ②  ③  ④  ⑤

02 대화를 듣고, 여자가 찾고 있는 가방으로 가장 적절한 것을 고르시오.

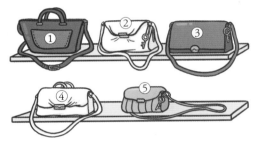

03 대화를 듣고, 남자가 받을 거스름돈으로 가장 적절한 것을 고르시오.

① $4　　　② $4.50　　　③ $5.50　　　④ $7.50　　　⑤ $10

04 대화를 듣고, 남자의 심정으로 가장 적절한 것을 고르시오.

① 외로움　　　　　② 기쁨　　　　　③ 속상함
④ 만족함　　　　　⑤ 지루함

05 대화를 듣고, 두 사람이 대화하는 장소로 가장 적절한 것을 고르시오.

① hospital　　　　② bank　　　　③ classroom
④ police station　　⑤ gym

06 대화를 듣고, 두 사람이 방과 후에 갈 곳을 고르시오.

① 병원   ② 도서관   ③ 공원   ④ 양로원   ⑤ 고아원

07 대화를 듣고, 여자가 전화를 건 목적으로 가장 적절한 것을 고르시오.

① 예약을 확인하려고   ② 식당을 예약하려고
③ 식당 위치를 물어보려고   ④ 예약 시간을 변경하려고
⑤ 인원수를 변경하려고

08 대화를 듣고, 대화를 마친 후 두 사람이 할 일로 가장 적절한 것을 고르시오.

① 친구 집 가기   ② 생일 선물 사러 가기
③ 친구에게 선물 주기   ④ 집에 가기
⑤ 생일 파티 가기

09 대화를 듣고, 두 사람의 관계로 가장 적절한 것을 고르시오.

① 조종사 — 승무원   ② 승객 — 승객   ③ 점원 — 손님
④ 교사 — 학생   ⑤ 은행원 — 고객

10 다음을 듣고, 남자가 언급하지 <u>않은</u> 것을 고르시오.

① 이름   ② 나이   ③ 고향
④ 가족 수   ⑤ 장래 희망

11 대화를 듣고, 여자가 남자에게 부탁한 일로 가장 적절한 것을 고르시오.

① 자리 맡아 주기   ② 표 예매하기
③ 간식 사다 주기   ④ 돈 빌려 주기
⑤ 함께 식사하기

12 대화를 듣고, 여자가 남자에게 해 준 충고로 가장 적절한 것을 고르시오.

① 잠자기 1시간 전에는 전자 기기를 사용하지 마라.
② 잠자기 1시간 전에는 운동을 하지 마라.
③ 잠자기 전에 따뜻한 우유를 마셔라.
④ 평소보다 1시간 일찍 잠자리에 들어라.
⑤ 잠자기 전에 음악을 들어라.

13 대화를 듣고, 여자가 원하는 것으로 가장 적절한 것을 고르시오.

① 식료품 계산   ② 식료품 배달   ③ 식료품 교환
④ 식료품 반품   ⑤ 식료품 무게 측정

14 다음을 듣고, 메모의 내용과 일치하지 <u>않는</u> 것을 고르시오.

Jennie's Plan for her Trip

When	This Friday
Where	Jeju Island
How	By plane
Why	To visit her aunt
How long	2 nights and 3 days
Things to do	Have a pajama party with her cousins, ride a horse

①   ②   ③   ④   ⑤

15 대화를 듣고, 대화 직후에 남자가 할 일로 가장 적절한 것을 고르시오.

① 농구 하기   ② 심부름 하기   ③ 숙제 하기
④ 배구 하기   ⑤ 친구 만나기

16 다음을 듣고, 두 사람의 대화가 <u>어색한</u> 것을 고르시오.

①   ②   ③   ④   ⑤

17 다음을 듣고, 내용과 일치하지 <u>않는</u> 것을 고르시오.

① 두 사람은 오늘 밤 뮤지컬을 보기로 했다.

② 공연은 오후 6시에 시작한다.

③ Lyric 극장은 Darling Harbor에 위치해 있다.

④ 남자는 공연 3시간 전에 만나기를 원한다.

⑤ 남자는 여자의 전화를 기다릴 것이다.

18 다음을 듣고, Sam이 Gloria에게 할 말로 가장 적절한 것을 고르시오.

① It isn't that bad.

② It takes about 30 minutes.

③ How many does she have?

④ Can I borrow some money from you, please?

⑤ Do you have enough money to pay for them all?

[19-20] 대화를 듣고, 남자의 마지막 말에 이어질 여자의 응답으로 가장 적절한 것을 고르시오.

19
① I'm still hungry.

② Don't make me sad.

③ Don't worry. Everything is okay.

④ It tastes fantastic. You're a really good cook.

⑤ It sounds wonderful. You will be a good cook.

20
① That's too bad.

② What do you have in mind?

③ Her hair is so long and pretty.

④ Just shampoo my hair, please.

⑤ She has very short blond hair.

● 다음은 **Listening Test 08**의 주요 지문입니다. 녹음을 다시 듣고, 질문에 대한 답을 완성하세요.

Q1

1 What is the man's son wearing?

 ↳ He is wearing _____, _____, _____, and

 _____.

Q2

2 Describe the woman's bag. You have to write at least 3 things.

 ↳ Her bag is _____ with _____ that has

 _____.

Q3

3 What is the second step when you use the parking machine?

 ↳ The second step is _____.

Q7

4 What is the woman doing?

 ↳ She is _____.

Q11

5 What does the man want the woman to do?

 ↳ He wants her to _____.

Q15

6 What did the man want to do?

 ↳ He wanted to _____.

Q17

7 What are Jennie and Tom going to do tonight?

 ↳ They _____.

Q18

8 Why do Sam and Gloria need to buy a clear file folder?

 ↳ The reason is that _____.

자신의 상황에 맞게 내용을 완성하고 말해 보세요.

A What are you going to do after school? Fill in the table below and tell your classmates about it.

Things to Do after School	
(1) Where are you going to go?	
(2) What are you going to do there?	
(3) Why are you going to do that?	
(4) Who are you going to do that with?	
(5) How long will it take you to do that?	

I am going to talk about what I am going to do after school today. After school,
I am going to go (1)_____ and (2)_____. The
reason why I am going to do it is that (3)_____. I am
going to do that with (4)_____. I think it will take me (5)_____
to do that.

B Do you have any plans for a trip? Fill in the table below and tell your classmates about it.

Planning a Trip	
(1) Where are you going to go?	
(2) Who are you going there with?	
(3) When are you going there?	
(4) How are you going to get there?	
(5) What are you going to do there?	① ② ③
(6) How long are you going to stay there?	

I am going on a trip to (1)_____ with (2)_____ (3)_____.
I am going there (4)_____. I am going to ①_____
there. I am also going to ②_____ and ③_____
_____. I am going to stay there for (5)_____. I
hope to have a great time there.

01

W Which is your son?

M My son is _____ _____ _____ and _____.

W Is he wearing blue _____ with a _____ _____?

M No, he is wearing blue jeans with a _____ jacket.

W Oh, I see. He is _____.

02

M How may I help you?

W I'm _____ _____ my bag. I left it on the _____ this morning.

M I see. We've had _____ lost _____ today, so _____ _____ yours.

W It is a _____ _____ with a long _____.

M What _____ is it? We have _____, _____, and _____ bags.

W Mine is black with a _____ _____ _____.

03

W Do you need any help?

M Yes, I want to _____ my _____ _____, but I don't know how to use this _____ _____.

W First, press this _____. Then, _____ the _____ _____ into the parking machine.

M Okay. It says $5.50.

W Then, _____ five _____ and _____ _____ into the machine.

M Okay. But I only have a $10 _____.

04

W _____ _____?

M I had a _____ _____ _____.

W Why? What happened to you?

M I lost my _____ _____ while I was _____ _____ _____ in the park.

W That's too bad. _____ _____ _____ call your phone?

M I will.

05

M May I help you?

W Yes. I'd like to _____ _____ _____.

M You mean a _____ _____?

W Yes. What should I do?

M Please _____ me your identification card and _____ _____ this _____.

W Okay.

06

W What are you _____ _____ _____ after school?

M I have no plans. Why?

W Would you like to _____ _____ in doing _____ _____?

M Are you going to a _____ _____?

W No, we are going to an _____ this time.

M Okay. I will _____ you.

07

[Telephone rings.]

M Susan's Restaurant. _____ _____

_____ _____ _____?

W I'd like to _____ _____ _____

for dinner at 6:30 p.m.

M For _____ _____ people?

W _____ _____ and a 7-year-old

_____.

M I see. What's your family name, please?

W My _____ _____ is Kim.

08

M Did you buy a _____ _____

_____ Billy?

W Yes, I did. _____ _____ _____

one, too?

M _____ _____. I'm on my way to get

one now. _____ _____ _____

_____ me?

W Sure.

M _____ _____ to the store, then.

09

M Excuse me.

W Yes? Is there _____ _____?

M I _____ you are _____ in my seat.

W Oh, really? Let me _____ my seat number

on my _____ _____.

M Okay. Go ahead.

W Oh, I'm sorry. I'm in the _____ _____.

10

M Hello, _____. It's very _____

_____ _____ _____ _____.

My name is Brian Johnson and I'm 16 years old.

_____ _____ Seattle and I want to be

a _____ when I _____ _____.

I like this school and I want to make many

_____ _____ here.

11

W Tom, could you _____ my _____,

please? I'll be back soon.

M Sure. Oh, can I ask you a _____?

W What is it?

M When you come back, could you _____

some _____ for me?

W Okay. What do you want to have?

M _____ and _____, please. Here's some

_____.

12

W Hey, Eddie. What's wrong?

M Hi, Sue. I'm so _____. I _____

_____ very well these days.

W What do you usually do before going to bed?

M I _____ on my _____ and my friend's

blogs _____ _____.

W If you want to _____ well, you should not

use electronic devices _____ _____

_____ one hour before going to bed.

M Oh, I see. I'll try that.

13

M What can I do for you?

W I'd like to have these _____ _____.

M Could you _____ _____ this form, please?

W No problem. _____ _____ is it?

M It _____ on their _____. Let me check.

14

① Jennie will _____ _____ _____ on Jeju Island.

② Jennie will take an _____ to Jeju Island this _____.

③ Jennie wants to have a _____ _____ with her cousins.

④ Jennie also wants to ride a _____.

⑤ Jennie will be back on _____.

15

M Mom, can I _____ _____ and _____ _____ with Jake?

W Did you do your _____?

M Not yet. I will do it _____ playing _____. I'll be back in _____ _____.

W Sorry, Tom. Why don't you do your _____ with Jake first and then go out?

M Okay, I will.

16

① M Why don't we _____ _____ _____?

W Sounds great.

② M I wish you _____ _____.

W Thank you very much.

③ M Where are you from?

W I _____ _____ _____ Sydney, Australia.

④ M What do you _____ _____ *bulgogi*?

W I think it's _____ _____.

⑤ M I think she's beautiful.

W I don't _____.

17

[Beep]

M Hi, Jennie. This is Tom. I'm just _____ to _____ you that we're going to _____ the _____, *Mamma Mia* tonight. The musical _____ at 6 p.m. at the Lyric Theater in Darling Harbor. Why don't we _____ _____ 4 p.m. and have an _____ _____ nearby? Please _____ _____ _____ as soon as you get this _____.

18

M At the _____ _____, Gloria meets her classmate, Sam. They _____ _____ a clear file folder for their project. They have to collect _____ _____ in the file folder. Sam picks one up and pays for it. But Gloria picks up a file folder and several _____ _____ such as a _____, a _____, and a mug. They look _____. Sam is _____ about how much money she has. In this situation, what would Sam say to

Gloria?

19

M Hi, Jennie. Come on _____ .

W Hi, Tom. _____ were you doing?

M I was making _____ _____ sauce.

W I didn't know that you could make _____

_____ . It smells great. May I _____ it?

M Of course. Go ahead. _____ is it?

W It tastes fantastic. You're a really good cook.

20

M Hi, Jennie. You have had a _____ . I like

your new _____ _____ .

W Thank you.

M Where did you get your _____ ?

W I go to the Barbie Shop in The Rocks.

M I feel like _____ my hair style, too.

W What do you have in mind?

Listening Test

01 대화를 듣고, 내용과 일치하는 그림을 고르시오.

① ② ③ ④ ⑤

02 대화를 듣고, 여자가 마실 것으로 가장 적절한 것을 고르시오.

①  ② ③ ④ ⑤

03 대화를 듣고, 남자가 감량한 몸무게로 가장 적절한 것을 고르시오.

① 6kg   ② 7kg   ③ 8kg   ④ 9kg   ⑤ 10kg

04 대화를 듣고, 남자의 심정으로 가장 적절한 것을 고르시오.

① 기쁨   ② 슬픔   ③ 지루함
④ 감동함   ⑤ 미안함

05 대화를 듣고, 두 사람이 대화하는 장소로 가장 적절한 것을 고르시오.

① airport   ② subway station   ③ bus stop
④ movie theater   ⑤ taxi stand

06 대화를 듣고, 여자의 기분으로 가장 적절한 것을 고르시오.

①   ②   ③   ④   ⑤

07 대화를 듣고, 여자가 도서관에 가는 목적으로 가장 적절한 것을 고르시오.
① 책을 빌리려고   ② 학교를 안내하려고
③ 시험공부를 하려고   ④ 친구를 만나려고
⑤ 책을 반납하려고

08 대화를 듣고, 여자가 중요하게 생각하는 것을 고르시오.
① 건강   ② 협동   ③ 학업 성적
④ 솔선수범   ⑤ 우선순위

09 대화를 듣고, 남자의 직업으로 가장 적절한 것을 고르시오.
① flight attendant   ② tour guide   ③ teacher
④ cook   ⑤ hotel receptionist

10 대화를 듣고, 여자가 구입할 신발의 종류로 가장 적절한 것을 고르시오.
① 플랫슈즈   ② 샌들   ③ 운동화
④ 하이힐   ⑤ 장화

11 대화를 듣고, 여자가 남자에게 부탁한 것으로 가장 적절한 것을 고르시오.

① 체크아웃 시간 연장하기　　　　② 짐 보관해 주기
③ 시내 관광 시켜 주기　　　　　　④ 공항에 짐 부치기
⑤ 공원까지 태워 주기

12 대화를 듣고, 여자가 남자에게 제안한 것으로 가장 적절한 것을 고르시오.

① 친구와 함께 연습해라.　　　　　② 보조 바퀴를 달고 연습해라.
③ 매일 자전거를 타라.　　　　　　④ 균형 감각을 먼저 익혀라.
⑤ 작은 자전거를 구입해라.

13 대화를 듣고, 여자가 남자를 찾아온 이유로 가장 적절한 것을 고르시오.

① 비행기에 가방을 두고 내려서　　② 다른 사람과 가방이 바뀌어서
③ 가방이 파손되어서　　　　　　　④ 가방이 도착하지 않아서
⑤ 새 가방을 구입하려고

14 다음을 듣고, 초대장의 내용과 일치하지 <u>않는</u> 것을 고르시오.

Halloween Party Invitation

Date	Friday, October 31st
Time	5 p.m. – 8 p.m.
Place	the community center
Activities	1. A Halloween costume contest
	2. Making jack-o'-lanterns
	3. Going trick or treating

①　　　　　②　　　　　③　　　　　④　　　　　⑤

15 대화를 듣고, 대화를 마친 후 두 사람이 갈 곳으로 가장 적절한 것을 고르시오.

① 놀이공원　　　　　　② 공원　　　　　　③ 식당
④ 백화점　　　　　　　⑤ 영화관

16 다음을 듣고, 두 사람의 대화가 <u>어색한</u> 것을 고르시오.

①   ②   ③   ④   ⑤

17 다음을 듣고, 내용과 일치하지 <u>않는</u> 것을 고르시오.

① 코알라는 호주의 유명한 동물이다.
② 사람들이 '코알라 곰'이라고 부르지만 곰은 아니다.
③ 코알라는 유칼립투스 나뭇잎을 주식으로 먹는다.
④ 코알라는 하루에 12시간 정도 잔다.
⑤ 코알라는 대개 10년 정도 산다.

18 다음을 듣고, Bill이 Susan에게 할 말로 가장 적절한 것을 고르시오.

① I agree with you.
② I'm glad to hear that.
③ I'd like to have sweets.
④ I'm not happy with the food.
⑤ I really enjoyed all the dishes.

[19-20] 대화를 듣고, 남자의 마지막 말에 이어질 여자의 응답으로 가장 적절한 것을 고르시오.

19
① I think I'm lost.
② You can't miss it.
③ It's very kind of you.
④ It's about 10 miles from here.
⑤ It takes about fifteen minutes.

20
① Are you tired?
② No, it's on me, today.
③ It's good for your health.
④ What does she want to have?
⑤ Don't eat too much junk food.

● 다음은 **Listening Test 09**의 주요 지문입니다. 녹음을 다시 듣고, 질문에 대한 답을 완성하세요.

Q1

1 Why is the woman happy?

↳ The reason is that _____.

Q3

2 How much did the man weigh before going on a diet?

↳ He weighed _____.

Q7

3 Why did the girl say "Welcome to our school"?

↳ The reason is that _____.

Q10

4 What did the woman say about the sandals?

↳ She said they are _____.

Q11

5 Why does the man want to keep his luggage in the hotel after he checks out?

↳ The reason is that _____.

Q12

6 What does the man think of learning to ride a bike?

↳ He thinks _____.

Q18

7 Why did Bill and Susan choose the Thai restaurant?

↳ The reason is that _____.

Q20

8 What does the man do to be healthy?

↳ To be healthy, _____.

● 자신의 상황에 맞게 내용을 완성하고 말해 보세요.

A   What was your most memorable vacation? Fill in the table below and tell your classmates about it.

My Most Memorable Vacation	
(1) When was it?	
(2) Where did you go?	
(3) Who did you go there with?	
(4) What did you do?	
(5) How was it?	

My most memorable vacation happened (1)_____. I went to

(2)_____ with (3)_____. While I was there, I

(4)_____. It was very (5)_____. I hope

vacation comes soon so that I can go there again.

B   You are going to have a Halloween party. Fill in the blanks and tell your classmates about it.

Join US for a Halloween Party!

(1) Date: _____

(2) Time: _____

(3) Place: _____

(4) Activities: _____

_____

_____

We are going to have a Halloween party. It will be on (1)_____

at (2)_____. The party will be at (3)_____. There will be fun

activities like (4)_____

_____. It will be a great party.

Don't miss it!

01

M _____ _____ your _____

_____.

W Thank you very much.

M _____ _____ _____ _____?

W I still _____ _____ I won it. I'm very

_____.

M I hope you will _____ _____

_____ in your next competition.

W I'll _____ my _____.

02

W It's very hot _____. I'm _____.

M Would you like to _____ _____?

W Yes. I'd like to drink _____ _____.

No. I will have _____ _____

_____ chocolate milk.

M Okay. I will _____ it for you. I will have a

_____, I think.

W Actually, I'll just _____ _____. That

would be _____.

M Alright.

03

W _____ _____. Are you Tony?

M YES! Do I _____ that _____?

W Yes! I almost didn't _____ you.

M Nice to hear that. I really _____

_____ to lose weight during the

_____. My _____ was 85kg, and now

I _____ 79kg.

W Wow! You look like you've lost _____

_____ 10kg.

M Thanks.

04

W _____ _____? Why are you crying?

M I'm _____ _____ this movie. The

_____ _____ is very _____.

W Oh, come on. It's just a _____.

M I know. But I can't _____ _____

_____ _____ my eyes.

W I didn't know that you're such a _____

_____.

05

W How can I _____ _____ this

_____ _____?

M You can buy a ticket at the _____

_____ or you can _____ your

_____ _____ here.

W I see. By the way, this station is _____

_____ line number two and line

_____ _____. Which way should

_____ _____ if I'd like to _____

line number two?

M _____ _____ _____. Line

number two is green.

W Thank you.

06

M _____!

W Thank you very much. Without your _____,

I wouldn't be able to _____ _____ _____ as a school _____.

M You're welcome. _____ _____ _____ _____?

W I feel like I'm _____ _____ _____. I can't stop smiling.

M I can tell. Anyway, you _____ it.

07

M Oops! I'm sorry. Are you okay?

W Yes. Thank you for helping me to _____ _____ my books.

M It was my _____. _____ _____ _____, do you know where the _____ is?

W Yeah. I'm _____ _____ _____ there now to _____ these books.

M Good. I'll go with you. I'm a _____ _____ from Miami, so _____ is _____.

W _____ _____ our school.

08

W Where are you going?

M I'm going to _____ _____ with my friends.

W Did you _____ your _____?

M I'll finish it when I _____ _____.

W Oh, boy. You have to finish your homework _____, if not you _____ _____ _____. You should _____ the things you have to do according to _____, and finish them _____ _____ _____.

M Okay, Mom.

09

M _____ _____ _____ Korea! Do you have _____ _____ _____?

W I think I'm fine.

M Good. Let me tell you _____ _____. We will go to _____ _____ now to _____ _____. After that I will take you to a _____ _____. Then we will have Korean food _____ _____. Lastly, we will come back to the hotel.

W _____ _____.

M Shall we _____ _____ _____?

W Sure.

10

W Are these _____ _____?

M Yes. There's 50% _____ _____ sandals, 35% off _____ _____ _____, 25% off on _____, and 10% off on _____.

W I see. Can I try these sandals _____ _____ _____?

M Sure. Here you are.

W [Pause] Thank you. They are _____ _____ and _____. I will take them.

11

W Excuse me, but can I _____ you a _____?

M Sure. What can I do for you?

W After I _____ _____, could you _____ my luggage here in the hotel? I'd like to _____ _____ the city before I go to the _____.

M Sure. When are you coming back to _____

it _____?

W In about _____ _____ _____.

Thank you.

M My pleasure.

12

W It's a good day, isn't it?

M Yeah, it is.

W Let's go _____ _____ _____ the
Han Riverside Park!

M Sorry, I can't. It's _____ _____ for
me to learn _____ _____ _____
_____. I think I don't have any _____
_____ _____.

W Oh, I didn't know that. Why don't you
_____ _____ a bike with _____
_____ for about a month, and then
_____ _____ _____ _____
without them?

M Okay, I'll try.

13

W Excuse me. _____ of my _____ hasn't
arrived.

M Can I see your _____, please? [Pause]
Okay, so you were _____ _____
ZY123 from London?

W Yes, that's right.

M Can you give me a _____ of your bag?

W Yes, it is a _____ sized _____ bag
with a red ribbon _____ _____ the
handle.

14

① M The party will be at _____ p.m.
_____ _____, October 30th.

② M The party will be _____ for _____
hours.

③ M The party will _____ _____ at the
community center.

④ M There will be a Halloween _____
contest.

⑤ M People can _____ jack-o'-lanterns.

15

W Tom, are you _____ now?

M Yes. Why?

W Why don't we _____ a 4D _____ in
the CYJ Theater?

M What's a 4D movie?

W I heard that the _____ you sit on
_____ and you can even _____ the
_____ in the scene.

M Wow! That's _____. Let's go _____
now.

16

① M What _____?

W I'll have a party _____.

② M Can you help me with _____
_____?

W Sorry, but I can't.

③ M _____ me _____ _____ again.

W Okay, I will.

④ M _____ _____ shall we _____
it?

W How about _____ p.m.?

⑤ M _____ are you going to _____ this winter?

W I plan to learn _____ snowboard.

17

W Have you ever _____ _____ koalas? The koala is one of Australia's _____ animals. They have small bodies with _____ _____. Sometimes people call them '_____ _____' but they are not _____. They live in _____. They only eat eucalyptus _____. They spend about _____ _____ a day _____ in trees. They usually live about 10 _____.

18

M Bill and Susan like to visit _____ restaurants to _____ their food. Today they went to a Thai restaurant which was _____ by many reviewers. Susan said the food was great. However, Bill _____ _____ with her because all the _____ he tried was too _____, too _____ or too _____. In this situation, what would Bill say to Susan?

19

W Excuse me. Are you _____ _____ _____?

M Yes, I am. Do you need _____ _____?

W Yes, please. Would you _____ showing me _____ _____ _____ the Opera House?

M No, _____ _____ _____. It's about _____ _____ that way.

W It's very kind of you.

20

M I feel so _____ these days. To be _____, what should I do?

W Do you _____ regularly?

M No. But I'm trying not to use _____ and walk to _____.

W Good job! Just _____ _____ _____.

M Aren't you hungry? I'd like to have _____.

W Don't eat too much junk food.

01 대화를 듣고, 내일의 날씨로 가장 적절한 것을 고르시오.

① ② ③ ④ ⑤

02 대화를 듣고, 대화를 마친 후 남자가 갈 곳으로 가장 적절한 것을 고르시오.

① ② ③ ④ ⑤

03 대화를 듣고, 여자에게 추가로 필요한 금액으로 가장 적절한 것을 고르시오.

① $8　　　② $9　　　③ $10　　　④ $11　　　⑤ $12

04 대화를 듣고, 남자의 심정으로 가장 적절한 것을 고르시오.

① glad　　　　　② worried　　　　　③ surprised
④ jealous　　　　⑤ excited

05 대화를 듣고, 두 사람이 대화하는 장소로 가장 적절한 것을 고르시오.

① police station　　　② bank　　　③ fire station
④ post office　　　⑤ lost and found center

06 대화를 듣고, 두 사람이 가게 될 장소로 가장 적절한 것을 고르시오.

①   ②   ③   ④   ⑤

07 대화를 듣고, 여자가 약속을 지키지 <u>못하는</u> 이유로 가장 적절한 것을 고르시오.

① 남동생을 돌봐야 해서   ② 시험공부를 해야 해서
③ 엄마를 도와야 해서   ④ 급한 볼일이 생겨서
⑤ 병원에 가야 해서

08 대화를 듣고, 여자의 마지막 말의 의도로 가장 적절한 것을 고르시오.

① 조언   ② 거절   ③ 수락   ④ 제안   ⑤ 감사

09 대화를 듣고, 두 사람의 관계로 가장 적절한 것을 고르시오.

① classmate — classmate   ② mother — son
③ artist — reporter   ④ teacher — student
⑤ boss — worker

10 대화를 듣고, 남자가 구입할 과일을 고르시오.

① 바나나   ② 사과   ③ 배
④ 오렌지   ⑤ 감

11 대화를 듣고, 남자가 도서관에서 책을 빌리려는 이유로 가장 적절한 것을 고르시오.

① 과학 시험이 있어서   ② 과학 과제 주제를 선정하려고

③ 주말 동안 읽을 책이 필요해서   ④ 여자의 과제를 도우려고

⑤ 지구 온난화의 심각성을 알아보려고

12 대화를 듣고, 여자가 남자에게 해 준 조언으로 가장 적절한 것을 고르시오.

① 여행 계획 세우기   ② 사진 많이 찍기

③ 사진 액자 구입하기   ④ 전자 앨범 구입하기

⑤ 인터넷에 사진 올리기

13 대화를 듣고, 남자가 전화를 건 목적으로 가장 적절한 것을 고르시오.

① 가져갈 피자를 주문하려고   ② 피자를 배달시키려고

③ 주문을 취소하려고   ④ 주문을 추가하려고

⑤ 가격을 알아보려고

14 다음을 듣고, 그래프의 내용과 일치하지 <u>않는</u> 것을 고르시오.

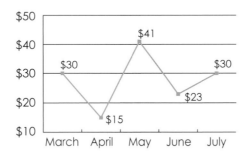

How Much Money Jim Spent Every Month

①   ②   ③   ④   ⑤

15 대화를 듣고, 대화를 마친 후 남자가 할 일로 가장 적절한 것을 고르시오.

① 자필 서명하기   ② 보안 카드 수령 하기

③ 비밀번호 등록하기   ④ 온라인뱅킹 신청하기

⑤ 신분증 가지러 가기

16 다음을 듣고, 두 사람의 대화가 <u>어색한</u> 것을 고르시오.

①   ②   ③   ④   ⑤

17 다음을 듣고, 자원봉사에 대해 언급되지 <u>않은</u> 것을 고르시오.

① 자원봉사는 어렵지 않다.
② 누구나 할 수 있지만 최소한 8살은 넘어야 한다.
③ 자원봉사는 당신과 다른 사람들에게 행복을 준다.
④ 자원봉사는 간단하고 작은 것일 수도 있다.
⑤ 양로원에서 노인들과 이야기하는 것도 자원봉사가 될 수 있다.

18 다음을 듣고, Peter가 Jenny에게 할 말로 가장 적절한 것을 고르시오.

① Let's have some ice cream.
② I'll go home and take a rest.
③ I think you should see a doctor.
④ Why don't you borrow this book?
⑤ If you study hard, you will get a good grade.

[19-20] 대화를 듣고, 남자의 마지막 말에 이어질 여자의 응답으로 가장 적절한 것을 고르시오.

19 ① No, I can't.
② Yes, I'm very exhausted.
③ I am good at taking photos.
④ Yes, I'm looking forward to it.
⑤ I don't like the long wait for rides.

20 ① It's on July 2nd.
② She's wearing a hat.
③ When is your birthday?
④ Okay. This one goes on the card.
⑤ Okay, here are two photos of my family.

● 다음은 Listening Test 10의 주요 지문입니다. 녹음을 다시 듣고, 질문에 대한 답을 완성하세요.

Q2 **1** Where is the man going now?

↳ He is on the way to _____.

Q5 **2** Why did the woman lose her bag?

↳ The reason is that _____.

Q7 **3** Why did the woman call the man?

↳ The reason is that she has to _____.

Q8 **4** When is the project due?

↳ It is due _____.

Q11 **5** What will the man and the woman do to collect some information on global warming?

↳ They will _____.

Q12 **6** What is the man going to do this weekend?

↳ He _____.

Q13 **7** What did the man order and how long will it take to be ready to pick it up?

↳ The man ordered _____ and it will take

_____.

Q20 **8** What does the woman want to do with her invitations for her birthday party?

↳ She wants _____.

● 자신의 상황에 맞게 내용을 완성하고 말해 보세요.

A Imagine you are a weather forecaster. Complete the sentences by using the information in the table below.

(1) Weather I	(2) Weather II	(3) Temperature (°C)	(4) Advice
warm / sunny / cool / cloudy / windy / foggy	hot / humid / cold / chilly / rainy / snowy	30 20 10 -5 -10	take an umbrella bring your jacket wear a hat wear sunglasses wear a heavy coat

Good morning. This is today's weather report. This morning, it is (1)_____

and (1)_____. The temperature is about (3)_____ degrees.

However, it will be (2)_____ and (2)_____ this afternoon. The

temperature will go (up/down) to (3)_____ degrees. So (4)_____

_____ if you're going out. The (2)_____, (2)_____

weather will continue till tonight. This is Amy Han, and this has been your daily

weather update. Thank you.

B How much is your monthly allowance? How do you spend it? Fill in the blanks and tell your classmates about it.

How I Spend My Monthly Allowance

(1) How much allowance do you get every month?	
(2) How do you usually spend it?	① _____ won: _____ ② _____ won: _____ ③ _____ won: _____
(3) How much do you save every month?	
(4) What do you want to do with the money you save?	

Every month, I get (1)_____ won for my allowance. I usually spend about

①_____won on _____, and about ②_____

won on _____. I also spend ③_____ won on

_____. I usually save (3)_____ won of my

allowance every month. I want to (4)_____ with the money.

10 Dictation Test

01

W It's _____. I don't like _____.

M I love winter, _____ when it _____.

W Oh, I heard _____ _____ _____ that it's going to snow _____.

M _____? I hope it snows _____ _____ so that I can _____ _____ _____.

W Sounds _____. I'll _____ you.

02

M Are you okay?

W Yes. I went to the _____ _____, so I'm okay now.

M Good. I'm on the way to the _____ to _____ this book.

W Didn't you say you are _____ _____ go to a _____ _____ today?

M I will go right after _____ this book.

W I see. I'll _____ _____ and _____ _____ _____.

03

W Oh, _____ _____ this dress. It's so _____.

M _____ _____ _____ _____ try it on?

W Let me _____ the _____ _____. [Pause] Hmm... I don't think I can buy it.

M _____?

W It is $57 but I only have $45. _____, I didn't _____ my _____ _____.

M I can _____ you some money if you _____.

04

W _____ _____ _____ your packing?

M _____. But I am wondering _____ I have to _____ an umbrella _____ _____.

W Why? Is it going to _____?

M According to the _____, yes. I hope it won't rain _____ the trip. If it rains, there won't be many things to _____.

W You're right. I hope the _____ _____ fine.

05

W [Urgency in voice] _____ _____ _____.

M _____ _____?

W A man _____ _____ _____. Please help me _____ my bag. There are many _____ _____ inside it.

M Okay. _____ _____. Did you see the _____? Do you remember _____ _____ _____?

W Well. He is _____ 175cm _____, and _____.

06

M Did you hear where we are _____

_____ _____ _____ _____?

W No, _____ _____. Where are we
  going?

M It's a secret. _____ _____?

W A _____? A _____? A _____?

M None of them. It's a place where we _____
  _____ a roller coaster.

W Really? Hooray! I will ride a _____
  _____ there.

07

[Telephone rings.]

W Hello. _____ _____ Junsu?

M Yes. Is this Jiseon?

W Yes. I'm calling to _____ _____
  but I'm going to have to _____ our
  appointment for _____. My parents can't
  come home early today, so I have to _____
  _____ _____ my _____
  _____.

M It's okay. I will just go to your home then. I'll
  play with your brother.

W Really? Thank you. He'll be _____
  _____ to see you.

08

W Are you done with your _____?

M Not yet. I haven't even _____ _____
  _____ yet.

W Oh, no. The project is _____ _____.
  You only have _____ _____
  _____.

M I know. If you have time now, could you help me
  with _____ _____ _____ and

_____ _____?

W Sure. Why not?

09

W _____, Tim. _____ _____ the
  _____ _____ _____ the final
  exam in my class.

M Really? I _____ _____ it. I'm so
  happy.

W I'm so _____ _____ you. I hope you
  will _____ _____ the good work.

M Thank you, ma'am. I made it _____
  _____ _____. I really appreciate
  _____ _____.

W Thanks for saying so.

10

W May I help you?

M I'd like to buy some _____ _____.

W All my fruit is fresh. What would you like?
  _____, _____, persimmons, oranges
  or _____?

M Which fruits are _____ _____ now?

W Apples and persimmons are in season.

M Okay. Then I will _____ _____
  persimmons. I like the _____ _____.

11

W Tom, I need your _____.

M What is it?

W Would you mind _____ me with my
  _____ _____?

M Of course not. What is the _____ about?

W It's about _____ _____.

M Wow, that's an interesting topic. Let's go to the _____ to borrow _____ _____ related to it.

12

W What are you going to do _____ _____?

M I'm going to make a _____ _____ of my trip to Europe.

W You must have _____ _____ _____, right?

M You're right. Actually a book is not enough.

W Why don't you buy an _____ _____ and put the pictures in it?

M That's a good idea. I might just do that.

13

[Telephone rings.]

W Hello. ABC Pizza. May I help you?

M Hi. I'd _____ _____ _____ a large BBQ chicken pizza.

W Would you like it _____?

M No. I'll _____ and _____ it _____.

W Okay. It'll be _____ _____ 15 minutes.

14

① W This graph _____ how much money Jim _____ every month.

② W Jim _____ $30 _____ in March and July.

③ W Jim only spent _____ _____ his allowance in April.

④ W Jim _____ the most money in May.

⑤ W Jim _____ 23 dollars in June.

15

W May I help you?

M I'd like to _____ _____ _____.

W Which would you _____, a checking account or a savings account?

M A _____ _____, please.

W Could you fill out _____ _____ and show me _____ _____, please?

M Oh, I _____ it _____ my office desk. I'll go _____ _____.

16

① M _____ _____ does it take to get there?

W It takes about _____ _____.

② M I can't believe it. I _____ _____ _____.

W Yes, I'm sure that you'll enjoy it.

③ M Would you like to _____ _____ _____?

W No, thank you. I'll call again.

④ M Can you _____ _____ _____ 3 o'clock?

W I'm afraid I can't. How about 4?

⑤ M How about _____ _____ tonight?

W Why not? I know a nice place.

17

M What do you think of _____ _____?

It's not hard. Everyone, even 8-year-old kids,

can do it. _____ _____ _____,

volunteering gives you and others _____. It

could be a _____, _____ _____.

For example, you can talk with _____

_____ at a nursing home or _____

_____ _____. Why don't you start

_____ today, and give _____ to you

and other people?

18

W Jenny has _____ _____. She has

_____ _____ and she even has

_____ _____ _____. However,

she goes to _____ _____ with Peter to

prepare for their _____ _____.

2 hours later, she tells Peter that she wants to

_____ _____ because her symptoms

are _____ _____. In this situation,

what would Peter say to Jenny?

19

M What are you going to do _____

_____?

W I'm going to an _____ _____ with my

family.

M Sounds like fun. _____ do you want to ride

the _____?

W I _____ _____ _____ the roller

coaster the most. I _____ _____.

M Sounds great. You look really _____.

W Yes, I'm looking forward to it.

20

M What are you doing, Jennie?

W I'm _____ _____ for my birthday

party.

M They _____ good. Do you want to

_____ one of these _____?

W Yes. Just pick one _____ _____

_____. Which one do you like most?

M I like _____ _____.

W Okay. This one goes on the card.

11 Listening Test

01 대화를 듣고, 남자가 가장 좋아하는 겨울 스포츠를 고르시오.

① 스케이트   ② 썰매   ③ 스키

④ 스노보드   ⑤ 스키 점프

02 대화를 듣고, 내용과 일치하는 그림을 고르시오.

03 대화를 듣고, 남자가 받은 포인트는 총 몇 점인지 고르시오.

① 500점   ② 1,000점   ③ 2,000점

④ 3,000점   ⑤ 4,000점

04 대화를 듣고, 두 사람의 심정으로 가장 적절한 것을 고르시오.

① proud   ② tired   ③ disappointed

④ nervous   ⑤ happy

05 대화를 듣고, 두 사람이 대화하는 장소로 가장 적절한 것을 고르시오.

① 동물 병원   ② 공원   ③ 수족관

④ 박물관   ⑤ 영화관

06 대화를 듣고, 여자가 구입할 신발로 가장 적절한 것을 고르시오.

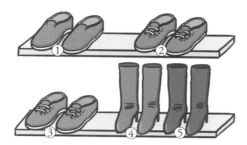

07 대화를 듣고, 남자가 여자를 만나려는 목적으로 가장 적절한 것을 고르시오.

① 생일 선물을 사 주려고 ② 목도리 반품하러 같이 가려고
③ 할인 기간에 물건을 구입하려고 ④ 숙제를 도와 달라고 부탁하려고
⑤ 선물 사러 같이 가자고

08 대화를 듣고, 여자의 마지막 말의 의도로 가장 적절한 것을 고르시오.

① 걱정 ② 사과 ③ 경고 ④ 격려 ⑤ 축하

09 대화를 듣고, 두 사람의 관계로 가장 적절한 것을 고르시오.

① professor — student ② girlfriend — boyfriend
③ friend — friend ④ photographer — traveler
⑤ traveler — traveler

10 대화를 듣고, 여자가 구입할 준비물이 아닌 것을 고르시오.

① 도화지 ② 물감 ③ 붓
④ 크레용 ⑤ 팔레트

11 대화를 듣고, 여자가 남자에게 부탁한 것으로 가장 적절한 것을 고르시오.

① 지도 검색하기   ② 항공권 예약하기
③ 숙소 추천하기   ④ 관광 안내하기
⑤ 관광 명소 알려 주기

12 대화를 듣고, 남자의 고민으로 가장 적절한 것을 고르시오.

① 친구와의 화해   ② 발표 자료 만들기
③ 발표에 대한 두려움   ④ 발표 주제 선정
⑤ USB를 잃어버린 일

13 대화를 듣고, 여자가 오늘 저녁 식사를 거르는 이유로 가장 적절한 것을 고르시오.

① 배탈이 나서   ② 입맛이 없어서
③ 다이어트 중이라서   ④ 건강 검진 때문에
⑤ 군것질을 많이 해서

14 다음을 듣고, 표의 내용과 일치하지 <u>않는</u> 것을 고르시오.

What Jennie Did Last Week						
Sun	Mon	Tue	Wed	Thu	Fri	Sat
Did the volunteer work	Played the piano	Played basketball	Played the piano	Played basketball	Went shopping	Went to the library
①	②		③		④	⑤

15 대화를 듣고, 두 사람이 점심 식사 후 할 일로 가장 적절한 것을 고르시오.

① 서류 작업하기   ② 사무실 정리하기
③ 식당 예약하기   ④ TV 시청하기
⑤ 영화 관람하기

16 다음을 듣고, 두 사람의 대화가 <u>어색한</u> 것을 고르시오.

①   ②   ③   ④   ⑤

17 다음을 듣고, 내용과 일치하지 <u>않는</u> 것을 고르시오.

① 프로젝트는 지구와 관련된 문제를 연구하는 것이다.
② 이 프로젝트는 5개의 그룹으로 진행된다.
③ 그룹 회원의 명단과 선정된 주제를 내일까지 제출해야 한다.
④ 연구 수행 후 1,000 단어 분량의 보고서를 작성해야 한다.
⑤ 보고서의 마감일은 다음 주 금요일이다.

18 다음을 듣고, Wendy가 Sue에게 할 말로 가장 적절한 것을 고르시오.

① Never mind.
② It's very boring.
③ Stop saying that.
④ Please be on time.
⑤ Turn off your mobile phone, please.

[19-20] 대화를 듣고, 남자의 마지막 말에 이어질 여자의 응답으로 가장 적절한 것을 고르시오.

19
① I'll try again.
② That's too bad.
③ It looks strange.
④ What should we do?
⑤ Oh, I'm lucky. I'll take it.

20
① I feel awful.
② It was really exciting.
③ That sounds like fun.
④ I think that's impossible.
⑤ I think that's a better idea.

● 다음은 Listening Test 11의 주요 지문입니다. 녹음을 다시 듣고, 질문에 대한 답을 완성하세요.

Q1 1 Which season does the man like best and why?

↳ He likes _____.

Q2 2 Why did the man say "It's so hard"?

↳ The reason is that he has to _____.

Q8 3 Why did the woman say, "My goodness."?

↳ The reason is that the man _____.

Q10 4 What is the boy going to buy at the art supplies store?

↳ He is going to buy _____, _____, _____, and

_____.

Q11 5 Where is the woman going to visit?

↳ She _____.

Q12 6 What mistake did the man make on his presentation?

↳ He _____.

Q15 7 What and where will the man and the woman have lunch?

↳ They will _____.

Q19 8 How much money does the woman have to pay for the neck warmer?

↳ She has to pay _____.

● 자신의 상황에 맞게 내용을 완성하고 말해 보세요.

A What do you want for your birthday? Why do you want it? Complete the sentences by using the information in the table below.

(1) What	(2) Reason I	(3) Reason II
a book	I love reading	read it when I am bored
a cat/dog	I want to have a pet	stay warm in cold weather
a coat	I can't stand the cold	play with it when I feel lonely
a new smartphone	mine is too old	use the Internet anywhere
a new bike	my old one is too little	ride my bike to school every day

I'd like to get (1)_____ for my birthday. The reason is that

(2)_____. If I get (1)_____, I will be able to

(3)_____. I hope my birthday comes soon.

B What did you do last week? Fill in the table below and tell your classmates about it.

Monday	Tuesday	Wednesday

Thursday	Friday	Weekend

I did a lot of thing last week. On Monday, I _____.

On Tuesday, I _____. On Wednesday,

I _____. On Thursday, I _____

_____. On Friday, I _____. On the

weekend, I _____. It was a very busy week for

me.

01

W I _____ _____, it's too _____ in _____. Which _____ do you like best?

M I like winter _____ _____ because it snows.

W Are you _____ _____ any winter sports?

M I like _____ the most. But I enjoy _____, sledding, and _____, too.

W Wow! You're _____ a _____.

02

W _____ _____! Go!

M Do you want to _____ _____? Do you want to _____ _____? If so, come on to JJ Fitness Center.

W Cut! You should say that with a _____ _____. Don't look so _____ or _____.

M Sorry. It's so _____ to run and talk _____ _____ _____ _____, though.

W I know, but let's try that _____ _____ _____.

03

W Did you buy _____ _____ _____?

M Yes. Please _____ _____ Mom.

W Oh, _____ _____. Why do you _____ _____ your _____ _____?

04 *(column 2)*

M Because there was a _____. If you _____ 1,000 won, they give you 500 points _____ _____.

W So, _____ _____ did you _____?

M I spent _____ won.

04

W How was the _____ _____? I don't think I did very well on it.

M _____ _____. I couldn't understand some of the _____. I think I'm going to _____.

W We studied _____ _____ this time, though, didn't we?

M You're right. _____ _____ _____ it and study for the _____ _____.

W Okay. I will try.

05

W Look at the sign. _____ _____ _____.

M What? No way. [Pause] Oh, _____ _____ _____ _____ more carefully. It says _____ aren't allowed without a _____.

W I see. Our _____ will be fine, then.

M Right. _____ _____ _____. Look at the children _____ on the _____. They look happy.

W The people lying on the grass _____ _____.

06

W This store has many _____ _____ .

M _____ _____ _____ go in and try some on?

W Let's do it. [Pause] The _____ _____ are pretty. I think the ones with _____ are better.

M I prefer the _____ _____ with shoelaces.

W I like these _____ . Winter is _____ _____ , I think I'll take the brown ones.

M Okay.

07

M Do you _____ _____ this _____ ?

W Yes. Why?

M I have to _____ _____ _____ for my mom's birthday. I want you to help me _____ _____ _____ her.

W Okay. What do you want to buy?

M I'm _____ _____ getting her a scarf because it's getting _____ .

W _____ _____ _____ _____ !

08

W _____ _____ _____ _____ the test this _____ ?

M A test? Do we have a test today?

W _____ _____ . Did you _____ we have a test in _____ _____ ?

M Oh, no! What should I do?

W We have _____ _____ to study. You can do it. _____ _____ .

09

W Excuse me. Could you please _____ _____ _____ for me and my boyfriend?

M Sure. _____ _____ . Ready! Three! Two! One!

W Thank you. _____ _____ _____ _____ to take one, too?

M Okay, thanks.

W This place is _____ _____ _____ _____ than I thought.

M I think so too.

10

M Mom, please go to the _____ _____ _____ with me. I have to buy _____ _____ my art class.

W Alright. What do you need?

M _____ _____ , watercolor paints, brushes, and crayons.

W You need _____ _____ ?

M Yes. Those are the things that the _____ asked us to _____ .

W Okay. Let's go.

11

M What are you doing, Jennie?

W I'm looking for a _____ of _____ .

M Why? Are you going to _____ there?

W Yes. My dad is going to go there _____ _____ next week. I'm going with him.

M Sounds great. I'll tell you about many _____ _____ to _____ .

W Can you _____ _____ _____ on

my map, please?

12

M I didn't do very well on my _____ today.

W Why? What happened? It was _____ _____, wasn't it?

M Yes, that's right. I was responsible for _____ a PowerPoint presentation, but I _____ _____ _____ it on my USB memory stick. My partner is still _____ _____ me.

W Oh my god!

M What should I do?

W I think you should _____ _____ to your partner.

13

M Let's _____ _____ for dinner, Jennie.

W I'm _____ _____ dinner today.

M Why? What's wrong?

W I can't eat anything because I have a _____ _____ tomorrow.

M Oh, that's too bad. I hope there's _____ _____ with your health.

14

① W On Sunday, Jennie _____ her _____ _____.

② W On Monday and Wednesday, Jennie _____ _____ _____.

③ W On Tuesday and Thursday, Jennie _____ _____ _____.

④ W On Friday, Jennie _____ _____.

⑤ W On Saturday, Jennie _____ _____ _____ _____.

15

M I'm so _____.

W Me, too. We'd better finish this _____ after we eat. What do you want to have for lunch?

M _____ _____ _____ at the VVIPs Buffet?

W Oh, sounds great. My mouth is _____.

M Have you _____ their king prawn dish? _____ _____.

W Let's hurry.

16

① M I'm sure you'll do it _____ _____ _____.

  W It's nice _____ _____ _____ say so.

② M Do you have _____ _____ today?

  W No, I don't.

③ M Can I _____ this sweater, please?

  W What's _____ with it?

④ M _____ do you like to study?

  W I like to study _____ _____.

⑤ M Do you _____ me _____ the window?

  W Yes, of course. It's too hot here.

17

M Attention, students! We are going to have _____ _____ to research issues _____ to the Earth, for example,

_____ _____, the greenhouse effect, etc. This will be done _____ _____. Therefore, _____ _____ _____ five members and choose _____ _____. Please send me _____ _____ _____ group members and your topic _____ _____. After you _____ it, you should write a 1,000-word _____. Please hand it in _____ _____ _____.

18

W Sue goes to see a movie with Wendy. _____ _____ _____ _____ the movie, Sue's mobile phone _____. She hurries to _____ it to _____ _____. In this situation, what would Wendy say to Sue?

19

M Hi, how may I help you?

W I'm looking for a _____ _____. Can I have a look?

M Yes. We have _____ _____. Come _____ _____, please.

W [Pause] Oh, I like the _____ _____. How much is it?

M The _____ _____ was $30 but we now _____ a 50% _____ _____.

W Oh, I'm lucky. I'll take it.

20

M Jennie, let's go see _____ _____ _____ _____.

W Okay. Do you have a special thing _____ _____?

M _____ _____ the *Hunger Games 2*?

W Sorry, I saw it _____ _____.

M Oh, did you? What did you _____ _____ _____?

W It was really exciting.

01 대화를 듣고, 여자가 주문한 음식으로 가장 적절한 것을 고르시오.

① ② ③ ④ ⑤

02 대화를 듣고, 남자가 설명하는 것을 고르시오.

① ② ③ ④ ⑤

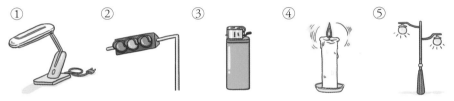

03 대화를 듣고, 여자가 자동차 수리를 위해 지불한 금액을 고르시오.

① $210   ② $220   ③ $225   ④ $230   ⑤ $235

04 대화를 듣고, 여자의 심정으로 가장 적절한 것을 고르시오.

① nervous   ② bored   ③ glad
④ excited   ⑤ tired

05 대화를 듣고, 두 사람이 대화하는 장소로 가장 적절한 것을 고르시오.

① restaurant   ② hospital   ③ hotel
④ office   ⑤ shopping mall

06 대화를 듣고, 여자의 직업으로 가장 적절한 것을 고르시오.

07 대화를 듣고, 여자가 남자에게 전화를 건 목적으로 가장 적절한 것을 고르시오.

① 풍선 구입을 부탁하려고   ② 파티에 초대하려고
③ 파티 일정을 알려 주려고   ④ 파티 준비를 도와 달라고
⑤ 파티 날짜 변경을 알려 주려고

08 대화를 듣고, 남자가 지난 주말에 한 일이 <u>아닌</u> 것을 고르시오.

① 대청소하기   ② 바닥 청소하기
③ 가구 재배치하기   ④ 가구 구입하기
⑤ 사우나 가기

09 대화를 듣고, 두 사람의 관계로 가장 적절한 것을 고르시오.

① 작가 — 배우   ② 점원 — 손님   ③ 친구 — 친구
④ 교사 — 학생   ⑤ 사장 — 비서

10 대화를 듣고, 여자가 구입할 물건으로 가장 적절한 것을 고르시오.

① 건강 팔찌   ② 티셔츠   ③ 웨딩 케이크
④ 책   ⑤ 상품권

11 대화를 듣고, 여자가 원하는 것을 고르시오.

① 에펠 탑 위치 확인　　　　　② 에펠 탑 폐장 시간 확인
③ 에펠 탑 입장권 예약　　　　④ 에펠 탑 사진 찍기
⑤ 에펠 탑 배경으로 사진 찍기

12 대화를 듣고, 여자의 마지막 말의 의도로 가장 적절한 것을 고르시오.

① 꾸중　　　② 추천　　　③ 축하　　　④ 허락　　　⑤ 거절

13 대화를 듣고, 여자가 물건을 받지 못한 이유로 가장 적절한 것을 고르시오.

① 원하는 사이즈가 다 팔려서　　② 배송이 지연되어서
③ 주문이 취소되어서　　　　　④ 원하는 색상이 다 팔려서
⑤ 배송지에 착오가 생겨서

14 다음을 듣고, 그래프의 내용과 일치하지 않는 것을 고르시오.

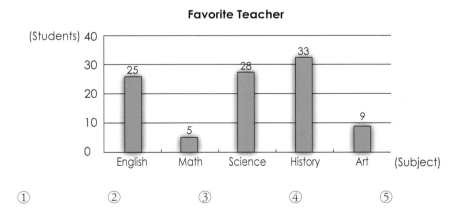

Favorite Teacher

(Students) 40 30 25 28 33 20 10 5 9 0
English　Math　Science　History　Art　(Subject)

①　②　③　④　⑤

15 대화를 듣고, 대화를 마친 후 두 사람이 할 일로 가장 적절한 것을 고르시오.

① 수영 모자 쓰기　　　　　② 수경 쓰기
③ 잃어버린 물건 찾기　　　④ 준비 운동하기
⑤ 샤워하기

16 다음을 듣고, 두 사람의 대화가 <u>어색한</u> 것을 고르시오.

①   ②   ③   ④   ⑤

17 다음을 듣고, 내용과 일치하지 <u>않는</u> 것을 고르시오.

① 퀸 메리 2호는 세계에서 가장 큰 유람선이다.
② 퀸 메리 2호의 승선 인원은 약 3,800명이다.
③ 퀸 메리 2호의 길이는 345미터이고 갑판은 14개가 있다.
④ 퀸 메리 2호의 최대 속도는 시간당 56km이다.
⑤ 퀸 메리 2호는 식당, 수영장, 영화관 등을 곧 갖출 예정이다.

18 다음을 듣고, Tom이 Jennie에게 할 말로 가장 적절한 것을 고르시오.

① It's not my style.
② I'm glad you like it.
③ I'm sure she likes it very much.
④ You already have a lot of T-shirts.
⑤ I like this one better than that one.

[19-20] 대화를 듣고, 남자의 마지막 말에 이어질 여자의 응답으로 가장 적절한 것을 고르시오.

19
① I'm a little nervous.
② I'm sorry to hear that.
③ It was nice to see her again.
④ Don't worry. You'll be fine.
⑤ Please say hello to your mom for me.

20
① That would be great.
② 10 a.m. would be great.
③ You might need more time.
④ I have a dental appointment that day.
⑤ Maybe we can get together another time.

다음은 **Listening Test 12**의 주요 지문입니다. 녹음을 다시 듣고, 질문에 대한 답을 완성하세요.

Q4
1 Why is the woman moving back and forth?

↳ She has an _____, but she

_____.

Q7
2 What did the woman ask the man to do for the party?

↳ She asked him to _____.

Q8
3 What did the man do on the weekend?

↳ He did _____.

Q10
4 What is the present for?

↳ It is for _____.

Q12
5 Why hasn't the man been to the Gustav Klimt exhibition yet?

↳ The reason is that _____.

Q13
6 What and when did the woman order?

↳ She ordered _____.

Q15
7 What do the man and the woman have to wear in the swimming pool?

↳ In the swimming pool, they have to wear _____.

Q18
8 Why did the man choose a trendy T-shirt for his sister's birthday present?

↳ The reason is that _____.

자신의 상황에 맞게 내용을 완성하고 말해 보세요.

A What kind of restaurant did you visit recently? Fill in the blanks in the table below and tell your classmates about it.

Restaurant Review	
(1) What kind of restaurant did you visit recently?	
(2) Who did you go with?	
(3) What did you order?	
(4) How did it taste?	
(5) Will you visit the restaurant again? Why?	

Recently, I visited a(n) (1)_____ restaurant with (2)_____. We

ordered (3)_____. It was (4)_____. I think I (will/

won't) visit the restaurant again because (5)_____

.

B Who is your favorite teacher? Fill in the blanks and tell your classmates about him/ her.

My Favorite Teacher	
(1) What subject does he/she teach?	
(2) What does he/she look like?	① ②
(3) Why do you like him/her?	③ ④ ⑤

My favorite teacher is my (1)_____ teacher. (He/She) is ①_____

_____. (He/She) also ②_____.

There are three reasons why (he/she) is my favorite teacher. First, (he/she) is

③_____. Second, (he/she) ④_____

_____. Lastly, (he/she) ④_____

_____. I am so glad that I have such a nice teacher.

01

W The food in this _____ is so good. _____ _____ now.

M I'm glad to hear you _____ our food.

W I _____ _____ _____ of my boyfriend's _____, and it was good. I also enjoyed my _____ and _____.

M _____ _____ _____ saying so.

W I will try _____ and _____ next time.

02

M Hey, Violet. _____! Look at the _____. It's _____.

W What does the red _____ _____, Dad?

M _____ _____ _____ and green means _____. So if you see the _____ _____, you have to stop and _____ _____ the green light.

W Okay. I will _____ _____ _____ _____, Dad.

M Good girl.

03

W Did you _____ _____ my car?

M Yes, I did. I _____ the _____, motor oil, and 2 windshield _____.

W Thanks. How much is it _____ _____?

M _____ the tires is $200, the motor oil is $25, and the windshield wipers _____ $5 _____.

W Okay. Here is my _____ _____.

04

W Oh, no. _____ _____ _____ _____?

M Why? Why are you _____ _____ _____ _____?

W I'll have an _____ _____ _____ tomorrow evening, but I _____ the text.

M Relax. You'll be fine. _____ _____ _____ _____. You'll feel much better.

W Okay. _____.

05

[Telephone rings.]

W Hello. _____ _____. How may I help you?

M Hello, this is Jack Adams in room 408. I'd like a _____ _____, please.

W Okay, sir. _____ _____ do you want it at?

M 6:30 in the morning. And I would like _____ _____ _____, please.

W Sure. They will be sent to your _____ _____ _____.

M Thank you.

06

W Please _____ _____ _____ hand higher, and _____ _____ the sky.

M Like this?

W Right. You'd better _____ more _____.

M Okay. I'll try.

W That's good now. _____ _____.
[Pause] _____ _____! Please
_____ _____ for the next picture
now.

07

[Telephone rings.]

W Hello. _____ _____ _____
_____ Jake, please?

M Hello, this is Jake. _____ _____ ?

W _____ _____, Jessie. I'd like to know
_____ you can help me to _____
_____ my party _____ _____.

M _____ _____ I can. What do you
want me to do?

W Please _____ _____ some balloons.

M No problem.

08

W How was your _____ ?

M I was busy doing a big _____. I dusted
rooms, _____ furniture, and _____
the _____.

W Wow. You must be _____ now.

M You're right. _____ _____ I went to
the sauna. I _____ _____ _____
now.

W Good.

09

M Can I have my _____ _____ ? I should
_____ _____ it again so that I won't
_____ any _____ in front of people.

W Here you are. I think you're _____ to
_____ it.

M Thank you for saying so. What time is
_____ _____ ?

W It will be at 2 p.m., sir. Do you want some
_____ or _____ ?

M Coffee, please.

10

W I'm _____ _____ a present for my
parents' 30th _____ anniversary. Can you
_____ me _____ ?

M These health bracelets and T-shirts are
_____. They have the same _____ but
are available in _____ _____.

W My parents already have the bracelets. The
T-shirts _____ good.

M Come here and _____ _____
_____.

W I like these _____ and _____
_____. I'll take them.

11

M _____ _____ do we have to go?

W Look, can you see the tower _____
_____ ? That is the Eiffel Tower.

M I can't wait to see _____ _____
_____.

W I'd like to get a _____ _____
_____ here.

M Why don't you ask that _____ ?

W Okay. [Pause] Excuse me, sir. Would you mind
_____ _____ _____ of us?

12

W Hi, Tom. You seem to be _____ _____ these days.

M Yeah, I've been busy with my _____ _____.

W You like Gustav Klimt, don't you? There's an _____ of his at the City Gallery now. Have you _____ _____ _____?

M No, not yet. How was it?

W It was _____. _____ _____ it.

13

W Do you _____ the Ugg boots that I ordered _____ _____ _____?

M Yes. Did you _____ them?

W No.

M Not yet? It's taking _____ _____.

W They said there's no more _____ in _____ _____.

M That's too bad.

14

① M This bar chart shows the _____ _____ of favorite teachers.

② M The most favorite teacher is the _____ _____.

③ M Students _____ the English teacher _____ the science teacher.

④ M Four more students like the art teacher better than the _____ _____.

⑤ M Only 5 students answered that their favorite teacher teaches _____.

15

W Why don't we have a _____ _____?

M Okay. Let's wear _____ _____ before we forget.

W That's a good idea. Here is mine. Wait a second. I think _____ is _____.

M What's wrong?

W Oh, I got it. We forgot to _____ _____ _____.

M Let's do it now.

16

① M _____ _____ is Jennie?

　 W She's _____ _____ talking with Sue.

② M Do you want _____ _____ _____?

　 W I think so, too.

③ W _____ _____ will you stay in New York?

　 M I'll stay there _____ _____ _____.

④ M What do you think of your _____ _____ _____?

　 W I think he's _____.

⑤ M Did you watch _____ _____ _____ last night?

　 W No, I didn't have _____ _____.

17

W Did you know? The Queen Mary 2 is the _____ _____ _____ in the world. It can _____ _____ 3,800 people. It is _____ meters long and it has

_____ decks. It has a maximum speed of
_____ km/h. It has restaurants, swimming
pools, and _____ _____. Many people
_____ _____ on this giant ship.

18

W Jennie is Tom's sister. She always tries to be
trendy. Her _____ is coming. Tom bought
_____ _____ _____ for her.
When she _____ the T-shirt, she says she
_____ it _____ _____. Tom is
really _____ about that. In this situation,
what would Tom say to Jennie?

19

M Jennie? Is _____ you? Jennie?
W Hi, Tom! How are you doing?
M _____. How about you?
W I'm _____. How's your mom?
M She's _____ _____ with her volunteer
work.
W Please say hello to your mom for me.

20

W I heard that you are going to have _____
_____ this Saturday. How's it going?
M I'm _____ _____ it. Can you come?
W I'd love to, but I _____.
M Oh, that's too bad. Why not?
W I have a dental appointment that day.

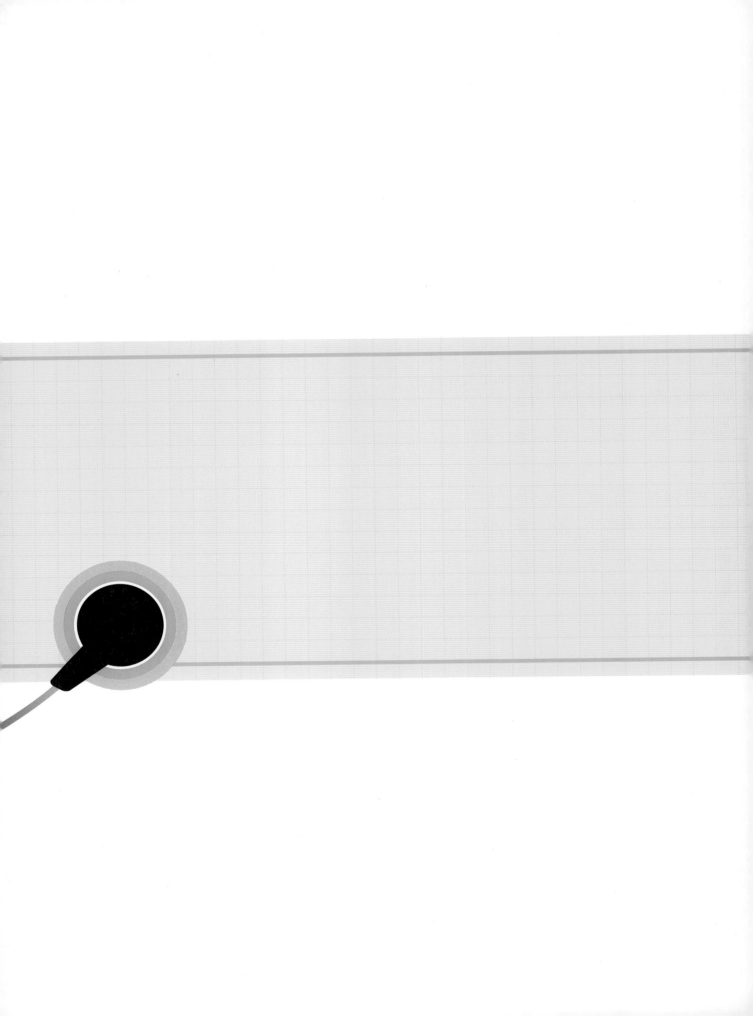

Actual Test
01~02회

01 대화를 듣고, 여자가 이용할 교통수단으로 가장 적절한 것을 고르시오.

①   ②   ③   ④  ⑤

02 대화를 듣고, 남자가 생일 선물로 받고 싶은 것으로 가장 적절한 것을 고르시오.

①  ②   ③   ④   ⑤

03 대화를 듣고, 현재 시각을 고르시오.

① 10:00 ② 10:30 ③ 11:00
④ 11:20 ⑤ 11:30

04 대화를 듣고, 남자의 심정으로 가장 적절한 것을 고르시오.

① surprised ② exhausted ③ scared
④ relieved ⑤ worried

05 대화를 듣고, 두 사람이 대화하는 장소로 가장 적절한 것을 고르시오.

① 은행 ② 체육관 ③ 우체국
④ 여행사 ⑤ 항공사

06 대화를 듣고, 두 사람이 하려는 일로 가장 적절한 것을 고르시오.

① 도서관 가기
② 영화 관람
③ 야구 경기 관람
④ 저녁 식사 준비
⑤ 컴퓨터 게임

07 대화를 듣고, 여자가 박물관에 가려는 이유로 가장 적절한 것을 고르시오.

① 그곳에서 약속이 있어서
② 좋아하는 전시회가 열려서
③ 미술 작품을 구입하려고
④ 보고서를 작성해야 해서
⑤ 무료 입장권이 생겨서

08 대화를 듣고, 남자가 주말에 한 일로 가장 적절한 것을 고르시오.

① 파티 준비하기
② 컴퓨터 게임하기
③ 사촌 돌봐 주기
④ 사촌 돌잔치 참석하기
⑤ 친구 생일 파티 참석하기

09 대화를 듣고, 남자의 직업으로 가장 적절한 것을 고르시오.

① taxi driver
② pilot
③ bus driver
④ police officer
⑤ passenger

10 대화를 듣고, 두 사람이 구입할 식료품이 <u>아닌</u> 것을 고르시오.

① 계란
② 베이컨
③ 빵
④ 과일
⑤ 우유

11 대화를 듣고, 여자가 남자에게 부탁한 것으로 가장 적절한 것을 고르시오.

① 뉴스 확인하기　　　　　　② 학교 신문 기사 작성하기
③ 비밀 지키기　　　　　　　④ 자신을 지지해 주기
⑤ 학생 회장 출마하기

12 대화를 듣고, 여자가 남자에게 조언한 것으로 가장 적절한 것을 고르시오.

① 엄마 말씀을 따라라.　　　　② 네가 원하는 것을 해라.
③ 선생님과 상의해서 결정해라.　④ 영어 원서를 읽어라.
⑤ 영어 공부에 집중해라.

13 대화를 듣고, 여자가 재즈 페스티벌에 가지 <u>못하는</u> 이유로 가장 적절한 것을 고르시오.

① 친구와 선약이 있어서　　　　② 숙제를 해야 해서
③ 라이브 재즈 공연이 아닐 것 같아서　④ 너무 늦게 시작해서
⑤ 할아버지 생신 잔치에 가야 해서

14 다음을 듣고, 표의 내용과 일치하지 <u>않는</u> 것을 고르시오.

Tom's Weekly Activities							
	Sun	Mon	Tue	Wed	Thu	Fri	Sat
Walk the dog	✓	✓	✓		✓		✓
Clean his room							
Do his homework	✓	✓	✓	✓	✓	✓	✓
Go to the library			✓	✓			✓
Do voluntary work	✓						

①　　　　②　　　　③　　　　④　　　　⑤

15 대화를 듣고, 대화를 마친 후 남자가 가장 먼저 할 일로 가장 적절한 것을 고르시오.

① 〈누가 내 치즈를 옮겼을까?〉 읽기　② 〈어린 왕자〉 읽기
③ 요약문 쓰기　　　　　　　　④ 줄거리 듣기
⑤ 숙제 제출하기

16 다음을 듣고, 두 사람의 대화가 <u>어색한</u> 것을 고르시오.

①   ②   ③   ④   ⑤

17 다음을 듣고, 내용과 일치하지 <u>않는</u> 것을 고르시오.

① CYJ 미술관은 가족 프로그램을 유료로 제공하고 있다.
② 티켓 배부는 오전 10시부터 시작된다.
③ 티켓은 선착순으로 배부된다.
④ 프로그램들이 종종 정원이 찬다.
⑤ 프로그램 참가를 위해서는 10시 이전에 도착하기를 권장한다.

18 다음을 듣고, Sam이 Sally에게 할 말로 가장 적절한 것을 고르시오.

① Help yourself.
② I'm full. I had enough.
③ Don't drink too many soft drinks.
④ Would you like to have some more snacks?
⑤ You must throw your trash in the trash can.

[19-20] 대화를 듣고, 남자의 마지막 말에 이어질 여자의 응답으로 가장 적절한 것을 고르시오.

19
① That sounds easy.
② You look terrible.
③ I'm so sad though.
④ I'm really proud of you.
⑤ He'll be glad to hear that.

20
① I have no idea.
② Wish me good luck.
③ I don't think that's fair.
④ Now I know I can do this.
⑤ I hope both of you can join us.

01

W It's 2 o'clock already.

M Do you _____ _____ _____?

W Yes, I do. Since I am running late, I will not _____ . I will use a _____ _____ .

M Are you thinking of _____ the _____?

W No. If I take it, I would have to walk a lot. I'll _____ _____ _____ .

M Okay.

02

W Andrew, your _____ is _____ _____ . What present do you want?

M Well. I _____ _____ about it.

W Last year I gave you an _____ _____ , and your parents gave you a _____ _____ .

M Right. And _____ _____ _____ gave me a _____ . I wish I had a new smartphone.

W I'm sorry but I _____ _____ that. I'll think about something else.

M Don't take it _____ , anything is fine.

03

W _____ _____ _____ _____? Do you live far from here?

M I live in Mokdong. It _____ 10 minutes by bus to get there.

W That's good. I live quite _____ _____ . If I leave now, I'll probably _____ _____ at 11:30.

M _____ _____? Does it take an hour and a half to get home?

W That's right.

04

W Did you watch the _____ _____ _____ last night?

M No. How was it?

W It was very _____ . I think I've _____ _____ _____ with it.

M Oh, come on. You're a _____ _____ _____ . You should study harder than ever before. _____ _____ TV. You can watch _____ _____ TV _____ you want after _____ the _____ .

W Okay. I'll stop watching it.

05

W I'd like to _____ _____ _____ to England.

M Okay. Please _____ it _____ _____ _____ . How would you like to _____ it? _____ _____ or surface _____?

W By air, please.

M Alright. Would you like _____ _____ or standard shipping?

W Standard, please.

06

W I'm very _____ . Which team do you _____ _____ , Noah?

M I _____ _____ the Tigers. What about you?

W I'm _____ _____ _____ _____ the Lions.

M I see. Looks like some people are _____

_____ _____ while waiting for the

_____ _____ _____.

W Look at the _____ _____. They are

very _____.

07

W _____ _____ _____ _____

go to the museum with me?

M Yes, I am. But _____ are you going to the

museum?

W Because I _____ _____ write a report

about _____ _____ _____ art.

M Does it _____ that you have to _____

_____ _____?

W Right. I have to _____ my entrance ticket

to _____ I _____ _____.

08

W How was your _____?

M I went to my _____ _____ to

_____ my cousin's 1st birthday.

W Oh, really? Who does the baby _____

_____, his mom or dad?

M I think he _____ his dad more. He's so

_____.

W What did you _____ _____

_____?

M I gave him a T-shirt.

09

W Excuse me. Does this bus go to Gimpo Airport?

M No. You _____ _____ the _____

651 bus. It will be _____ in 7 minutes.

W Thank you. _____ _____ _____,

how long does it usually _____ to

_____ there?

M It will _____ take 35 minutes _____

_____.

W Thank you. _____ _____!

10

M What do we have to buy?

W _____ _____ _____ the grocery

list. We have to buy eggs, milk, bacon, bread,

and fruit.

M I think we have some milk in the _____.

W Do we?

M Yes. I bought it _____ on the way home.

W I see. Let's _____ that then.

11

M Hey, Jennie. What's up?

W Did you hear the _____? Kate has a new

boyfriend. _____ _____ it is?

M I have no idea.

W William Smith, the _____ _____.

M Oh, I can't believe it.

W Can you _____ _____ _____?

12

M What are you planning to do during the

_____ _____, Jennie?

W I'm going to _____ _____ in

_____. What about you?

M I haven't decided yet. _____ wants me to

go to an _____ _____ like you but I

_____ _____ to.

W Then, what do you want to do?

M I just want to _____ a lot of _____ at

a book club.

W If I were you, I would do _____ _____

_____ _____.

13 · Dictation Test **137**

13

M Let's go to the _____ _____
_____ night. I have two tickets for it.

W Sounds great. I like _____ _____.

M It starts at 6 p.m. _____ _____ shall
we meet?

W _____ _____ at 5 p.m.? Wait. Sorry, I
_____ _____ with you.

M Why?

W I have to go to a _____ _____ for
_____ _____.

14

① W Tom _____ walks his dog

② W Tom _____ cleans his room.

③ W Tom _____ does his homework.

④ W Tom _____ goes to the library.

⑤ W Tom only does voluntary work _____
_____.

15

M Jennie, have you read the books, _____
_____ My Cheese? and The Little Prince?

W Yes, a _____ _____ _____.
Why?

M I have to read and write _____ _____
of them. Do you remember the _____?

W Sorry. Unfortunately, I don't remember them
well.

M _____ do you think is more _____?
I'll read that first.

W I think The Little Prince is _____
_____ than Who Moved My Cheese.

16

① M What do you do in your _____

_____?

W I _____ with _____ _____.

② M I don't like this song.

W _____ do I.

③ M I _____ _____ _____ on the
final exam.

W Don't mention it.

④ M Why are you so _____?

W I _____ _____ in the race.

⑤ M Do you remember _____ _____,
Joe?

W Yes, I remember him well.

17

W Hello, _____ to CYJ Art Gallery! We are
providing _____ _____ for family
programs at the _____ _____. Ticket
distribution starts at 10:00 a.m. on a _____,
_____ basis. Programs often _____
_____ so we recommend _____
_____ _____ before 10:00 a.m.

18

W Sam and Sally are drinking a cola _____
_____ _____. After drinking her
cola, Sally looks around to find _____
_____ _____. Unfortunately, there's
no _____ _____ nearby. There is only
a _____ saying 'NO TRASH' near a tree.
Sally runs to the tree then puts her empty can
_____ it. In this situation, what would Sam
say to Sally?

19

M Mom, look at this! It's my _____
_____.

W Congratulations, son!

M Thank you. I didn't _____ to get this runner's up award.

W I thought your painting was _____ _____.

M I didn't win, but I _____ _____ _____.

W I'm really proud of you.

20

W Anne, Jake and I are going to do _____ _____ at an orphanage tomorrow. Why don't you _____ _____?

M It's up to Tom. We're supposed to do our _____ _____.

W Do you think he wants to join us?

M I'm sure he does. Anyway I'll ask him _____ _____.

W I hope both of you can join us.

Actual Test

01 대화를 듣고, 여자가 구입할 쿠키로 가장 적절한 것을 고르시오.

① ② ③ ④ ⑤

02 대화를 듣고, 남자가 말하는 표지판으로 가장 적절한 것을 고르시오.

① ② ③ ④ ⑤

03 대화를 듣고, 여자가 책을 받을 수 있는 날짜로 가장 적절한 것을 고르시오.

① 3일 ② 8일 ③ 11일
④ 12일 ⑤ 13일

04 대화를 듣고, 남자의 심정으로 가장 적절한 것을 고르시오.

① 만족함 ② 지루함 ③ 긴장함
④ 외로움 ⑤ 기대함

05 대화를 듣고, 두 사람이 대화하는 장소로 가장 적절한 것을 고르시오.

① 사진관 ② 영화 촬영소 ③ 공항
④ 여행사 ⑤ 식당

06 대화를 듣고, 여자가 원하는 머리 모양으로 가장 적절한 것을 고르시오.

① ② ③ ④ ⑤

07 대화를 듣고, 남자가 환전하려는 이유로 가장 적절한 것을 고르시오.

① 해외에 송금하려고　　　　② 해외 쇼핑을 하려고
③ 해외 출장을 가려고　　　　④ 화폐 수집을 하려고
⑤ 환율이 하락해서

08 대화를 듣고, 두 사람이 할 일로 가장 적절한 것을 고르시오.

① 저녁 식사 준비하기　　　　② 꿀 구입하기
③ 저녁 메뉴 고르기　　　　　④ 음식 주문 전화하기
⑤ 외식하기

09 대화를 듣고, 두 사람의 관계로 가장 적절한 것을 고르시오.

① dad — daughter　　　　② teacher — student
③ doctor — nurse　　　　④ clerk — customer
⑤ dentist — patient

10 대화를 듣고, 두 사람이 구입할 비상 약품이 아닌 것을 고르시오.

① 두통약　　　　② 복통 약　　　　③ 1회용 밴드
④ 치통약　　　　⑤ 소독용 알코올

11 대화를 듣고, 남자가 여자에게 부탁한 것으로 가장 적절한 것을 고르시오.

① 중고 가방 구입하기　　　② 재활용품 분리수거하기
③ 청바지 수선하기　　　　④ 쓰레기 버리기
⑤ 바느질 도와주기

12 대화를 듣고, 여자가 남자에게 조언한 것으로 가장 적절한 것을 고르시오.

① 걱정 인형을 이용해라.　　　② 일찍 잠자리에 들어라.
③ 잠자리에 들기 전 체조를 해라.　　④ 커피는 오전에만 마셔라.
⑤ 커피 대신 허브 차를 마셔라.

13 대화를 듣고, 남자가 여자에게 전화를 건 목적으로 가장 적절한 것을 고르시오.

① 전화를 설치해 달라고　　　② 인터넷을 설치해 달라고
③ 전화번호를 물어보려고　　　④ 피자를 배달시키려고
⑤ 콜택시를 부르려고

14 다음을 듣고, 항공권의 내용과 일치하지 <u>않는</u> 것을 고르시오.

Boarding Pass		
Passenger Name	From	To
SMITH/TOM MR	**SYDNEY**	**SEOUL**
Flight No.　　Date	Boarding Time　　Gate No.	Seat
OZ857　　**07 JUN**	**15:10**　　**Gate 6**	**39F**

①　　　②　　　③　　　④　　　⑤

15 대화를 듣고, 두 사람이 할 일로 가장 적절한 것을 고르시오.

① 저녁 식사하기　　　② 식당 예약하기
③ 메뉴 선정하기　　　④ 약속 변경하기
⑤ 가족 회의하기

16 다음을 듣고, 두 사람의 대화가 <u>어색한</u> 것을 고르시오.

① ② ③ ④ ⑤

17 다음을 듣고, 내용과 일치하지 <u>않는</u> 것을 고르시오.

① 규칙적인 식사의 중요성을 말하고 있다.
② 한 끼를 거르면 신진대사가 빨라진다.
③ 한 끼를 거른 후 식사를 하면 그 음식을 빠르게 분해하지 못한다.
④ 분해되지 못한 음식은 지방으로 축적된다.
⑤ 식사를 거르지 않아야 한다.

18 다음을 듣고, Tom이 그의 엄마에게 할 말로 가장 적절한 것을 고르시오.

① How do you like it?
② Can you find my bag?
③ I can't wait for the trip.
④ I don't want to go on a trip.
⑤ I'm not happy with the color.

[19-20] 대화를 듣고, 여자의 마지막 말에 이어질 남자의 응답으로 가장 적절한 것을 고르시오.

19
① It's nice to see you.
② Don't make me sad.
③ What are friends for?
④ I'm sorry to hear that.
⑤ That would be a big help.

20
① I don't have any problem.
② I hope he will be okay soon.
③ Don't worry too much about it.
④ Why don't you take him to the vet?
⑤ Look on the bright side. He won't feel pain any more.

01

W There are so many _____ _____

_____ . I can't pick one.

M _____ _____ this bear shaped one?

It's our best-seller. This heart shaped one is

_____ , too.

W Are these ones _____ _____ ?

M Yes. The _____ _____ in the

_____ one is strawberry _____ , too.

W I see. Oh, tomorrow is _____ 11th. I will

take these long sticks _____ _____

chocolate.

M Okay.

02

W Why is _____ _____ moving so

slowly?

M _____ _____ _____ _____ .

There is a school, so this is a _____

_____ . You have to _____ _____ .

W Oh, that's why.

M The _____ _____ is 30kph and you

can see _____ _____ on the ground.

W I see. I will drive _____ _____ and

_____ .

03

W _____ _____ . I'm looking for the

book *Chicken Soup for the Soul*.

M I'm sorry but it is _____ _____

_____ now.

W When will you get new stock in?

M If I _____ it now, it will _____

_____ 3 days. It will be _____ to our

on _____ the 11th.

W Okay. I'll _____ a copy.

04

W What are you _____ _____ ?

M I'm thinking about _____ _____ .

I will have a _____ _____ with my

_____ .

W That _____ _____ _____ . What

are you going to do?

M We will _____ _____ , watch a movie,

and _____ _____ . I can't wait for

tomorrow.

W _____ _____ !

05

M How may I help you?

W I need an _____ _____ for my

_____ .

M Okay, _____ _____ _____

here in this _____ and keep your back

_____ .

W Like this?

M Yes. Look into the _____ and _____ .

One! Two! Three!

06

M How would you like your _____

_____ ?

W My hair is _____ _____ . I'd like it cut

shoulder-length.

M Okay. Are you going to _____ this

_____ hair style?

W _____ _____ it. I want to

have my hair _____.

M Alright. _____ _____ your hair color?

W I _____ brown _____ black.

07

W What are you doing?

M I'm _____ _____ the best bank to _____ _____ _____ exchange rates.

W Why are you _____ _____? Are you _____ _____?

M Yes. I will go to Hong Kong for a _____ _____.

W I see. _____ _____ _____.

08

W Oh! It's _____ 5 p.m.

M Why? Did you forget what you _____ _____ do?

W It's not that. I'll just _____ _____ _____ us.

M _____. Why don't we _____ _____ _____? I've wanted some for the past _____ _____.

W Really? Okay. I'll get the phone book. Please _____ _____ what you'd like to order.

09

M _____ _____ _____ _____. Say "Ah!"

W "Ah!"

M Good. You have a lot of _____. Have you been eating a lot of _____?

W Yes. But I _____ my _____ three times a day.

M Brushing _____ _____ a day is important but you have to brush your teeth _____ _____ _____ of eating sweets. Okay?

W I _____.

10

W Let's prepare some _____ for _____. Our first-aid kit is _____.

M That's a good idea. What do we have to buy?

W Let's buy some _____ for _____, stomachaches, and _____.

M What about _____ _____ and band-aids?

W I bought band-aids _____ when I got a _____ _____.

M I see.

11

W What are you doing with that _____, Tom?

M I'm doing _____ _____. It's not easy.

W What's _____ _____?

M _____ _____ _____ from old jeans. It's a method of _____.

W Why don't you _____ _____ _____ for help?

M She's out now. Could you give me _____ _____?

12

W You look really tired. _____ _____?

M I can't seem to get much _____ at the _____.

W Do you have _____ _____ _____ _____?

M No. I think I am drinking too much _____

because of my new _____ _____.

W Try not to drink too much _____. Why
don't you drink herb tea _____ _____
coffee?

M Okay, I will try to.

13

W Hello, 411 _____ _____. How may I
help you?

M I'd like to _____ _____ _____
_____ in my house. Could you _____
_____ _____ the number to call?

W _____ _____, please. The number you
have asked is _____-_____. It's TNT
Telecom.

M Thank you. Have a nice day.

W _____ _____ _____.

14

① W This is a _____ _____ for Tom
Smith.

② W The flight is _____ leaving on
_____ _____.

③ W Tom Smith will be seated in _____
_____ traveling from _____ to
_____.

④ W The flight has a boarding time of _____
_____.

⑤ W Tom Smith has to board at _____
_____.

15

M Mom, let's eat out this _____ _____.

W That's a good idea, but every restaurant will be
really _____ that day.

M We can _____ _____ _____ in

advance.

W What do you want to have?

M I have no idea. Oh, _____ _____
Mexican food? There's a famous Mexican
restaurant that's just a 15 minute _____
from our house.

W First, let's _____ for _____
_____ _____ _____ on the
Internet. Then we can think about what we will
_____ _____.

16

① M Why are you so _____?
   W I got the latest _____.
② M I like _____ _____ very much.
   W _____ _____ _____.
③ M Can you tell me _____ you are
   _____?
   W I _____ _____ _____.
④ M May I see your _____?
   W Sure. _____ it is.
⑤ M How's it going?
   W I'll go _____ _____.

17

M Do you know how important it is to have 3
_____ a day _____? When you
_____ a meal, your metabolism begins to
_____ _____. Then, the next time you
eat something, your metabolism is _____
_____ to _____ the food _____
as quickly. As a result, the food is _____
as _____. So please, don't _____
_____. It is a small but _____ thing
you can do to be _____.

18

W Tom is going to take a _____ _____
_____ this summer vacation. Today, his
mom bought _____ _____ for him at
the department store. He is very _____ but
he has to _____ _____ a _____.
It feels like that he _____ _____ until
then. In this situation, what would Tom say to
his mom?

19

W I'd like to _____ _____ _____.
Can you _____ me yours? Mine is
_____.

M Okay. Let's go bike riding together. You can use
_____ and I'll use my _____.

W _____ and _____ shall we meet?

M How about _____ _____ tomorrow at
_____ _____?

W Okay, Peter. I'm glad to have a _____
_____ _____.

M What are friends for?

20

M Hey, Alice. You _____ quite _____.
What happened?

W My cat went to _____ last night.

M Oh, I'm _____ to hear that. Was it
_____?

W Yes, he had a _____ _____.

M Look on the bright side. He won't feel pain any
more.

Vocabulary **R**eview

01 Vocabulary Review

01	favorite	가장 좋아하는
	choose	선택하다
02	in the future	미래에
	be interested in	~에 흥미가 있다
	be good at	~에 소질이 있다
03	in front of	~앞에
	entrance	입구
04	glad	기쁜
	can't wait to-V	~을 기다릴 수 없다, 정말 ~하고 싶다
	go inside	안으로 들어가다
	have a seat	자리에 앉다
05	backpack	배낭
	subway	지하철
	around	대략
	on one's way to	~로 가는 길에
	look like	~처럼 생기다
	stripe	줄무늬
06	comfortable	편안한
	lie down	눕다
07	book report	독후감
	due	마감 기한
08	visit	방문하다
	province	지방
	farm	농장
09	late	늦은
	be able to-V	~할 수 있다
	be late for	~에 늦다
10	weather report	일기 예보
	cloudy	흐린
	rain	비가 오다

11	right	옳은, 맞은
	have a party	파티를 열다
12	a little	약간
	overweight	과체중의
	sweet	단것, 사탕
	meat	(소·돼지) 고기
	vegetable	채소
13	go shopping	쇼핑하러 가다
	favorite store	단골가게
	a lot of	많은
	clothes	옷, 의류
14	get up	일어나다
	walk one's dog	개를 산책시키다
15	color	색, 색깔
16	busy	바쁜
	weekend	주말
	volunteer work	자원봉사 활동
17	tell great jokes	농담을 잘하다
	patient	환자
	hold	열다, 개최하다
18	back	등
	hurt	아프다
	get worse	점점 악화되다
	medicine	약
19	lesson	수업
	magic	마술
	swan	백조
20	put on	~을 입다
	life jacket	구명조끼

02 Vocabulary Review

01	sweet	달콤한
	transfer	이동하다
02	sunny	맑은
	until	~까지
	information	정보
03	go hiking	하이킹 가다
	forget	잊다
	math	수학
04	What's up?	무슨 일이니?
	speech contest	말하기 대회
	win a medal	메달을 따다
05	look for	~을 찾다
	section	구역
	easily	쉽게
06	try on	~을 입어 보다
	fitting room	탈의실
	on sale	할인 중인
	offer	제공하다
07	yet	아직
	make it	만나다
08	sick	아픈
	have a cold	감기에 걸리다
	How about -ing?	~하는 게 어때?
09	the day after tomorrow	내일모레
	Parents' Day	어버이날
	wallet	지갑
	scented candle	향초
10	be ready to-V	~할 준비가 되다
	order	주문하다
	dessert	디저트, 후식

11	absent	결석한
	serious	심각한
	by the way	그건 그렇고
	borrow	빌리다
12	eat out	외식하다
	passed	지나간
	anyway	어쨌든
13	interesting	재미있는
	unfortunately	불행하게도
	beginning	시작, 도입
	fall asleep	잠들다
14	free time	여가 시간
	quite often	꽤, 자주
15	take out	가지고 나가다
	trash	쓰레기
	light bulb	전구
16	introduce	소개하다
	neither	(둘 중) 어느 쪽도 아니다
17	captain	기장
	land	착륙하다
	local time	현지 시각
	document	서류
18	a piece of	한 조각의 ~
	enough	충분한
	delicious	맛있는
19	have no idea	전혀 모르다
	lost	길을 잃은
	get to	~에 도착하다
	on time	제시간에, 정각에
20	upset	화가 난

03 Vocabulary Review

01	rainy	비가 오는
	continue	계속되다
02	cute	귀여운
	art festival	예술제
	cap	야구 모자
03	How much ~ ?	~은 얼마인가요?, 얼마나 많은 양의 ~?
	adult	성인
	need	필요하다
04	playground	운동장
	excited	신난, 흥분한
	runner	달리기 선수
05	pharmacy	약국
	turn left	좌회전하다
	on one's right	~의 오른편에
06	think about	~에 대해 생각하다
	scarf	스카프, 목도리
	broach	브로치
	wear	매다, 입다
07	free	한가한
	take	시간이 걸리다
	jump rope	줄넘기
	try out	시험 삼아 해 보다
08	stay home	집에 머무르다
	have fun	재미있게 보내다
09	score	점수, 성적
	be proud of	~을 자랑스럽게 여기다
	keep up	계속하다
	effort	노력
10	sure	확실한, 확신하는
	report	보고서

11	favor	부탁
	package	소포
	take a look at	~을 살펴보다
12	cost	비용이 들다
	repair	수리하다, 고치다
	suggest	제안하다
	fix	~을 고치다
13	wait for	~을 기다리다
	exit	출구
14	popular	인기 있는
	among	~ 가운데
15	presentation	발표
	shortage	부족
	topic	주제
16	work out	운동하다
	date	날짜
17	attention	주의, 집중
	right now	지금, 당장
18	save	저장하다
	turn on	~을 켜다
	work	작동하다
	matter	문제, 사건, 일
19	meal	식사
	change	거스름돈
	next to	~옆에
20	introduce	소개하다
	be from	~ 출신이다
	pleased	기쁜

04 Vocabulary Review

01	check	확인하다
	pack	(짐을) 싸다
	thick	두꺼운
02	be famous for	~로 유명하다
	on top of	~의 꼭대기에
	dot	점
03	public	공공의
	check out	확인하다
	stripe	줄무늬
04	not at all	전혀 ~이 아닌
	horrible	끔찍한
	messy	지저분한
05	turn right	우회전하다
	post office	우체국
06	a glass of	(유리컵) 한 잔의 ~
07	bookshelf	책장, 책꽂이
08	look	~하게 보이다
	terrible	끔찍한
	headache	두통
	medicine	약
09	neighbor	이웃
	next door	옆집
	noisy	시끄러운
	house warming party	집들이
10	class	수업
	stay	머무르다
	most of the time	대부분의 시간

11	on the way home	집에 오는 길에
	drop by	~에 들르다
	cucumber	오이
12	yummy	맛 있는
	be crazy about	~을 정말 좋아하다
	tooth	이
	hurt	아프다
	painkiller	진통제
13	borrow	빌리다
	about	~에 관한
	typhoon	태풍
14	take a message	메시지를 받다
	practice	연습하다
	play	연극
15	honey	여보, 자기
	outdoor	야외의
16	look around	둘러보다
	invite	초대하다
17	breaking news	뉴스 속보
	final round	결승전
18	do one's best	최선을 다하다
	get a perfect score	만점을 받다
	make a mistake	실수하다
	perfect	완벽한
19	take pictures	사진 찍다
	photographer	사진작가
20	plan	계획
	special	특별한
	join	함께 하다
	unfortunately	불행하게도

05 Vocabulary Review

01	talk to	~와 이야기하다
	shine	빛나다
02	live in	~에 살다
	fur	털
	circle	원
	cute	귀여운
03	strange	이상한
	according to	~에 따르면
	timetable	시간표
	run	운행하다
04	classmate	급우, 학급 친구
	car accident	차 사고
05	product	제품
	dinosaur	공룡
	a lot	많이
06	present	선물
	recommend	추천하다
	perfume	향수
	necklace	목걸이
	ring	반지
07	leave a message	메시지를 남기다
	understand	이해하다
08	refrigerator	냉장고
	starve	굶주리다
09	finish	끝내다
	do one's homework	숙제를 하다
10	spring break	봄 방학
	several	몇몇의
	exercise	운동하다
	gym	체육관

11	download	내려받다
	heal	치료하다
	pick	고르다
	choose	고르다
12	select	고르다, 선택하다
	suitable	적당한
	without	~없이
13	stay up all night	밤을 꼬박 새우다
	poster	포스터
14	look like	~처럼 생기다
	spot	점
15	near	근처의
	can't wait to-V	빨리 ~하고 싶다
16	pass	건네다
	My pleasure.	도움이 되어 기뻐요.
17	shopper	쇼핑객
	next	다음의
	bunch	다발, 송이
	free	무료인, 공짜인
18	nervous	긴장한
	make a mistake	실수하다
	make fun of	~을 놀리다
	down	의기소침한, 우울한
19	lose	지다
	relay	이어달리기
	sprain	삐다, 삐끗하다
	ankle	발목
20	colorful	다채로운
	artist	화가, 예술가

Vocabulary Review

01	jog	조깅하다
	headphone	헤드폰
02	puppy	강아지
	collar	(개 등의 목에 거는) 목걸이
	while	반면
03	arrange	정하다
	be supposed to-V	~하기로 되어 있다
	public library	공공 도서관
	place	장소
	far away	먼
	both	둘 다
04	talk about	~에 대해 말하다
	regularly	규칙적으로
	nowadays	요즈음
	all the time	항상
05	necktie	넥타이
	prefer	선호하다
	expensive	비싼
06	work out	운동하다
	stay healthy	건강을 유지하다
07	knee	무릎
	length	길이
08	make a snowman	눈사람을 만들다
	have a snowball fight	눈싸움을 하다
09	special	특별한
	offer	제공(하다)
10	pretty good	아주 좋은
	Poor you!	안됐다!

11	favor	부탁
	borrow	빌리다
	battery	배터리
12	lose	잃어버리다
	leave	남겨 두다
	Lost and Found	분실물 센터
13	customer service	고객 센터
	item	물건, 품목
	receive	받다
14	the number of	~의 수
	same	같은
15	in mind	염두에 둔
	chili	칠리고추의, 매운
	grocery	식료품점
	mushroom	버섯
16	toothache	치통
17	passenger	승객
	book	예약하다
	proceed	이동하다, 나아가다
	immediately	속히, 즉시
	complete	마치다, 완료하다
18	mid-term exam	중간고사
	advice	조언
	solve	풀다
	not ~ anymore	더 이상 ~아니다
19	after school	방과 후에
20	since	~이래로
	bite	물다

07 Vocabulary Review

01	ticket booth	매표소
	line	줄
	purse	(여성용) 지갑, 핸드백
	curly	곱슬거리는
02	careful	조심스러운, 신중한
	slippery	미끄러운
	dangerous	위험한
	warn	경고하다
	danger	위험
03	play	연극
04	soon	곧
	go inside	안으로 들어가다
	seat	좌석
	rank	(지위를) 차지하다
05	terrible	심한, 끔찍한
	drugstore	약국
	on time	제시간에, 정각에
06	in the middle of	~의 중간에
	across from	~ 건너편에
07	join	함께 하다, 합류하다
	surprise party	깜짝 파티
08	weekend	주말
	grandparents	조부모
09	hungry	배고픈
	ready	준비된
	call	부르다
	worry	~을 깨우다
10	available	이용 가능한
	turn on	~을 켜다

	do ~ a favor	부탁하다
11	wake up	~을 깨우다
	see off	배웅하다
12	windy	바람이 부는
	blue	우울한
	miss	놓치다, 빠지다
	volunteer work	자원봉사 활동
13	broken	고장 난, 깨진
	reasonable	적당한, 합리적인
14	activity	활동
15	overeat	과식하다
	dish	요리, 접시
	fireworks	불꽃놀이
	hurry up	서두르다
16	mind	~을 꺼려하다
	upset	화가 난
17	cut A into B	A를 B로 자르다
	piece	조각
	freeze	얼리다
	frozen	얼린
	blender	믹서기, 분쇄기
	add	첨가하다
	blend	섞다, 혼합하다
18	clerk	점원
	towards	~ 쪽으로
19	amazing	놀라운
	autograph	사인, 서명
20	go abroad	해외로 가다
	decide	결정하다

01	mittens	벙어리 장갑
	cute	귀여운
02	several	여러 개의
	lost	잃어버린
	describe	묘사하다
	strap	끈
03	pay	지불하다
	fee	요금
	machine	기계
	press	누르다
	insert	집어 넣다
	bill	지폐
04	take a walk	산책하다
05	open an account	계좌를 개설하다
	savings account	예금 계좌
	identification card	신분증
	fill out	~을 채우다
	form	양식
06	plan	계획
	nursing home	양로원
	orphanage	고아원
07	make a reservation	예약하다
	adult	성인
08	gift	선물
	on one's way to	~로 가는 길에
09	seat number	좌석 번호
	boarding pass	탑승권
10	be from	~출신이다
	grow up	자라다

11	save a seat	자리를 맡다
	these days	요즘
	write on the blog	블로그에 글을 쓰다
12	as well	또한
	electronic device	전자 기기
	at least	적어도
13	grocery	식료품
	deliver	배달하다
	depend on	~에 달려 있다
	weight	무게
14	ride a horse	말을 타다
	2 night 3 days	2박 3일
15	go out	외출하다
	luck	운
16	tasty	맛있는
	agree	동의하다
	remind	~을 상기시키다
17	nearby	근처에
	as soon as	~하자마자
	stationery store	문구점
	project	프로젝트
18	collect	모으다
	article	기사
	expensive	비싼
19	smell	~한 냄새가 나다
	haircut	이발, 머리 깎기
20	feel like -ing	~하고 싶다
	shampoo	(머리를 샴푸로) 감다
	blond hair	금발머리

01	congratulations on	~을 축하하다
	competition	경기, 시합
02	thirsty	목마른
	a carton of	한 팩의 ~
	grab	재빨리 손에 넣다
	actually	실은
03	recognize	알아보다, 인식하다
	weight	무게
	weigh	무게가 나가다
04	move	감동시키다
	scene	장면
	touching	감동시키는
	tear	눈물
	sensitive	감성적인, 예민한
05	go through	~을 통과하다
	ticket gate	개찰구
	scan	~을 스캔하다
	transportation card	교통 카드
06	support	지지(하다)
	elect	선출하다
	deserve	~을 받을 만하다
07	pick up	~을 집다
	fault	잘못
	transfer student	전학생
08	rank	순위를 매기다
	importance	중요성
	order	순서
09	jet lag	시차증, 시차로 인한 피로
	tourist spot	관광 명소

10	comfortable	편안한
	fashionable	유행하는
11	check out	(호텔에서) 체크아웃하다
	luggage	(여행용) 짐
	look around	둘러보다
12	difficult	어려운
	sense of balance	균형 감각
	give ~ a try	~을 시도해 보다
	without	~없이
13	flight	항공편, 항공기
	description	묘사, 설명
	handle	손잡이
14	costume	의상
	jak-o'-lantern	호박등
	invitation	초대장
15	amazing	놀라운
16	give ~ a call	~에게 전화하다
	snowboard	스노보드를 타다
17	best-known	가장 잘 알려진
	gray	회색의
	fur	털
	call	~라고 부르다
18	reviewer	비평가, 평론가
	salty	짠
	spicy	매운
19	show ~ the way to	~에게 …로 가는 길을 알려 주다
	exercise	운동하다
20	regularly	규칙적으로
	give up	포기하다
	junk food	정크푸드(인스턴트 음식 혹은 패스트푸드)

10 Vocabulary Review

01	freezing	몹시 추운
	especially	특히
02	return	반납하다
	right after	곧 바로
	take a rest	휴식을 취하다
03	try on	입어 보다, 신어 보다
	price	가격
	moreover	게다가
	credit card	신용 카드
	lend	빌려 주다
04	almost	거의
	whether	～인지 아닌지
05	snatch	강탈하다
	calm down	진정하다
	thief	도둑
	slim	날씬한
06	secret	비밀
	guess	추측하다
07	appointment	약속
	take care of	～을 돌보다
08	gather	모으다
	due	만기가 된
09	final exam	기말고사
	be proud of	～을 자랑스럽게 여기다
	keep up	계속하다
	because of	～ 때문에
	appreciate	고마워하다, 감사하다
10	pear	배
	persimmon	감
	in season	제철인

11	global warming	지구 온난화
	related to	～와 관련된
12	plenty of	많은 ～
	enough	충분한
	electronic album	전자 앨범
13	deliver	배달하다
	ready	준비가 된
14	allowance	용돈
	save	저축하다
15	open an account	계좌를 개설하다
	checking account	당좌 예금
	savings account	저축 예금
	fill out	～을 작성하다
16	leave a message	메시지를 남기다
	volunteer work	자원봉사 활동
17	happiness	행복
	the elderly	어르신들, 노인들
	nursing home	양로원
18	fever	열
	runny nose	콧물
	prepare for	～을 준비하다
	symptom	증상
19	amusement park	놀이공원
	ride	～을 타다; 놀이 기구
	look forward to -ing	～을 고대하다
20	invitation	초대장
	photo	사진

01	be good at	~을 잘하다	
	sled	썰매를 타다	
02	lose weight	살을 빼다	
	stay healthy	건강을 유지하다	
	exhausted	지친	
	at the same time	동시에	
03	item	항목, 품목	
	point	점, 점수	
	for free	무료로	
04	fail	낙제하다	
	disappointed	낙담한	
05	allow	허락하다	
	grass	잔디	
	peaceful	평화로운	
06	shoelace	신발 끈	
07	choose	선택하다	
	think about	~에 대해 생각하다	
08	be ready for	~할 준비가 되다	
	My goodness.	어머나, 이런.	
09	take a picture	사진을 찍다	
	still	움직이지 않는	
10	material	재료	
	drawing paper	도화지	
	brush	붓, 솔	
	map	지도	
11	on business	사업차	
	mark	표시하다	

	presentation	발표
12	be responsible for	~에 책임이 있다
	partner	짝, 파트너
13	medical check-up	건강 검진
14	Tuesday	화요일
	Thursday	목요일
15	rib	갈비
	buffet	뷔페
	watering	침이 고이는
	fantastic	환상적인
16	exchange	교환하다
	in groups	그룹으로
	attention	주의, 집중
	research	연구; 연구하다
	issue	문제, 쟁점
17	topic	주제
	list	명단
	report	보고서
	hand in	제출하다
	in the middle of	~의 중간에
18	ring	울리다
	turn off	(전원을) 끄다
	kind	종류
19	original	원래의
	discount	할인
	lucky	운이 좋은
20	awful	끔찍한, 지독한
	impossible	불가능한

12 Vocabulary Review

01	full	배부른
	take a bite	한 입 깨물다
02	keep ~ in mind	~을 명심하다
03	repair	고치다, 수리하다
	in total	전체; 합
	cost	비용이 들다
	each	각각의
04	back and forth	앞뒤로
	text	원문
	relax	긴장을 풀다
	take a deep breath	숨을 깊이 쉬다
05	wake-up call	모닝콜
	right away	즉시, 당장
06	raise	들어 올리다
	point to	~을 가리키다
	naturally	자연스럽게
	pose	포즈를 취하다
07	blow up	~을 불다
	balloon	풍선
08	busy	바쁜
	cleanup	청소
	rearrange	재배치하다, 재배열하다
	furniture	가구
	mop	대걸레질하다
09	manuscript	원고
	look through	~을 검토하다
10	wedding anniversary	결혼 기념일
	bracelet	팔찌
	popular	인기 있는
	available	구할 수 있는

11	far	먼
	close	가까이
	picture	사진
12	seem	~처럼 보이다
	exhibition	전시회
	awesome	굉장한
13	order	주문하다
	ago	~ 전에
	stock	재고
14	survery	설문 조사
	result	결과
	prefer A to B	B보다 A를 더 선호하다
15	missing	빠뜨린, 놓친
	warm up	준비 운동하다
16	stay	머물다
17	cruise ship	유람선
	carry	실어 나르다
	deck	갑판
	maximum speed	최대 속도
	giant	거대한
18	trendy	최신 유행의
	glad	기쁜
19	say hello to	~에게 안부를 전하다
	bazaar	바자회
	work on	~에 노력을 들이다, 착수하다
20	dental	치과의
	appointment	약속
	get together	만나다

13 Vocabulary Review

01	public transportation	대중교통
02	laptop computer	노트북 컴퓨터
	novel	소설
	afford	여유[형편]가 되다
	seriously	심각하게
03	far from	~로부터 멀리
	quite	꽤
04	soap opera	연속극
	fall in love with	~와 사랑에 빠지다
	relieved	안도한
05	package	소포
	scale	저울
	surface mail	일반 우편물
	express delivery	특급 배송
	standard shipping	일반 배송
06	root for	~을 응원하다
	a big fan of	~의 광팬
07	submit	제출하다
	entrance ticket	입장권
	prove	증명하다
08	celebrate	축하하다
	cousin	사촌
	resemble	닮다
	cute	귀여운
09	probably	아마도
	safely	안전하게
10	refrigerator	냉장고
	skip	건너뛰다

	guess	추측하다
11	class president	반장
	secret	비밀
12	decide	결정하다
13	live	생방송의, 살아 있는
	start	시작하다
14	rarely	거의 ~않는
	weekly	주간의
15	summary	요약
	storyline	줄거리
	unfortunately	불행하게도
16	neither	(부정문) ~도 마찬가지이다
	do well on	~을 잘하다
	mention	언급하다, 말하다
17	provide	제공하다
	distribution	배부
	on a first-come, first-served basis	선착순으로
	fill up	(정원이) 차다, 가득 채우다
	recommend	추천하다, 권유하다
18	trash can	쓰레기통
	nearby	근처에
	trash	쓰레기
	empty	빈
19	expect	기대하다
	runner's up award	2등상
	terrible	안 좋은, 심한, 형편없는
20	orphanage	고아원
	be up to	~에 달려 있다
	be supposed to-V	~하기로 되어 있다

14 Vocabulary Review

01	shape	모양
	popular	인기 있는
	round	둥근
	flavor	향
02	traffic	차량, 교통
	suddenly	갑자기
	slow down	속도를 줄이다
	speed bump	과속 방지 턱
03	out of stock	재고가 없는
	reserve	예약하다
	copy	(책·신문 등의) 한 부, 한 권
04	exchange	교환하다
05	ID picture	증명사진
	passport	여권
	straight	곧게
06	be tired of	~에 질리다
	prefer A to B	B보다 A를 선호하다
	take advantage of	우대 받다, ~을 이용하다
07	exchange rate	환율
	business trip	출장
08	already	이미, 벌써
	phone book	전화번호부
09	cavity	충치
	sweet	단것
	brush one's teeth	양치하다
10	medicine	약
	emergency	응급 사태
	pill	알약
	stomachache	복통

11	needle	바늘
	method	방법
	recycling	재활용
	give ~ a hand	~을 도와주다
12	at up the moment	지금
	machine	기계
13	set the Internet	인터넷을 설치하다
	hold on	전화를 끊지 않고 기다리다
14	boarding pass	탑승권
	seat	좌석; 자리에 앉히다
	from A to B	A에서부터 B까지
	board	타다, 탑승하다
	crowded	붐비는, 복잡한
15	make a reservation	예약하다
	in advance	미리
	book	예약하다
16	excited	흥분한, 신난
	passport	여권
17	meal	식사
	regularly	규칙적으로
	metabolism	신진대사
	break down	~을 분해하다
	as a result	그 결과로
	store	저장하다
18	backpack	배낭
19	broken	고장 난
20	down	우울한, 의기소침한
	heaven	천국
	pain	고통, 통증

MEMO

MEMO

MEMO

MEMO

MEMO

내신 및 시·도 교육청 영어듣기평가 완벽 대비

Listening 올리고

Level **1**

중학영어듣기 모의고사

정답 및 해석

DARAKWON

내신 및 시·도 교육청 영어듣기평가 완벽 대비

Listening 올리고

Level **1**

중학영어듣기 모의고사

정답 및 해석

DARAKWON

01 ③	02 ③	03 ③	04 ①	05 ①
06 ③	07 ⑤	08 ④	09 ④	10 ④
11 ⑤	12 ⑤	13 ④	14 ②	15 ①
16 ④	17 ③	18 ④	19 ③	20 ①

01

W   Tony, do you like sports?

M   Of course. I love sports.

W   What's your favorite sport, then?

M   It's hard to choose one, but I like basketball best. How about you?

W   I like badminton. It's very exciting.

- -

여   Tony, 너 스포츠 좋아하니?

남   물론이지. 정말 좋아해.

여   그러면 네가 가장 좋아하는 스포츠는 무엇이니?

남   하나를 고르기 어려운데, 농구를 가장 좋아해. 너는?

여   나는 배드민턴을 가장 좋아해. 정말 재미있거든.

●●
favorite 가장 좋아하는   **choose** 선택하다   **exciting** 재미있는

02

M   What do you want to be in the future?

W   I'm interested in teaching, singing, drawing, and baking.

M   Wow! Does it mean that you want to be a teacher, singer, painter, and a baker?

W   Yes.

M   If you had to pick one, what would it be?

W   Well. I think I'm really good at drawing.

- -

남   너는 장래에 무엇이 되고 싶니?

여   나는 가르치는 것, 노래 부르는 것, 그림 그리는 것, 그리고 빵을 굽는 것에 관심이 있어.

남   우와! 너는 선생님, 가수, 화가, 그리고 제빵사가 되고 싶다는 뜻이니?

여   응.

남   만일 네가 하나를 선택해야 한다면, 그게 무엇이니?

여   글쎄. 나는 내가 정말로 그림에 소질이 있다고 생각해.

●●
in the future 미래에   **be interested in** ~에 흥미가 있다   **baker** 제빵사   **be good at** ~에 소질이 있다, ~을 잘하다

03

M   I have two tickets for this afternoon's baseball game. Do you want to go?

W   Of course. What time shall we meet?

M   Let's meet an hour before the game starts.

W   When does it start?

M   It starts at 2:30 p.m. Where are we going to meet?

W   Right in front of Entrance A.

- -

남   나 오늘 오후 야구 경기 표가 두 장 있어. 갈래?

여   물론이지. 몇 시에 만날까?

남   경기 시작 한 시간 전에 만나자.

여   언제 시작하는데?

남   오후 2시 30분. 어디에서 만날까?

여   A번 입구 바로 앞에서.

●●
Let's ~하자   **in front of** ~앞에   **entrance** 입구

04

W   I'm very glad to be here.

M   Me, too. I can't wait to see this movie.

W   Let's go inside and have a seat.

M   Oh, no! Where are the tickets?

W   What? Where did you put them?

M   I think I left them in the car. I'm so sorry.

- -

여   여기 와서 정말 기뻐.

남   나도 그래. 이 영화 정말 보고 싶었거든.

여   안에 들어가서 자리에 앉자.

남   오, 이런! 표가 어디에 있지?

여   뭐라고? 어디에 두었는데?

남   차 안에 놓고 온 것 같아. 정말 미안해.

●●
glad 기쁜   **can't wait to-V** ~을 기다릴 수 없다, 정말 ~하고 싶다   **go inside** 안으로 들어가다   **have a seat** 자리에 앉다

05

M Hello, how may I help you?

W I think I left my backpack on the subway.

M When was it?

W It was around 8 a.m. I was on my way to school.

M What does it look like?

W It's red with white stripes.

남 안녕하세요. 어떻게 도와드릴까요?

여 지하철 안에 제 배낭을 두고 온 것 같아요.

남 언제였나요?

여 오전 8시쯤이었어요. 학교에 가는 길이었거든요.

남 어떻게 생겼나요?

여 그것은 흰색 줄무늬가 있는 빨간색이에요.

backpack 배낭 **subway** 지하철 **around** 대략 **on one's way to** ~로 가는 길에 **look like** ~처럼 생기다 **stripe** 줄무늬

06

W When I sit on it, it makes me feel very comfortable. It is usually in the living room. I sometimes lie down on it and watch TV. What is it?

여 내가 이 위에 앉아 있을 때, 그것은 나를 무척 편안하게 해 준다. 그것은 보통 거실에 있다. 나는 가끔 그 위에 누워 TV를 본다. 그것은 무엇인가?

sit on ~위에 앉다 **comfortable** 편안한 **usually** 일반적으로, 보통 **living room** 거실 **sometimes** 때때로 **lie down** 눕다

07

[Telephone rings.]

W Hello?

M Hello, Susie. Do you have plans for this evening?

W Not really. But I have to finish my book report, it's due tomorrow. I will be free after that. Why?

M I'm going to have a potluck party. Can you come?

W Definitely. I'd love to.

[전화벨이 울린다.]

여 여보세요?

남 여보세요. Susie. 너 오늘 저녁에 무슨 계획 있어?

여 꼭 그렇진 않아. 그렇지만 독후감 쓰는 것을 끝내야 해. 내일까지 끝내야 하거든. 그 이후에는 자유야. 왜?

남 나 포틀럭 파티를 하려고 해. 올 수 있어?

여 당연하지. 정말 그러고 싶어.

plan 계획 **Not really.** 꼭 그렇지는 않다. **book report** 독후감 **due** 마감 기한 **potluck party** 음식을 각자 준비해 와서 하는 파티 **definitely** 당연하게, 확실하게

08

M What are you going to do this weekend?

W I'm going to visit my uncle.

M Where does he live?

W He lives in Gangwon Province. I'm going to help him on his farm.

M That sounds great.

남 너 이번 주말에 뭐 할 거니?

여 삼촌을 방문할 거야.

남 어디에 사시는데?

여 강원도에 사셔. 농장 일을 도와드리려고.

남 재미있겠다.

be going to-V ~할 예정이다 **visit** 방문하다 **province** 지방 **farm** 농장

09

W Eunseong, you're late again today. What's wrong with you?

M I helped a little boy find his mom on the way to school.

W Really? Were you able to find his mom?

M No. But I took him to the police station.

W I'm proud of you. Please don't be late for class again, though.

여 은성아. 너는 오늘도 또 늦었구나. 무슨 일이니?

남 학교 오는 길에 어린 소년의 엄마 찾는 것을 도와주었어요.

여 정말? 그의 엄마를 찾을 수 있었니?

남 아니요. 하지만 그를 경찰서에 데려다 주었어요.

여 네가 자랑스럽구나. 그렇지만 다시는 수업에 늦지 마라.

late 늦은 **What's wrong with you?** 무슨 일이니? **help + 목적어 + (to)동사원형** ~가 …하는 것을 도와주다 **on the way to** ~로 오는 [가는] 길에 **be able to-V** ~할 수 있다 **take** 데려다 주다 **police station** 경찰서 **be proud of** ~을 자랑스럽게 여기다 **be late for** ~에 늦다 **class** 수업

10

W Where are you going?

M I am going to a bookstore.

W Did you see a weather report? What's the weather like outside?

M It's not very good. It's cloudy. I think it's going to rain soon.

W Oh, no. Really?

- -

여 너 어디 가니?

남 서점에 가.

여 일기 예보 들었니? 밖에 날씨가 어때?

남 썩 좋지는 않아. 흐려. 곧 비가 올 것 같아.

여 오, 이런. 정말?

bookstore 서점 **weather report** 일기 예보 **cloudy** 구름이 낀, 흐린 **rain** 비가 오다

11

[Telephone rings.]

M Hello, John speaking.

W Hi, John. It's Liz. I'm calling about Ann's birthday.

M Ann's birthday? Oh, it's this Friday, right?

W Yes, it is. Let's have a party for her. Can you help me?

M Yeah, sure. Good idea. What can I do?

W I want you to bring your camcorder.

- -

[전화벨이 울린다.]

남 여보세요. John입니다.

여 안녕, John. 나 Liz야. Ann의 생일 때문에 전화했어.

남 Ann 생일? 아. 이번 주 금요일이지, 맞지?

여 그래. 맞아. 그녀를 위해 파티를 하자. 나를 도와줄 수 있니?

남 그럼. 물론이지. 좋은 생각이다. 내가 무엇을 할까?

여 네가 비디오카메라를 가져와 주면 좋겠어.

birthday 생일 **Friday** 금요일 **right** 옳은, 맞은 **have a party** 파티를 열다 **sure** 물론 **bring** 가지고 오다 **camcorder** 비디오카메라

12

M I'm a little overweight but I can't stop eating sweets like candies and chocolate. I really like meat but I don't like eating vegetables. What should I do?

- -

남 저는 약간 과체중이지만 사탕, 초콜릿 같은 단것들 먹는 것을 끊을 수가 없어요. 저는 정말 고기를 좋아하지만 채소를 먹는 것을 싫어해요. 저는 어떻게 해야 할까요?

① 일찍 잠자리에 들어야 한다.

② 설탕을 많이 먹어서는 안된다.

③ 매일 이를 닦아야 한다.

④ 규칙적인 운동을 위해 체육관에 가야 한다.

⑤ 단것을 줄이고 균형 잡힌 식사를 해야 한다.

a little 약간 **overweight** 과체중의 **stop -ing** ~하는 것을 멈추다 [그만두다] **sweet** 단것, 사탕 **meat** (소·돼지) 고기 **vegetable** 채소 **brush one's teeth** 이를 닦다

13

M Where do you usually go shopping?

W I usually go shopping at Dongdaemun Market.

M Do you have a favorite store?

W Yes. The name of my favorite store is Full-Coordi.

M Why do you like it?

W It has a lot of nice large clothes.

- -

남 너는 보통 쇼핑하러 어디에 가니?

여 나는 보통 동대문 시장에 쇼핑하러 가.

남 네 단골가게가 있니?

여 응. 내 단골가게 이름은 Full-Coordi야.

남 왜 그 곳을 좋아하니?

여 멋진 큰 치수 옷들이 많아.

go shopping 쇼핑하러 가다 **favorite store** 단골가게 **a lot of** 많은 **clothes** 옷, 의류

14

① M Tom gets up at 7:00 a.m.

② M After breakfast Tom walks his dog in the park.

③ M Tom goes to school at 8:30 in the morning.

④ M Tom plays basketball at 3:00 in the afternoon.

⑤ M Tom does his homework before he has dinner.

Tom의 하루 일과	
오전 7시	기상하기
오전 7시 30분	공원에서 개 산책시키기
오전 8시	아침 식사 하기
오전 8시 30분	등교하기
오후 12시 30분	점심 식사 하기
오후 3시	농구 하기
오후 5시	숙제 하기
오후 6시	저녁 식사 하기

① 남 Tom은 아침 7시에 일어납니다.

② 남 아침 식사 후 Tom은 공원에서 개를 산책시킵니다.

③ 남 Tom은 오전 8시 30분에 학교에 갑니다.

④ 남 Tom은 오후 3시에 농구를 합니다.

⑤ 남 Tom은 저녁을 먹기 전에 숙제를 합니다.

get up 일어나다 **breakfast** 아침 식사 **walk one's dog** 개를 산책시키다 **before** ~전에

15

① M Where do they live?

   W They are in the living room.

② M What's your favorite color?

   W My favorite color is black.

③ M What're those in your hand?

   W They're our movie tickets.

④ M Let's watch *Music Live* on Channel 9.

   W Okay. I'm interested in music.

⑤ M What's your favorite day of the week?

   W I love Saturday.

① 남 그들은 어디에 사니?

   여 그들은 거실에 있어.

② 남 네가 가장 좋아하는 색은 뭐니?

   여 내가 가장 좋아하는 색은 검정색이야.

③ 남 네 손의 그것들은 뭐니?

   여 우리 영화 표야.

④ 남 9번 채널에서 〈Music Live〉 보자.

   여 좋아. 나는 음악에 관심 있어.

⑤ 남 일주일 중에 네가 가장 좋아하는 요일이 뭐니?

   여 나는 토요일이 좋아.

color 색 **be interested in** ~에 관심이 있다

16

W Tom, let's go to the movies this Saturday.

M Sorry, I can't. I'm busy on the weekend.

W What do you do on the weekend?

M I do volunteer work at Seoul Metropolitan Library.

W Wow, that sounds great. Can I join you?

M Sure.

여 Tom, 이번 토요일에 영화 보러 가자.

남 미안. 안 돼. 나는 주말에 바빠.

여 주말에 뭐 하는데?

남 서울 시립 도서관에서 자원봉사를 해.

여 우와, 근사하게 들린다. 너와 함께 해도 될까?

남 물론이지.

go to the movies 영화 보러 가다 **busy** 바쁜 **weekend** 주말 **volunteer work** 자원봉사 **sound + 형용사** ~하게 들리다

17

W Hello, everyone. The man in this picture is my grandfather. He's 60 years old, but he still works. He's a doctor. He tells great jokes so his patients like him. He plays the violin very well. Every December he holds a violin concert at his hospital. I want to grow up to be like him.

여 안녕하세요, 여러분. 이 사진 속의 남자는 우리 할아버지이십니다. 그는 60세이지만, 여전히 일하고 계십니다. 그는 의사이십니다. 그는 농담을 잘해서 환자들이 좋아합니다. 그는 바이올린을 아주 잘 켜십니다. 매년 12월, 그는 자신의 병원에서 바이올린 연주회를 여십니다. 저는 우리 할아버지처럼 자라고 싶습니다.

picture 사진, 그림 **tell great jokes** 농담을 잘하다 **December** 12월 **hold** 열다, 개최하다 **concert** 연주회

18

M <u>On his way home</u>, Jake met Jennie. She <u>didn't</u> look <u>so good</u>. She said that her <u>back</u> <u>hurt</u> a lot and was <u>getting</u> worse. In this situation, what would Jake say to Jennie?

남 집으로 오는 길에, Jake는 Jennie를 만났습니다. 그녀는 그리 좋아 보이지 않았습니다. 그녀는 허리가 많이 아픈데 점점 심해지고 있다고 말했습니다. 이 상황에서, Jake는 Jennie에게 뭐라고 말할까요?

① 그리 좋지 않아.
② 어떻게 지내니?
③ 나는 점점 더 악화되고 있어.
④ 안됐구나. 병원에 가는 것이 낫겠다.
⑤ 나는 병원에 가서 약을 좀 타왔어.

•• **back** 등 **hurt** 아프다 **get worse** 점점 나빠지다 **had better** ~하는 게 낫다 **see a doctor** 진찰 받다 **medicine** 약

19

W Look, Mike! Here are the new <u>after-school</u> <u>programs</u>.

M What kind of <u>lessons</u> are there?

W <u>Magic</u>, hip-hop dancing, <u>flute</u>, and soccer lessons. What are you <u>interested</u> in?

M I'm interested in <u>hip-hop dancing</u>. How about you?

W Me, too. Then, let's take lessons <u>together</u>.

M <u>That's a good idea.</u>

여 Mike, 이거 봐! 여기 새로운 방과 후 프로그램들이 있어.
남 어떤 수업들이 있니?
여 마술, 힙합댄스, 플루트, 그리고 축구 수업. 너는 무엇에 관심이 있니?
남 나는 힙합댄스에 관심 있어. 너는 어때?
여 나 역시도. 그럼 우리 같이 그 수업 듣자.
남 <u>좋은 생각이야.</u>

① 나는 그렇게 생각하지 않아.
② 천만에.
③ 좋은 생각이야.
④ 지금은 바쁘지 않아.
⑤ 재미 있는 수업 같아.

•• **after-school** 방과 후의 **lesson** 수업 **magic** 마술 **flute** (악기) 플루트

20

M Wow, this is <u>the</u> <u>first</u> <u>time</u> I have been in <u>a</u> <u>boat</u> shaped like a swan.

W <u>Wait</u> a moment!

M What's wrong?

W Look at this <u>sign</u>. You have to put on <u>a</u> <u>life</u> <u>jacket</u> in this boat.

M <u>Oh, I see.</u>

남 우와, 백조 모양의 배를 타는 게 이번이 처음이야.
여 잠깐만 기다려 봐!
남 무슨 일이니?
여 이 표지판 좀 봐. 배 안에서는 구명조끼를 입어야 해.
남 <u>오, 알았어.</u>

① 오, 알았어.
② 나중에 그것을 할게요.
③ 내가 어떻게 하면 좋을까?
④ 우리 수영해서 강을 건너자.
⑤ 네 구명조끼를 벗는 게 어때?

•• **shaped like** ~처럼 생긴 **swan** 백조 **sign** 표지판 **put on** ~을 입다
life jacket 구명조끼 **take off** ~을 벗다

Further **S**tudy 정답 p. 14

1 She likes <u>badminton best</u>.
2 She is interested in <u>teaching</u>, <u>singing</u>, <u>drawing</u>, and <u>baking</u>.
3 They are going to <u>see a movie</u>.
4 It is due <u>tomorrow</u>.
5 They are going to <u>have a birthday party for Ann</u>.
6 She usually goes shopping <u>at Dongdaemun Market</u>.
7 She wants to <u>go to the movies with Tom</u>.
8 He <u>has never tried it</u>. It is <u>the first time he has been on it</u>.

A

I'm going to talk about my favorite sport. My favorite sport is (1)soccer. I like it because it is (2)fun and exciting. I play it (3)once a week. I usually play it (4)after school. My (5)P.E. teacher taught me how to play (1)soccer.

(1) 운동	(2) 이유	(3) 얼마나 자주	(4) 언제	(5) 누가 가르쳐 주었는가?
야구 농구 배구 축구 테니스	재미있는 흥미진진한 흥미로운 매력적인	거의 매일 일주일에 한 번 한 달에 한 번 일주일에 두 번 일주일에 세 번	방과 후에 주말에 아침에	친구 체육 선생님 코치 엄마 / 아빠 형 / 누나

저는 제가 가장 좋아하는 스포츠에 대해 이야기하려고 합니다. 제가 가장 좋아하는 스포츠는 축구입니다. 저는 그것이 재미있고 흥미진진하기 때문에 좋아합니다. 저는 일주일에 한 번 그것을 합니다. 저는 보통 방과 후에 그것을 합니다. 우리 체육 선생님께서 축구 하는 법을 가르쳐 주셨습니다.

B

Time	Things to do
6:00 a.m.	Get up
6:10 a.m.	Work out
7:00 a.m.	Have breakfast
8:00 a.m.	Go to school
3:30 p.m.	Do my homework
6:30 p.m	Have dinner
7:00 p.m.	Use the Internet
11:00 p.m.	Go to bed

I get up at 6:00 a.m. every day. I work out at 6:10 a.m. Usually I have breakfast at 7:00 in the morning. Then, I go to school at 8:00 a.m. I always do my homework at 3:30 p.m. I have dinner at 6:30 p.m. After dinner, I use the Internet for an hour. I go to bed at 11:00 p.m.

시간	할 일
오전 6:00	기상하기
오전 6:10	운동하기
오전 7:00	아침 식사 하기
오전 8:00	등교하기
오후 3:30	숙제하기
오후 6:30	저녁 식사하기
오후 7:00	인터넷 하기
오후 11:00	잠자리에 들기

저는 매일 아침 6시에 일어납니다. 저는 아침 6시 10분에 운동을 합니다. 보통은 아침 7시에 아침 식사를 합니다. 그런 다음, 저는 8시에 학교에 갑니다. 저는 항상 오후 3시 30분에 숙제를 합니다. 저는 오후 6시 30분에 저녁을 먹습니다. 저녁 식사 후, 저는 한 시간 정도 인터넷을 이용합니다. 저는 11시쯤에 잠자리에 듭니다.

02 Listening Test 정답 p. 20

01 ①	02 ①	03 ④	04 ⑤	05 ③
06 ②	07 ⑤	08 ②	09 ①	10 ⑤
11 ⑤	12 ②	13 ④	14 ③	15 ②
16 ①	17 ②	18 ④	19 ⑤	20 ②

01

M I am very sweet and brown. Bees transfer from one flower to another flower and make me. People sometimes use me instead of sugar when they cook. Some people drink me as a tea. What am I?

남 나는 매우 달콤하고 갈색이야. 벌들이 이 꽃에서 저 꽃으로 이동하며 나를 만들어. 사람들은 때때로 요리할 때 설탕 대신 나를 사용해. 어떤 사람들은 나를 차로 마셔. 나는 무엇일까?

sweet 달콤한 **transfer** 이동하다 **instead of** ~대신에 **sugar** 설탕 **as** ~로써 **tea** (마시는) 차

02

W Did you listen to the news this morning?

M What news?

W I mean the weather forecast for tomorrow.

M Yeah. I heard that it's going to be sunny until tomorrow morning. It will be cloudy in the afternoon, and will rain in the evening, though.

W I see. Thank you for the information.

여 너 오늘 아침 뉴스 들었어?

남 어떤 뉴스?

여 내일 일기 예보 말하는 거야.

남 응. 내일 아침까지는 맑을 거래. 그렇지만 오후에는 흐리고, 저녁에는 비가 올 거래.

여 알았어. 알려 줘서 고마워.

weather forecast 일기 예보 **sunny** 맑은 **until** ~까지 **thank ~ for** …에 대해 ~에게 고맙다 **information** 정보

03

[Beep]

W Hello, Tim. This is Kathy. I'm very sorry, but I can't go hiking on Thursday. I forgot that I have a math test then. Are you free on Saturday? If you are, let's go on Saturday. Please call me back. My number is 010-1234-5678.

여 안녕, Tim. 나 Kathy야. 정말 미안한데, 목요일에 등산을 못 갈 것 같아. 그때 수학 시험이 있는 것을 깜박했어. 토요일에 한가하니? 만일 그렇다면, 토요일에 가자. 답신 전화해 줘. 내 번호는 010-1234-5678이야.

go hiking 하이킹 가다 **forget** 잊다 **math** 수학 **free** 한가한 **call ~ back** 답신 전화하다

04

M You look very happy today. What's up?

W I was worried about the speech contest, but…

M But what? Did you win a medal?

W Right! I won the gold medal.

M Wow, congratulations!

W Thank you.

남 너 오늘 매우 행복해 보여. 무슨 일이니?

여 말하기 대회 때문에 걱정했었는데….

남 그런데 뭐? 메달 딴 거야?

여 맞아! 금메달 땄어.

남 우와, 축하해!

여 고마워.

What's up? 무슨 일이니? **be worried about** ~에 대해 걱정하다 **speech contest** 말하기 대회 **win a medal** 메달을 따다 **Congratulations!** 축하해!

05

W May I help you?

M I'm looking for a novel.

W What is the title of the book?

M It is *Who Moved My Cheese?*

W Oh, it is in section 7. You will find it easily.

M Thanks.

여 도와드릴까요?

남 소설책을 찾고 있어요.

여 책 제목이 무엇인가요?

남 〈누가 내 치즈를 옮겼을까?〉예요.

여 오, 그것은 7번 구역에 있어요. 쉽게 찾으실 수 있을 거예요.

남 고마워요.

look for ~을 찾다 **novel** 소설 **section** 구역 **easily** 쉽게

06

M Excuse me. Can I try this shirt on?

W Sure. The fitting room is over there.

M Thanks. Is it on sale?

W Yes. We're offering a 20% discount. The original price of this shirt was $30.

M Okay. I will take it.

남 실례합니다. 이 셔츠를 입어 봐도 될까요?

여 물론이죠. 탈의실은 저쪽에 있습니다.

남 고맙습니다. 이것은 할인 중인가요?

여 네. 20% 할인해 드리고 있어요. 이 셔츠의 원래 가격은 30달러였습니다.

남 알겠습니다. 이것으로 할게요.

try on ~을 입어 보다 **fitting room** 탈의실 **on sale** 할인 중인 **offer** 제공하다 **discount** 할인 **original** 원래의 **take** 사다

07

w David, what are you going to do after school?

m I have no plans yet. Why?

w I bought a tennis racket last week, so I'd like to play tennis. Can you play with me?

m Nice. I'd love to. When do you want to meet?

w Let's make it at 5 p.m.

여 David, 너 방과 후에 뭐 할 거니?

남 아직 계획 없는데. 왜?

여 나 지난주에 테니스 라켓을 샀거든. 그래서 테니스를 치고 싶어. 나랑 같이 칠래?

남 좋아. 그러고 싶어. 언제 만나고 싶니?

여 오후 5시에 만나자.

after school 방과 후에 **plan** 계획 **yet** 아직 **racket** 라켓 **make it** 만나다

08

w Mom doesn't look well today. Is she sick?

m She has a cold. How about doing some house chores for her?

w Great. What can we do?

m Let's clean the house.

w That's a good idea. She will really like that.

여 엄마가 오늘 안 좋아 보이시더라. 아프시니?

남 감기 걸리셨어. 엄마를 위해 집안일을 하는 게 어때?

여 멋지다. 무얼 할까?

남 집 청소를 하자.

여 좋은 생각이야. 엄마가 정말 좋아하실 거야.

look well 좋아 보이다 **sick** 아픈 **have a cold** 감기에 걸리다 **How**

about -ing? ~하는 게 어때? **house chore** 집안일 **clean** 청소하다

09

w The day after tomorrow is Parents' Day.

m I know. What should we buy for Mom and Dad?

w Last year, we bought them wallets.

m Then, how about buying scented candles this year?

w That's a great idea.

여 내일모레는 어버이날이야.

남 알아. 엄마랑 아빠께 무얼 사 드리지?

여 작년에 지갑 사 드렸는데.

남 그럼. 올해는 향초를 사는 게 어때?

여 멋진 생각이야.

the day after tomorrow 내일모레 **Parents' Day** 어버이날 **wallet** 지갑 **scented candle** 향초

10

w Are you ready to order?

m Yes. I'd like spaghetti and a coke. What about you?

w I'll have a hamburger with an orange juice.

m What do you want for dessert?

w I will have an ice cream.

여 주문할 준비 됐니?

남 응. 나는 스파게티랑 콜라 마실래. 너는?

여 나는 오렌지 주스랑 햄버거로 할게.

남 디저트는 뭘 원하니?

여 아이스크림 먹을래.

be ready to-V ~할 준비가 되다 **order** 주문하다 **dessert** 디저트, 후식

11

m Hi, Jennie. What happened? Why were you absent today?

w Hi, Tom. I had to visit my grandma in the hospital.

m It must be serious. Is she okay now?

w Not yet. Thanks for asking. By the way, I need your help.

m What can I do for you?

w Can I borrow your notes for today's lessons if it is okay?

남 안녕, Jennie. 무슨 일이니? 오늘 왜 결석했어?

여 안녕, Tom. 할머니 문병 가야 했어.

남 심각했던 게 틀림없구나. 지금은 좀 괜찮으시니?

여 아직. 물어봐 줘서 고마워. 그건 그렇고, 나 네 도움이 필요해.

남 뭘 해 줄까?

여 괜찮다면 오늘 수업 노트들 좀 빌릴 수 있을까?

•• **What happened?** 무슨 일이니? **absent** 결석한 **visit ~ in the hospital** ~을 문병 가다 **must** ~임에 틀림없다 **serious** 심각한 **by the way** 그건 그렇고 **need** 필요하다 **borrow** 빌리다

12

M Sue, do you want to eat out? I know a nice new restaurant. I'll buy you lunch.

W Sure, but why?

M Today is your birthday. It's May 30th.

W Hahaha, Tony. My birthday is May 13th. It's already passed, but thank you anyway.

남 Sue, 외식하고 싶니? 내가 새로 문을 연 멋진 식당을 하나 아는데. 내가 너에게 점심 살게.

여 그래, 그런데 왜?

남 오늘이 네 생일이잖아. 5월 30일.

여 하하하, Tony. 내 생일은 5월 13일이야. 이미 지났어. 하지만 어쨌든 고마워.

•• **eat out** 외식하다 **restaurant** 식당 **lunch** 점심 식사 **May** 5월 **already** 이미 **passed** 지나간 **anyway** 어쨌든

13

M Which one do you want to see?

W What about this movie?

M Didn't you see this movie last week with Ann?

W Yes, I did, but I want to see it one more time.

M Was it that interesting?

W Yes, it was. Unfortunately, I missed the beginning when I saw it with Ann because I fell asleep.

남 어느 걸로 보고 싶니?

여 이 영화 어때?

남 Ann이랑 지난주에 이 영화 보지 않니?

여 응, 그랬지. 그런데 한 번 더 보고 싶어.

남 그렇게 재미있었니?

여 응, 그랬어. 불행하게도, Ann과 그것을 볼 때 잠이 들어서 시작 부분을 놓쳤어.

•• **one more time** 한 번 더 **interesting** 재미있는 **unfortunately** 불행하게도 **miss** 놓치다 **beginning** 시작, 도입 **at that time** 그때 **fall asleep** 잠들다

14

① M Bill likes to go in-line skating in his free time.

② M Jennie plays badminton in her free time.

③ M Jake uses the Internet in his free time but he doesn't play computer games.

④ M Kate plays the piano in her free time.

⑤ M Frank goes in-line skating or walks his dog in the park in his free time.

여가 활동	
Tom:	인라인스케이트 타러 가기
Jennie:	배드민턴 치기
Jake:	인터넷 사용하기 혹은 컴퓨터 게임 하기
Kate:	피아노 치기
Frank:	인라인스케이트 타러 가기 혹은 공원에서 개 산책시키기

① 남 Bill은 여가 시간에 인라인스케이트 타러 가는 것을 좋아합니다.

② 남 Jennie는 여가 시간에 배드민턴을 칩니다.

③ 남 Jake는 여가 시간에 인터넷을 하지만 컴퓨터 게임은 하지 않습니다.

④ 남 Kate는 여가 시간에 피아노를 칩니다.

⑤ 남 Frank는 여가 시간에 인라인스케이트를 타러 가거나 공원에서 개를 산책시킵니다.

•• **go in-line skating** 인라인 스케이트 타러 가다 **free time** 여가 시간 **play + 운동명** (운동)을 하다 **play + the + 악기명** (악기)를 연주하다 **activity** 활동

15

W Does your dad help your mom around the house?

M Yes, quite often.

W What does he usually do for her?

M He takes out the trash and cleans the bathroom.

What about your dad?

W The only thing he does for my mom is to <u>change</u>
<u>light bulbs</u>.

여 너희 아빠는 너희 엄마를 도와드리니?

남 응, 꽤 자주.

여 아빠는 엄마를 위해 주로 무엇을 하시니?

남 쓰레기를 내다 버리고 욕실을 청소하셔. 너희 아빠는 어때?

여 엄마를 위해 아빠가 하는 유일한 일은 전구를 갈아 끼우는 거야.

•• **quite often** 꽤, 자주 **take out** 가지고 나가다 **trash** 쓰레기 **change**
교체하다 **light bulb** 전구

16

① M Let me <u>introduce</u> <u>myself</u>.

W Me <u>neither</u>.

② M Hi, Jennie. <u>What</u> are you <u>doing</u>?

W I'm <u>cleaning</u> my room.

③ M <u>How</u> have you been?

W Not bad.

④ M I'd like you <u>to meet</u> my brother, Tom.

W Hi, Tom. Nice to meet you.

⑤ M <u>What</u> do you <u>think</u> it is?

W It <u>might</u> <u>be</u> a cat.

----

① 남 제 소개를 하겠습니다.

여 저도 아닙니다.

② 남 안녕, Jennie. 뭐 하고 있니?

여 내 방을 청소하고 있어.

③ 남 어떻게 지냈어?

여 나쁘지 않아.

④ 남 내 남동생 Tom이야.

여 안녕, Tom. 만나서 반가워.

⑤ 남 그게 뭐라고 생각해?

여 고양이일 거야.

•• **introduce** 소개하다 **neither** (둘 중) 어느 쪽도 아니다 **might** ~일지도
모른다

17

M Good morning, everyone. This is your <u>captain</u>
<u>speaking</u>. We will be <u>landing</u> at Los Angeles Airport

in about <u>30 minutes</u>. The weather in Los Angeles
is <u>rainy</u> and the <u>local time</u> is 7:30 a.m. Before we
<u>land</u> at the airport, please <u>check</u> that you have all of
your <u>personal belongings</u> and have all of your travel
<u>documents</u> ready. Thank you.

남 여러분. 안녕하세요. 기장입니다. 저희 비행기는 30분 후 로스앤젤레스
공항에 착륙하겠습니다. 로스앤젤레스의 날씨는 비가 오고 있으며
현지 시각은 오전 7시 30분입니다. 공항에 착륙하기 전에, 개인
소지품을 확인해 주시고 모든 여행 서류들을 준비해 주십시오.
감사합니다.

•• **captain** 기장 **land** 착륙하다 **rainy** 비가 오는 **local time** 현지 시각
check 확인하다 **personal belongings** 개인 소지품 **document** 서류

18

M On Halloween, Peter had a great <u>dinner</u> at Susan's
house. After having the <u>main course</u>, Susan gave
him <u>a piece of</u> chocolate cake and a cup of coffee
<u>for dessert</u>. He had had <u>enough</u> but the cake was
so <u>delicious</u> that he wanted to have some <u>more</u>. In
this situation, what would Peter say to Susan?

남 핼로윈에 Peter는 Susan의 집에서 근사한 저녁 식사를 했습니다.
주요리를 먹은 후, Susan은 그에게 후식으로 케이크 한 조각과 커피
한 잔을 주었습니다. 그는 배가 불렀지만 그 케이크가 너무 맛있어서
좀 더 먹고 싶었습니다. 이 상황에서 Peter는 Susan에게 뭐라고
말할까요?

① 케이크 맛있게 먹기를 바랄게.

② 초콜릿 케이크로 할게.

③ 케이크 좀 더 가져다줄까?

④ 케이크 좀 더 먹을 수 있을까?

⑤ 케이크 좀 더 먹을래?

•• **main course** 주요리 **a piece of** 한 조각의 ~ **a cup of** 한 잔의 ~
enough 충분한 **delicious** 맛있는

19

M <u>Where</u> are we?

W I have <u>no idea</u>. I think we're <u>lost</u>.

M Can we get to the station <u>by 9</u>?

W I'm not sure. Oh, look at <u>that sign</u>.

M It says the station is this way.

W Well, I'm sure we can make it on time now.

....

남 여기가 어디지?

여 모르겠어. 우리는 길을 잃은 것 같아.

남 9시까지 역에 도착할 수 있을까?

여 확실하지 않아. 저 표지판을 봐.

남 역은 이쪽이라고 하네.

여 음, 나는 우리가 제시간에 갈 수 있을 거라 확신해.

① 나는 그 결과에 대해 걱정했어.

② 저 표시판은 무슨 뜻이야?

③ 나는 그것을 하기에 너무 어렵다고 생각해.

④ 나는 시험에 대해 걱정하지 않아도 돼.

⑤ 음, 지금 나는 우리가 제시간에 갈 수 있다는 것을 확신해.

have no idea 모르다 **lost** 길을 잃은 **get to** ~에 도착하다 **by** ~까지
sign 표지판 **on time** 제시간에, 정각에

20

M I can't believe this!

W What can't you believe?

M I won the piano contest!

W Wow, congratulations! I told you so.

M I'm going to get $100.

W I am so happy for you.

....

남 믿을 수가 없어!

여 뭘 믿을 수 없다는 거야?

남 내가 피아노 경연 대회에서 우승했어!

여 우와, 축하해! 내가 그랬잖아.

남 나 100달러를 받게 돼.

여 정말 잘됐다.

① 알았어. 괜찮아.

② 정말 잘됐다.

③ 나는 네게 정말 화가 나.

④ 근사한 콘서트가 될 거야.

⑤ 오, 그건 좋은 생각이 아닌데.

believe 믿다 **contest** 경연 대회 **upset** 화가 난

Further **S**tudy 정답 p. 24

1 It is *Who moved my cheese?*.

2 She bought a tennis racket last week.

3 She has a cold.

4 They bought them wallets.

5 The reason is that she had to visit her grandma in the hospital.

6 Her birthday is on May 13th.

7 She saw the movie with Ann last week.

8 She is going to get $100 as prize money.

On **Y**our **O**wn 모범답안 p. 25

A

What I Did Last Parents' Day	
(1) What did you do last Parents' Day?	① made paper carnations ② wrote a card
(2) How did your parents feel?	surprised
(3) What did your parents say to you?	"Thank you."
(4) How did you feel?	proud of myself
(5) What will you do next Parents' Day?	sing a song for my parents

Today, I am going to talk about what I did last Parents' Day. I ①made paper carnations and ②wrote a card. My parents were very (2)surprised and said to me, "(3)Thank you." I felt very (4)proud of myself. Next Parents' Day, I think I will (5)sing a song for my parents.

....

지난 어버이날에 한 일	
(1) 지난 어버이날에 무엇을 했습니까?	① 종이 카네이션 만듦 ② 카드 씀
(2) 부모님은 기분이 어떠셨습니까?	놀람
(3) 부모님이 뭐라고 말씀했습니까?	"고맙구나."
(4) 당신은 기분이 어땠습니까?	나 자신에 대해 자랑스러움
(5) 다음 어버이날에는 무엇을 할 것입니까?	부모님께 노래를 불러 드림

저는 오늘 지난 어버이날 제가 한 일에 대해 이야기하겠습니다. 저는 종이 카네이션을 만들고 카드를 썼습니다. 부모님은 매우 놀라시며 저에게 "고맙구나"라고 말씀하셨습니다. 저는 제 자신이 매우 자랑스러웠습니다. 다음 어버이날에는 부모님을 위해 노래를 불러 드릴 생각입니다.

B

My Free-Time Activities	
Activities	Reasons I enjoy doing it
① play soccer	③ exciting, good for my health
② listen to music	④ makes me feel better, especially when I am depressed

I'm going to talk about what I like to do in my free time. In my free time, I like to ①play soccer. I enjoy doing it because ③it is exciting and good for my health. Besides ①playing soccer, I also like to ②listen to music. The reason is that ④it makes me feel better, especially when I am depressed.

나의 여가 활동	
활동	즐기는 이유
① 축구 하기	③ 신남, 건강에 좋음
② 음악 듣기	④ 특히 우울할 때 기분을 좋게 해 줌

저는 제가 여가 시간에 즐겨 하는 것에 대해 이야기하겠습니다. 여가 시간에 저는 축구 하는 것을 좋아합니다. 저는 그것이 신나고 건강에 좋기 때문에 그것을 하는 것을 즐깁니다. 축구 하는 것 외에도, 저는 또한 음악 듣는 것을 좋아합니다. 그 이유는 특히 우울할 때 음악을 들으면 기분이 좋아지기 때문입니다.

01 ③	02 ③	03 ④	04 ⑤	05 ③
06 ②	07 ①	08 ④	09 ④	10 ③
11 ④	12 ⑤	13 ④	14 ①	15 ①
16 ①	17 ①	18 ③	19 ②	20 ⑤

01

W Good morning. This is the weather report for today and tomorrow. It will be rainy and cold this afternoon, and the rain will continue tonight. Tomorrow, the rain will stop, and we'll have a sunny day. Thank you.

여 좋은 아침입니다. 오늘과 내일의 일기 예보입니다. 오늘 오후에는 비가 내리고 춥겠으며, 비는 오늘 밤까지 계속될 것입니다. 내일은 비가 그치겠고, 맑은 날이 될 것입니다. 감사합니다.

••
weather report 일기 예보 **rainy** 비가 오는 **cold** 추운 **continue** 계속되다

02

M What a cute face painting!
W Thank you for saying so. I got this flower painting at the art festival.
M Really? Did you buy your sunglasses there, too?
W Yes. I wanted to buy a cap, but I didn't.
M You look so good.

남 페이스 페인팅이 참 귀엽다!
여 그렇게 말해 줘서 고마워. 예술제에 갔다가 꽃 그림을 그렸어.
남 정말? 그곳에서 선글라스도 샀니?
여 응. 모자도 사고 싶었지만 그러지 않았어.
남 너 정말 멋지다.

••
cute 귀여운 **art festival** 예술제 **cap** 야구 모자 **look good** 멋져 보이다, 좋아 보이다

03

W How may I help you?

M I'd like to buy <u>tickets</u> for *Champion*. <u>How</u> <u>much</u> are the tickets?

W They are $7 for <u>adults</u> and $3 for <u>children</u>. How many do you <u>need</u>?

M <u>Two</u> adults and <u>one</u> child, please.

W Okay.

여 어떻게 도와드릴까요?

남 〈챔피언〉 표를 구매하고 싶습니다. 얼마죠?

여 성인은 7달러, 어린이는 3달러입니다. 몇 장 필요하세요?

남 성인 두 장과 어린이 한 장 주세요.

여 네.

●●
How much ~? ~이 얼마인가요?, 얼마나 많은 양의 ~?   **adult** 성인
How many ~? 얼마나 많은 ~?   **need** 필요하다

04

W Look at the children <u>in</u> <u>the</u> <u>playground</u>. They <u>look</u> so <u>excited</u>.

M Yes. Look at that boy <u>running</u>.

W You mean the boy with the <u>red</u> <u>cap</u> on?

M Yes. He's running very <u>fast</u>.

W Oh, that is my <u>son</u>.

M Wow! Your son is a <u>great</u> <u>runner</u>.

여 운동장에 있는 아이들을 보세요. 정말 신나 보여요.

남 맞아요. 저기 뛰고 있는 남자아이 좀 보세요.

여 빨간 모자 쓴 아이 말하는 거예요?

남 네. 정말 빨리 뛰네요.

여 오, 제 아들이에요.

남 우와! 당신 아들은 정말 훌륭한 달리기 선수네요.

●●
playground 운동장   **excited** 신난, 흥분한   **runner** 달리기 선수

05

W Excuse me, <u>how</u> <u>can</u> <u>I</u> <u>get</u> <u>to</u> a pharmacy?

M Go two blocks and turn left.

W Go <u>two</u> <u>blocks</u> and <u>turn</u> <u>left</u>?

M Yes. It's the second building <u>on</u> <u>your</u> <u>right</u>.

W Okay. Thank you.

여 실례지만, 약국에 어떻게 가나요?

남 두 블록 가서 좌회전하세요.

여 두 블록 가서 좌회전이요?

남 네. 오른편에 있는 두 번째 건물입니다.

여 알겠습니다. 감사합니다.

●●
pharmacy 약국   **turn left** 좌회전하다   **on one's right** ~의 오른편에

06

W Oh! Mom's birthday is <u>coming</u> <u>soon</u>.

M You're right. What are you going to buy for her?

W Well. I'm <u>thinking</u> <u>about</u> a <u>scarf</u>.

M Then, I will buy her a <u>broach</u>. It will be good if she wears it with the scarf.

W That's a <u>good</u> <u>idea</u>.

여 오! 엄마 생신이 곧 다가오네.

남 맞아. 엄마께 무얼 사 드릴 거니?

여 글쎄. 스카프를 생각하고 있는데.

남 그럼 나는 브로치를 사 드려야겠다. 스카프와 함께 달면 예쁠 거야.

여 좋은 생각이야.

●●
soon 곧   **think about** ~에 대해 생각하다   **scarf** 스카프, 목도리
broach 브로치   **wear** 매다, 입다

07

[Telephone rings.]

W Hello?

M Hello, Gloria. Are you free <u>this</u> <u>afternoon</u>?

W Well, I have to help my mom, but it won't <u>take</u> <u>so</u> <u>long</u>.

M Nice. I bought a new <u>jump</u> <u>rope</u> so I want to <u>try</u> <u>it</u> <u>out</u>. Can you do with me?

W Sure. I'll go to your house at 5.

M Okay. <u>See</u> <u>you</u>.

[전화벨이 울린다.]

여 여보세요?

남 여보세요. Gloria. 오늘 오후에 한가하니?

여 글쎄, 엄마를 도와드려야 하는데, 오래 걸리진 않을 거야.

남 잘됐다. 내가 줄넘기를 새로 샀는데 한 번 해 보고 싶어서. 나랑 같이 할래?

여 물론이지. 너희 집으로 5시까지 갈게.

남 알았어. 이따 봐.

•• **free** 한가한 **take** 시간이 걸리다 **jump rope** 줄넘기 **try out** 시험 삼아 해 보다

08

M What are you going to do on Sunday?

W I'm not sure. I may stay home and watch TV. How about you?

M I'm going to play soccer in the park.

W Sounds great. Have fun!

M Thank you.

남 일요일에 무엇을 할 거니?

여 잘 모르겠어. 집에서 TV 볼 것 같은데. 너는?

남 나는 공원에서 축구를 할 거야.

여 좋겠다. 재미있게 보내!

남 고마워.

•• **stay home** 집에 머무르다 **have fun** 재미있게 보내다

09

M Congratulations, Minji. Your English test score was the best in our school.

W Really? I can't believe it. I'm so happy now.

M I'm very proud of you. I hope you will keep up the good effort.

W Thank you. I will try my best, Mr. Hanks.

M Good girl.

남 민지야. 축하한다! 전교에서 네 영어 점수가 제일 높구나.

여 정말이요? 믿을 수가 없어요. 정말 기뻐요.

남 네가 정말 자랑스럽구나. 네가 계속 노력하기 바란다.

여 감사합니다. 최선을 다할게요. Hanks 선생님.

남 착하구나.

•• **score** 점수, 성적 **be proud of** ~을 자랑스럽게 여기다 **keep up** 계속하다 **effort** 노력

10

M What are you going to do this weekend?

W I'm not sure. I may go to the bookstore.

M For what?

W I want to buy some books to read. How about you?

M I'm going to the library to get some information for my report.

W Then, why don't we go together?

M Sounds good.

남 너 이번 주말에 무엇을 할 거니?

여 잘 모르겠어. 서점에 갈 것 같은데.

남 뭐 하려고?

여 읽을 책 좀 사려고. 너는?

남 나는 보고서를 쓰기 위해 정보를 수집하러 도서관에 갈 거야.

여 그럼 같이 가는 게 어때?

남 좋아.

•• **sure** 확실한, 확신하는 **may** (추측) ~일지도 모른다 **For what?** 뭐 하려고? **information** 정보 **report** 보고서

11

W Tom, are you busy now?

M Not really. Why?

W Can I ask you a favor?

M What is it?

W I have to send these two packages. Would you mind taking one of these to the post office for me?

M No problem. I'll take the heavy one.

여 Tom, 너 지금 바빠?

남 그렇지 않아. 왜?

여 내 부탁 좀 들어 줄래?

남 뭐니?

여 이 소포 두 개를 보내야 하는데. 날 위해 이 중 하나만 우체국까지 들어 줄 수 있을까?

남 문제없어. 내가 무거운 걸로 들게.

•• **busy** 바쁜 **favor** 부탁 **package** 소포 **Would you mind -ing?** ~해 줄래? **take A to B** A를 B까지 가져가다 **heavy** 무거운

12

M Would you take a look at this <u>MP3 player</u>?

W Yes, of course. Hmm... <u>How long</u> have you had it?

M About <u>4 years</u>. Can you tell me <u>how much</u> it'll cost <u>to repair</u> it?

W It'll be <u>more than</u> $100. I suggest you <u>buy a new one</u> instead of getting it <u>fixed</u>.

남 이 MP3 플레이어 좀 봐 주시겠어요?

여 네, 물론이죠. 음…. 이것을 가지고 계신 지는 얼마나 되었나요?

남 4년쯤요. 수리하는 데 얼마나 들까요?

여 100달러는 더 들 거예요. 이걸 고치기보다는 새것으로 사시는 걸 권해 드립니다.

••

take a look at ~을 살펴보다 **cost** 비용이 들다 **repair** 수리하다. 고치다 **more than** ~ 이상 **suggest** 제안하다 **instead of** ~대신에 **fix** ~을 고치다

13

W Hi, Sam. It's Kate. I <u>just arrived</u>. <u>When</u> are you arriving?

M Hi, Kate. I'm <u>already</u> there. I've been waiting for you.

W I <u>can't see</u> you. <u>Where</u> are you now?

M I'm <u>in front of</u> exit 1 at Gangnam Station.

W Oh, I'm sorry. I thought we <u>are going to meet</u> at exit 1 at Shinchon Station.

여 안녕, Sam. 나 Kate야. 나 방금 도착했어. 너 언제 도착하니?

남 안녕, Kate. 나 벌써 와 있어. 너 기다리고 있어.

여 안 보이는데. 너 지금 어디니?

남 강남역 1번 출구 앞이야.

여 오, 미안. 난 우리가 신촌역 1번 출구에서 만나기로 했다고 생각했어.

••

arrive 도착하다 **already** 이미 **wait for** ~을 기다리다 **in front of** ~ 앞에 **exit** 출구

14

① **W** This pie chart shows popular cities <u>to live in</u>.

② **W** Paris is <u>the most</u> popular city to visit.

③ **W** Rome is <u>more</u> popular <u>than</u> Berlin.

④ **W** New York is 12% <u>less</u> popular <u>than</u> Paris.

⑤ **W** Berlin is <u>the least popular</u> among five cities.

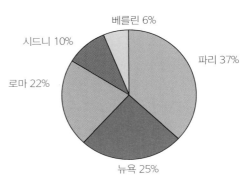

방문하고 싶은 도시

베를린 6%
시드니 10%
로마 22%
파리 37%
뉴욕 25%

---

① 여 이 원그래프는 살고 싶은 인기 도시를 보여 준다.

② 여 파리는 방문하고 싶은 가장 인기 있는 도시이다.

③ 여 로마는 베를린보다 더 인기 있다.

④ 여 뉴욕은 파리보다 12% 덜 인기 있다.

⑤ 여 베를린은 다섯 도시 가운데 가장 인기가 없다.

••

pie chart 원그래프 **popular** 인기 있는 **city** 도시 **less** 덜 ~한 **among** ~가운데

15

M Hi, Jennie. Come on in.

W Hi, Tom. Ann is <u>on her way</u>.

M Yeah, I know. She <u>called me</u> just <u>before</u> you arrived.

W <u>What</u> would you like to talk about for our <u>group presentation</u>?

M I'd like to talk about <u>water shortages</u>.

W Oh, I like <u>your topic</u> better than mine. Let's <u>have a vote</u> when Ann gets here.

남 안녕, Jennie. 들어와.

여 안녕, Tom. Ann은 오고 있어.

남 응. 나도 알아. 네가 도착하기 직전에 그녀가 내게 전화했어.

여 너는 우리 그룹 발표에서 무엇에 대해 얘기하고 싶니?

남 나는 물 부족에 대해 얘기하고 싶어.

여 오. 네 주제가 내 것보다 마음에 드는데. Ann이 도착하면 투표 하자.

••

come on in 들어오다 **on one's way** ~하는 중인 **call** 전화하다 **presentation** 발표 **shortage** 부족 **topic** 주제 **vote** 투표 **get** 도착하다

16

① M Why don't you come to my house?

W Because I'm sick.

② W What do you do in the morning?

M I work out and then have breakfast.

③ M How much is it?

W It's 2 dollars.

④ M What's the date today?

W It's October 27th.

⑤ M Help yourself.

W No, thanks. I have had enough.

. . . .

① 남 우리 집에 오는 거 어때?

여 왜냐하면 내가 아프기 때문이야.

② 여 너는 아침에 무엇을 하니?

남 운동하고 아침 식사를 해요.

③ 남 얼마예요?

여 2달러예요.

④ 남 오늘이 며칠이죠?

여 10월 27일입니다.

⑤ 남 마음껏 드세요.

여 고맙지만 사양할게요. 많이 먹었어요.

work out 운동하다 **date** 날짜 **October** 10월 **help oneself** 마음껏
먹다

17

W Ladies and gentlemen, can I have your attention, please? A girl named Cathy Johns is looking for her parents. She is six years old. She is wearing a red shirt with white pants. Will Cathy's parents please come to the information desk on the first floor right now?

. . . .

여 신사 숙녀 여러분, 주목해 주시겠어요? Cathy Johns라는 이름을
가진 여자아이가 부모님을 찾고 있습니다. 그녀는 6살입니다. 그녀는
빨간색 셔츠에 흰색 바지를 입고 있습니다. Cathy의 부모님은 지금
당장 안내 데스크로 와 주시겠습니까?

lady 숙녀 **gentleman** 신사 **attention** 주의, 집중 **named** ～라
고 이름 붙여진 **look for** ～을 찾다 **parents** 부모 **wear** ～을 입다
information desk 안내 데스크 **first floor** 1층 **right now** 지금 당장

18

M Jennie has a presentation tomorrow. Last night, she worked on her computer for more than five hours to make a handout. She saved the file on her computer. This morning when she turned on her computer, it didn't work. She told her teacher, Mr. Smith, about this matter. In this situation, what would Mr. Smith say to her?

. . . .

남 Jennie는 내일 발표가 있습니다. 어젯밤, 그녀는 유인물을 만들기
위해 5시간 이상 컴퓨터 작업을 했습니다. 그녀는 파일을 컴퓨터에
저장했습니다. 오늘 아침 그녀가 컴퓨터를 켰을 때, 컴퓨터가 작동하지
않았습니다. 그녀는 이 문제를 Smith 선생님께 말씀 드렸습니다. 이
상황에서 Smith 선생님은 그녀에게 뭐라고 말할까요?

① 근사하게 들리는 걸!

② 너 정말 잘했다!

③ 그 말을 들으니 유감이구나.

④ 미안해. 다시는 그러지 않을게.

⑤ 내가 실수를 하다니 정말 너무 화가 나.

work on one's computer 컴퓨터로 작업하다 **handout** 유인물
save 저장하다 **turn on** ～을 켜다 **work** 작동하다 **matter** 문제, 사건,
일 **make a mistake** 실수하다

19

M May I help you?

W Yes, please. I'd like a hamburger with fries.

M Anything to drink?

W A large coke, please.

M To go or for here?

W To go, please.

. . . .

남 도와드릴까요?

여 네, 감자튀김과 햄버거 주세요.

남 음료는요?

여 콜라 큰 거 주세요.

남 가져가시나요 아니면 여기서 드시나요?

여 가져갑니다.

① 여기 있습니다.

② 가져갑니다.

③ 식사 맛있게 하세요.

④ 여기 거스름돈 있습니다.

⑤ 네. 10달러 50센트입니다.

fries 감자튀김 **meal** 식사 **change** 거스름돈

20

w How are you doing, Billy?

M Great. How about you, Jane?

w Good. By the way, who is the man next to you?

M Oh, this is my English teacher, Mr. Brown. Mr. Brown, this is my friend, Jane.

w How do you do? Pleased to meet you, Mr. Brown.

여 어떻게 지내니, Billy?

남 아주 잘 지내. 너는 어때, Jane?

여 좋아. 그건 그렇고, 네 옆의 남자분은 누구시니?

남 오, 이분은 나의 영어 선생님인 Brown 선생님이셔. Brown 선생님. 이얘는 제 친구 Jane이에요.

여 처음 뵙겠습니다. 만나 뵙게 되어 기쁩니다, Brown 선생님.

① 오랜만입니다.

② 기분이 어떠세요?

③ 당신을 제 친구에게 소개하고 싶습니다.

④ 저는 한국 출신입니다. 어디 출신이세요?

⑤ 처음 뵙겠습니다. 만나 뵙게 되어 기쁩니다, Brown 선생님.

by the way 그건 그렇고 **next to** ~옆에 **introduce** 소개하다 **be from** ~출신이다 **pleased** 기쁜

Further **S**tudy 정답   p. 34

1 It is going to be rainy and cold this afternoon.

2 The reason is that her mom's birthday is coming soon.

3 He bought a new jump rope.

4 The reason is that her English test score was the best in their school.

5 He wanted her to fix it.

6 The reason is that Ann called him[Tom] just before Jennie arrived.

7 He wanted to eat a hamburger, fries, and a large coke.

8 They have never met before.

On **Y**our **O**wn 모범답안   p. 35

A

I am going to show you how you can get to the (1)church. First, (2)go straight for two blocks. Then, (3)turn left. It is (4)on your right.

길 안내하기	
(1) 교회 / 도서관 / 서점 / 약국 / 학교 / 미용실	(2) 한/두 블록 직진하세요
(3) 모퉁이에서 우회전/좌회전하세요	(4) 우측/좌측에 있는

당신에게 교회까지 어떻게 갈 수 있는지 알려 드리겠습니다. 먼저, 두 블록 직진하세요. 그다음에, 모퉁이에서 좌회전하세요. 교회는 당신 우측에 있습니다.

B

The City I Want to Visit	
City name	New York
Reason I want to visit the city	New York is the most famous city in the world.
Things to do	① have a cup of coffee in Times Square ② take a walk in Central Park ③ ride a ferry to see the Statue of Liberty ④ watch the musical *Phantom of the Opera* on Broadway ⑤ enjoy the night view at the top of the Empire State Building

(1)New York is the city I want to visit most. I really want to visit there because I think (2)New York is the most famous city in the world. I have many things to do when I visit there. First, I'll ①have a cup of coffee in Times Square. Second, I'll ②take a walk in Central Park. Third, I'll ③ride a ferry to see the Statue of Liberty. Then, I'll ④watch the musical *Phantom of the Opera* on Broadway. Finally, I'll ⑤enjoy the night view at the top of the Empire State Building.

내가 방문하고 싶은 도시	
도시 명	뉴욕
방문하고 싶은 이유	뉴욕은 세계에서 가장 유명한 도시이다.
할 것	① 타임스퀘어에서 커피 마시기 ② 센트럴 공원에서 산책하기 ③ 자유의 여신상을 보기 위해 페리 타기 ④ 브로드웨이에서 뮤지컬 〈오페라의 유령〉 보기 ⑤ 엠파이어스테이트 빌딩 꼭대기에서 야경 즐기기

뉴욕은 제가 가장 방문하고 싶은 도시입니다. 저는 뉴욕이 세계에서 제일 유명한 도시라고 생각하기 때문에 그곳에 정말 가 보고 싶습니다. 제가 그곳에 가게 되면 할 것들이 많이 있습니다. 첫 번째, 타임스퀘어에서 커피를 한 잔 할 거예요. 두 번째, 센트럴파크에서 산책을 할 겁니다. 세 번째, 자유의 여신상을 보기 위해 페리를 탈 겁니다. 그런 다음, 브로드웨이에서 뮤지컬 〈오페라의 유령〉을 볼 겁니다. 마지막으로, 엠파이어스테이트 빌딩 꼭대기에서 야경을 즐길 겁니다.

04 Listening Test 정답

p. 40

01 ②	02 ⑤	03 ④	04 ⑤	05 ⑤
06 ④	07 ⑤	08 ④	09 ①	10 ③
11 ⑤	12 ⑤	13 ⑤	14 ⑤	15 ④
16 ③	17 ⑤	18 ⑤	19 ③	20 ④

01

w When are you going to New York?

M On Saturday.

w Did you check the weather forecast?

M Yes. It said it's going to snow on the weekend.

w I see. You'd better pack a thick coat.

여 뉴욕에는 언제 갈 거니?

남 토요일에.

여 일기 예보는 확인했니?

남 그럼. 주말에 눈이 올 거라고 했어.

여 알겠어. 두꺼운 코트를 싸가는 것이 좋겠다.

check 확인하다 **weather forecast** 일기 예보 **snow** 눈이 오다 **had better** ~하는 게 더 낫다 **pack** (짐을) 싸다 **thick** 두꺼운

02

w This is the tallest animal you can see in the zoo. This animal is famous for its long neck. It eats leaves on top of trees. Its color is yellow and has brown dots all over its body. What is it?

여 이것은 동물원에서 볼 수 있는 가장 키가 큰 동물입니다. 이 동물은 긴 목을 가지고 있는 것으로 유명합니다. 그것은 나무 꼭대기에 있는 나뭇잎을 먹습니다. 그것의 색깔은 노란색이고 온 몸에 갈색 점들이 있습니다. 그것은 무엇일까요?

tall 키가 큰 **be famous for** ~로 유명하다 **on top of** ~의 꼭대기에 **brown** 갈색의 **dot** 점

03

[Telephone rings.]

w San Francisco Public Library. Can I help you?

M Hi. I think I left my MP3 player there. Have you seen it?

w What does it look like? I will check it out.

M It is a blue one with white stripes.

M Oh, it is here in the lost-and-found basket.

w Thanks. I'll be there soon.

[전화벨이 울린다.]

여 샌프란시스코 공공 도서관입니다. 도와드릴까요?

남 안녕하세요. 그곳에 제가 제 MP3 플레이어를 두고 온 듯한데요. 그것을 보셨나요?

여 어떻게 생겼나요? 확인해 보겠습니다.

남 흰색 줄무늬가 있는 파란색입니다.

여 아, 분실물 바구니에 있습니다.

남 감사합니다. 금방 가겠습니다.

public 공공의 **check out** 확인하다 **stripe** 줄무늬 **lost-and-found basket** 분실물 바구니

04

W Did you enjoy the party last night?

M It was not fun at all. I don't want to talk about it.

W Come on! What happened?

M It was horrible. The party place was messy, the food was cold, and the people came late.

W Oh, I'm sorry to hear that.

여 어젯밤 파티는 즐거웠어?

남 전혀 즐겁지 않았어. 말하기도 싫어.

여 어서! 무슨 일이 있었는데?

남 끔찍했어. 파티 장소는 지저분했고, 음식은 차가웠고, 사람들은 늦게 왔어.

여 어머나, 유감이다.

① 행복한　　　② 지루한　　　③ 걱정하는

④ 고마운　　　⑤ 화가 난

●●
enjoy 즐기다　**not at all** 전혀 ～이 아닌　**fun** 재미있는　**horrible** 끔찍한
messy 지저분한　**cold** 차가운

05

M Excuse me, how can I get to a flower store?

W Go one block and turn right.

M And then?

W It's on your right, next to the post office.

M Okay. Thank you very much.

남 실례합니다, 꽃 가게에 어떻게 갈 수 있나요?

여 한 블록을 가셔서 오른쪽으로 도세요.

남 그다음에는요?

여 당신의 오른편, 우체국 옆에 있습니다.

남 알겠습니다. 정말 감사합니다.

●●
get to ～에 도착하다　**flower shop** 꽃 가게　**turn right** 우회전하다
post office 우체국

06

M What do you want to order?

W I'll have a piece of cheese cake and a cola. How about you?

M I will have a piece of strawberry cake.

W What about a drink?

M I will have a glass of milk.

메뉴			
케이크		음료	
치즈케이크	$5.50	우유	$1.50
초콜릿 케이크	$4.00	사과 주스	$1.50
딸기 케이크	$3.00	콜라	$1.00

남 뭐 주문할래?

여 치즈케이크 한 조각과 콜라 먹을래. 너는?

남 나는 딸기 케이크 한 조각 먹을래.

여 음료수는?

남 우유 한 잔 마실게.

●●
order 주문하다　**a piece of** 한 조각의 ～　**a glass of** (유리컵) 한 잔의 ～

07

① W There is a sofa in the room.

② W There is a stand by the bed.

③ W A boy is sitting at the desk and using the computer.

④ W There is a bookshelf next to the desk.

⑤ W A boy is sitting at the desk and writing something.

---

① 여 방에 소파가 있다.

② 여 침대 옆에 스탠드가 있다.

③ 여 소년이 책상에 앉아서 컴퓨터를 사용하고 있다.

④ 여 책상 옆에 책장이 있다.

⑤ 여 소년이 책상에 앉아서 무언가를 쓰고 있다.

●●
stand 스탠드　**by** ～옆에　**bookshelf** 책장, 책꽂이　**next to** ～옆에

08

M Are you okay, Sumi? You look sick.

W I don't feel well. I have a terrible headache.

M I'm sorry to hear that. Did you take some medicine?

W Not yet. But I think I should. Thanks.

M You're welcome.

남 수미야, 괜찮니? 아파 보여.

여 별로 좋지 않아. 머리가 너무 아파.

남 안됐구나. 약은 먹었니?

여 아직. 그런데 먹어야겠어. 고마워.

남 아니야.

•• **look** ~하게 보이다 **terrible** 끔찍한 **headache** 두통 **medicine** 약

09

[Doorbell rings.]

M Who is it?

W I'm your <u>neighbor</u> from <u>next</u> <u>door</u>.

M Hello. <u>What's the matter</u>?

W I can't <u>sleep</u> because it's too <u>noisy</u>. What's going on in there?

M Oh, I'm very sorry. I <u>moved in</u> last week so I'm having a <u>housewarming</u> party.

W Please <u>keep quiet</u>. It's 1 a.m.

[초인종이 울린다.]

남 누구세요?

여 옆집에 사는 이웃입니다.

남 안녕하세요. 무슨 일이세요?

여 너무 시끄러워서 잠을 잘 수가 없습니다. 여기 무슨 일이 있나요?

남 어. 정말 죄송합니다. 제가 지난주에 이사를 와서, 집들이를 하고 있습니다.

여 제발 조용히 좀 해 주세요. 지금 새벽 1시예요.

•• **neighbor** 이웃 **next door** 옆집 **noisy** 시끄러운 **housewarming party** 집들이

10

W How was the class?

M It was fun. But the teacher gave <u>a lot of</u> <u>homework</u>.

W That's her <u>style</u>. You have to stay in the library <u>most of the time</u>.

M I think so. That's where I am going now.

W <u>Cheer up</u>! I will go with you.

여 수업은 어땠어?

남 재미있었어. 그런데 선생님이 숙제를 많이 내주셨어.

여 그분 스타일이셔. 도서관에서 대부분의 시간을 머물러야 할 거야.

남 나도 그렇게 생각해. 지금 거기에 가고 있어.

여 힘내! 나도 같이 가자.

•• **class** 수업 **a lot of** 많은 **stay** 머무르다 **most of the time** 대부분의 시간 **Cheer up!** 힘내!

11

W Can you help me <u>make dinner</u>, Tom?

M Of course, Mom. <u>What</u> can I do for you?

W On the way home, could you drop by <u>a grocery store</u>?

M Okay, <u>what</u> do we need?

W We need some <u>eggs</u>, cucumbers, and <u>lettuce</u>.

여 저녁 만드는 것 도와줄 수 있니, Tom?

남 물론이에요. 엄마. 뭘 도와 드릴까요?

여 집에 오는 길에 식료품 가게에 들를 수 있니?

남 네, 뭐 필요해요?

여 계란, 오이, 그리고 양상추가 좀 필요하구나.

•• **on the way home** 집에 오는 길에 **drop by** ~에 들르다 **grocery shop** 식료품 가게 **cucumber** 오이 **lettuce** 양상추

12

W Try some <u>chocolate</u>. It's so <u>yummy</u>.

M No, thanks. I'll try some <u>later</u>.

W Why? You love <u>chocolate</u>.

M Yeah, I'm <u>crazy</u> <u>about</u> it but my tooth really <u>hurts</u> now. I need a <u>painkiller</u>.

W Oh, you need to go <u>to</u> <u>the</u> <u>dentist</u>.

M Well, if you are okay, would you <u>take</u> me <u>to</u> <u>the</u> <u>dentist</u>?

여 이 초콜릿 좀 먹어 봐. 정말 맛있어.

남 고맙지만 사양할게. 나중에 먹어 볼게.

여 왜? 너 초콜릿 좋아하잖아.

남 응, 초콜릿을 정말 좋아하는데 지금은 이가 너무 아파. 진통제가 필요해.

여 오, 너 치과에 가 봐야겠다.

남 혹시, 괜찮다면 나 좀 치과에 데려다 줄래?

yummy 맛있는 **later** 나중에 **be crazy about** ~을 정말 좋아하다
tooth 이 **hurt** 아프다 **painkiller** 진통제 **go to the dentist** 치과에
가다

13

W Hey, Tom. Where are you going?

M I'm going to the library.

W Do you want to borrow some books?

M No. I need some information for my presentation.

W What's the presentation about?

M It's about typhoons.

- -

여 이봐, Tom. 어디 가는 중이니?

남 도서관에 가던 중이야.

여 책 좀 빌리려고?

남 아니. 발표를 위해 정보가 좀 필요해.

여 무엇에 관한 발표니?

남 태풍에 관한 거야.

borrow 빌리다 **information** 정보 **presentation** 발표 **about** ~에
관한 **typhoon** 태풍

14

[Telephone rings.]

M Hello. This is David. May I speak to Ann?

W Sorry, she's out. Can I take a message?

M Yes. Please tell her that we will practice the play in
classroom 303 at school at 3 p.m. on Thursday.

W Okay, I will.

M Thank you very much.

- -

전화 메시지	
찾는 사람:	① Ann
전화 건 사람:	② David
메모:	③ 연극 연습
	④ 학교 303호 교실
	⑤ 화요일 오후 3시

[전화벨이 울린다.]

남 여보세요, David인데요. Ann과 통화할 수 있을까요?

여 미안하지만 나갔는데. 메시지 남겨 줄까?

남 네, 저희가 목요일 오후 3시에 학교 303호 교실에서 연극 연습할

거라고 전해 주세요.

여 알겠다. 전해 줄게.

남 정말 감사합니다.

out 외출한 **take a message** 메시지를 받다[남겨 주다] **practice** 연습
하다 **play** 연극

15

W Honey, what are you doing?

M I'm looking for my outdoor jacket.

W Which one?

M My red windbreaker jacket.

W Oh, it is at the cleaners for dry cleaning.

M Then, let me know the shop number. I'll call and
check when it will be done.

- -

여 여보, 뭐 하고 있어요?

남 내 아웃도어 재킷을 찾고 있었어요.

여 어떤 거요?

남 빨간색 바람막이 재킷이요.

여 오, 그거 드라이클리닝하려고 세탁소에 맡겼어요.

남 그럼, 그 가게 전화번호 좀 알려 줘요. 전화해서 언제 다 되는지
알아볼게요.

honey 여보, 자기 **outdoor** 야외의 **windbreaker** 바람막이 **cleaner**
세탁업자 **check** 확인하다

16

① M May I help you?

   W No. I'm just looking around.

② M Thank you for coming.

   W Thank you for inviting me.

③ M How are you doing?

   W I go to school by bicycle.

④ M What do you think it is?

   W It might be a cat.

⑤ M I have a bad cold.

   W That's too bad.

- -

① 남 도와드릴까요?

   여 아니에요. 그냥 둘러보는 중이에요.

② 남 와 주셔서 감사합니다.

   여 초대해 주셔서 감사합니다.

③ 남 어떻게 지내니?
여 나는 학교에 자전거 타고 가.
④ 남 그게 뭐라고 생각해?
여 고양이일 거야.
⑤ 남 나 심한 감기에 걸렸어.
여 안됐다.

look around 둘러보다 **invite** 초대하다 **by bicycle** 자전거로 **bad cold** 심한 감기

17

M Hello. Welcome to Olympic Sports News. It is the fifth day of the London Winter Olympic Games. We have breaking news now. The Korean Skating team has made it to the final round. The final round is going to be at 10 a.m. on this Saturday. We hope the team will win the first gold medal in these Olympic Games.

남 안녕하십니까. 올림픽 스포츠 뉴스에 오신 걸 환영합니다. 런던 동계 올림픽 대회의 5일째 날입니다. 뉴스 속보를 말씀 드리겠습니다. 한국 스케이트 팀이 결승전에 진출했습니다. 결승전은 이번 주 토요일 아침 10시에 있을 예정입니다. 우리 스케이트 팀이 이번 올림픽 경기의 첫 금메달을 획득하기를 기원합니다.

Winter Olympic Games 동계 올림픽 **breaking news** 뉴스 속보 **final round** 결승전

18

M Kate is Bill's best friend. She studies very well. She always does her best. She got a perfect score on her English exam today. But she didn't do well on her math exam. She was very upset that she made so many mistakes. In this situation, what would Bill say to Kate?

남 Kate는 Bill의 절친입니다. 그녀는 공부를 아주 잘합니다. 그녀는 항상 최선을 다합니다. 그녀는 오늘 영어 시험에서 만점을 받았습니다. 하지만 수학 시험은 망쳤습니다. 그녀는 실수를 너무 많이 했다며 매우 화가 났습니다. 이 상황에서 Bill은 Kate에게 뭐라고 말할까요?

① 완벽한 것 같은데!
② 천만에.

③ 그것에 대해 잊지 마.
④ 너는 왜 그렇게 행복하니?
⑤ 기운 내! 다음에는 더 잘 할 수 있을 거야.

best friend 절친 **do one's best** 최선을 다하다 **get a perfect score** 만점을 받다 **exam** 시험 **do well on** ~을 잘하다 **upset** 화가 난 **make a mistake** 실수하다 **perfect** 완벽한

19

M What do you want to be, Jenny?
W Well, I don't know what I want to be.
M Well, what are you interested in?
W I'm interested in taking pictures.
M Then, what about becoming a professional photographer?
W That's a good idea. I'll think about that.

남 너는 장래에 뭐가 되고 싶니, Jenny?
여 글쎄요, 뭐가 되고 싶은지 잘 모르겠어요.
남 음, 무엇에 관심이 있니?
여 저는 사진 찍는 것에 관심이 있어요.
남 그럼 전문 사진작가가 되는 건 어떠니?
여 좋은 생각이에요. 그것에 대해 생각해 볼게요.

① 네가 그것을 좋아하기를 바라.
② 나는 네가 그것을 할 수 있다고 생각하지 않아.
③ 좋은 생각이에요. 그것에 대해 생각해 볼게요.
④ 나는 네가 훌륭한 사진사가 될 거라 생각해.
⑤ 저는 K-pop 스타들과 사진을 찍고 싶어요.

be interested in ~에 관심이 있다 **take pictures** 사진 찍다 **photographer** 사진작가

20

W Do you have any plans for this winter vacation?
M No, nothing special. How about you?
W I'm planning to go snowboarding. Do you want to join me?
M I'd like to, but unfortunately I can't snowboard.
W It doesn't matter. I can teach you.

여 이번 겨울 방학에 어떤 계획 있니?
남 아니, 특별한 건 없어. 너는 어때?
여 나는 스노보드 타러 갈 계획이야. 나랑 같이 갈래?

남 그러고 싶지만, 불행하게도 나는 스노보드를 못 타.

여 괜찮아. 내가 가르쳐 줄 수 있어.

① 그 말을 들으니 기뻐.
② 나는 스키 타는 것에도 관심 있어.
③ 그때는 안 될 것 같아.
④ 괜찮아. 내가 가르쳐 줄 수 있어.
⑤ 그럼 매표소 앞에서 만나자.

●●
plan 계획 **vacation** 방학 **special** 특별한 **go snowboarding** 스노보드 타러 가다 **join** 함께 하다 **unfortunately** 불행하게도 **matter** 문제가 되다 **ticket office** 매표소

Further Study 정답
p. 44

1 It is <u>famous for its long neck</u>.
2 (1) The party <u>place was messy</u>.
  (2) The food <u>was cold</u>.
  (3) The people <u>came late</u>.
3 She ordered <u>a piece of cheese cake</u> and <u>a cola</u>.
4 She has <u>a terrible headache</u>.
5 The reason is that she needs <u>some eggs, cucumbers, and lettuce to make dinner</u>.
6 He asked the woman <u>to take him to the dentist</u>.
7 He is going to <u>talk about typhoons</u>.
8 It is that <u>the Korean Skating team has made it to the final round</u>.

On Your Own 모범답안
p. 45

A

My Birthday	
(1) When is your birthday?	December 2nd
(2) Where do you usually have your birthday party?	at a restaurant
(3) Who do you usually celebrate your birthday with?	my friends and family
(4) What do you like to do on your birthday?	go to the movies with my friends
(5) What do you want to get for your birthday?	a new cell phone

I'm going to talk about my birthday. My birthday is on (1)<u>December 2nd</u>. I usually have my birthday party (2)<u>at a restaurant</u>. I also usually celebrate my birthday with (3)<u>my friends and family</u>. On my birthday, I like to (4)<u>go to the movies with my friends</u>. If I could get anything for my birthday, I would like to get (5)<u>a new cell phone</u>. I wish every day was my birthday.

나의 생일	
(1) 생일이 언제입니까?	12월 2일
(2) 보통 어디에서 생일 파티를 합니까?	식당에서
(3) 보통 누구와 생일을 축하합니까?	친구들과 가족
(4) 생일에 주로 무엇을 합니까?	친구들과 영화 보러 가기
(5) 생일 선물로 무엇을 받고 싶습니까?	새 휴대 전화

제 생일에 대해 이야기하겠습니다. 제 생일은 12월 2일입니다. 저는 보통 식당에서 생일 파티를 합니다. 저는 또한 친구들과 가족과 주로 생일을 축하합니다. 제 생일에 저는 친구들과 영화 보러 가는 것을 좋아합니다. 만약 생일 선물로 무엇이든지 받을 수 있다면, 저는 새 휴대 전화를 받고 싶습니다. 저는 매일이 제 생일이었으면 좋겠습니다.

B

My Future Job	
(1) What do you want to be?	a doctor
(2) Why do you want to be a(n) _____?	① find cures for cancer and other disease ② help sick and poor people
(3) To be a(n) _____, what do you need to do?	③ study math, science, English, and other subjects ④ get excellent grades at school to prepare for medical school

I want to be a (1)<u>doctor</u> when I grow up. There are two reasons why I want to be a (1)<u>doctor</u>. First, I want to ①<u>find cures for cancer and other diseases</u>. Second, I want to ②<u>help sick and poor people</u>. To be a (1)<u>doctor</u>, I need to ③<u>study math, science, English, and other subjects</u>. I also have to ④<u>get excellent grades at school to prepare for medical school</u>. I believe I will be able to be a great (1)<u>doctor</u> someday.

내 미래의 직업	
(1) 무엇이 되고 싶습니까?	의사
(2) 왜 _____가 되고 싶은가?	① 암과 다른 질병들의 치료법 찾기 ② 아프고 가난한 사람들 돕기
(3) _____가 되기 위해서는, 무엇을 해야 하는가?	③ 수학, 과학, 영어 등 공부하기 ④ 의대 진학을 위해 우수한 성적 받기

저는 커서 의사가 되고 싶습니다. 제가 의사가 되고 싶은 데는 두 가지 이유가 있습니다. 첫 번째로, 저는 암과 다른 질병들의 치료법을 찾고 싶습니다. 두 번째로, 저는 아프고 가난한 사람들을 돕고 싶습니다. 의사가 되기 위해서, 저는 수학, 과학, 영어 등을 공부해야 합니다. 저는 또한 의대에 진학하기 위해 학교 성적이 우수해야 합니다. 저는 제가 언젠가 훌륭한 의사가 될 수 있다고 믿습니다.

05 Listening Test 정답　　p. 50

01 ②	02 ①	03 ③	04 ③	05 ④
06 ③	07 ①	08 ②	09 ⑤	10 ④
11 ③	12 ②	13 ①	14 ⑤	15 ③
16 ②	17 ④	18 ⑤	19 ③	20 ⑤

01

[Telephone rings.]

M Hello, can I talk to Susie, please?

W Speaking. Who's this?

M Hi, Susie. It's Adam. I'm going to Seoul this afternoon for a meeting. How's the weather there?

W It's a little cloudy right now, but the sun will be shining this afternoon.

M Oh, thanks.

⋯⋯⋯⋯⋯⋯⋯⋯⋯⋯⋯⋯⋯⋯⋯⋯⋯⋯⋯⋯⋯⋯⋯

[전화벨이 울린다.]

남 여보세요. Susie와 통화할 수 있을까요?

여 전데요. 전화 거신 분은 누구시죠?

남 안녕. Susie. 나 Adam이야. 회의가 있어서 오늘 오후에 서울에 갈 거야. 거기 날씨가 어때?

여 지금은 흐린데, 오후에는 맑을 거야.

남 오, 고마워.

•• **talk to** ~와 이야기하다　**weather** 날씨　**a little** 약간　**shine** 빛나다

02

M I live in China. I am very big. I have black and white fur. I have big black circles around my eyes. People think I am very cute. I was in a movie called *Kung Fu*. What am I?

⋯⋯⋯⋯⋯⋯⋯⋯⋯⋯⋯⋯⋯⋯⋯⋯⋯⋯⋯⋯⋯⋯⋯

남 나는 중국에 살고 있습니다. 나는 정말 큽니다. 나는 검정색과 흰색 털이 있습니다. 나는 눈 주위로 큰 검정색 원이 있습니다. 사람들은 내가 정말 귀엽다고 생각합니다. 나는 〈쿵푸〉라는 영화에 나왔습니다. 나는 무엇일까요?

•• **live in** ~에 살다　**China** 중국　**fur** 털　**circle** 원　**around** ~ 주위에 **cute** 귀여운　**movie** 영화　**call** 부르다, 전화하다

03

M What time is it now?

W It's 4:50.

M That's strange. The subway is late.

W I don't think so. According to the timetable, it runs every 7 minutes. It arrives in 2 minutes.

M Oh, I see. I thought it ran every 5 minutes. Thank you.

⋯⋯⋯⋯⋯⋯⋯⋯⋯⋯⋯⋯⋯⋯⋯⋯⋯⋯⋯⋯⋯⋯⋯

남 지금 몇 시인가요?

여 4시 50분입니다.

남 이상하네요. 지하철이 늦네요.

여 아닌데요. 시간표에 따르면, 7분마다 운행합니다. 2분 후에 도착합니다.

남 오, 그렇군요. 저는 5분마다 운행하는 줄 알았습니다. 감사합니다.

•• **strange** 이상한　**subway** 지하철　**according to** ~에 따르 면　**timetable** 시간표　**run** 운행하다　**every** 매, ~마다　**minute** 분 **arrive** 도착하다

04

W Hey, Jaemin, <u>what's up</u>?

M I just got some <u>bad</u> <u>news</u>.

W Bad news? What is it?

M One of my classmates was in a <u>car</u> <u>accident</u>.

W Oh, really? I'm so sorry.

M I think I have to go to the <u>hospital</u> right now.

....

여 안녕, 재민아. 무슨 일이야?

남 방금 안 좋은 소식을 들었어.

여 안 좋은 소식? 뭔데?

남 같은 반 친구가 교통 사고를 당했대.

여 아, 정말? 안됐다.

남 지금 당장 병원에 가는 게 좋을 거 같아.

●●
one of + 복수 명사 ~들 중의 하나 **classmate** 급우. 학급 친구 **car accident** 차 사고

05

M May I help you?

W I'd like to buy a gift for my <u>younger</u> <u>brother's</u> <u>birthday</u>.

M How about this toy car? This toy car is the <u>best</u> <u>selling</u> <u>product</u> in our shop.

W Really? What about this dinosaur <u>water</u> <u>gun</u>?

M Kids like that <u>a lot</u>, too.

W Okay. I'll take <u>both</u> of them.

....

남 도와드릴까요?

여 남동생 생일 선물을 사려고요.

남 이 장난감 자동차는 어떠신가요? 이 자동차가 저희 가게에서 가장 잘 팔리는 제품입니다.

여 정말요? 이 공룡 물총은 어떤가요?

남 아이들은 그것도 정말 좋아하죠.

여 알겠습니다. 두 개 다 주세요.

① 애완동물 가게 ② 파티장 ③ 박물관 ④ 장난감 가게 ⑤ 주차장

●●
younger brother 남동생 **best selling** 가장 잘 팔리는 **product** 제품
dinosaur 공룡 **water gun** 물총 **a lot** 많이 **both** 둘 다

06

W May I help you?

M Yes. I'm <u>looking</u> <u>for</u> a present for my <u>girlfriend</u>. Can you <u>recommend</u> me one?

W Okay. Girls like to have <u>perfume</u>, <u>necklaces</u>, <u>rings</u>, or face lotion.

M Well, can you show me a ring?

W Sure. Which one do you like? The <u>ribbon</u> shaped or the <u>heart</u> shaped one?

M The heart <u>shaped</u> one, please.

....

여 도와드릴까요?

남 네. 여자 친구에게 줄 선물을 찾고 있습니다. 하나 추천해 주실 수 있을까요?

여 네. 여자들은 향수, 목걸이, 반지, 또는 로션을 갖고 싶어합니다.

남 음, 반지를 보여 주시겠어요?

여 네. 어느 것이 좋으세요? 리본 모양, 아니면 하트 모양?

남 하트 모양이요.

●●
look for ~을 찾다 **present** 선물 **recommend** 추천하다 **perfume**
향수 **necklace** 목걸이 **ring** 반지 **face lotion** 얼굴에 바르는 로션
show 보여 주다 **ribbon** 리본 **shaped** ~ 모양의 **heart** 하트, 심장

07

[Beep]

W Hi, Jerry. This is Alice. I'm so sorry to <u>leave a</u> <u>message</u>. I'm afraid I <u>can't</u> <u>come</u> to your <u>birthday</u> <u>party</u> tonight. My mom is <u>sick</u>. I think I have to be with her. I hope you <u>understand</u>. See you tomorrow <u>at</u> <u>school</u>.

....

여 안녕, Jerry. 나 Alice야. 메시지를 남겨서 미안해. 오늘 저녁 네 생일 파티에 못 갈 거야. 어머니께서 아프셔. 나는 어머니하고 같이 있어야 할 것 같아. 이해해 주기를 바라. 내일 학교에서 보자.

●●
leave a message 메시지를 남기다 **understand** 이해하다

08

M Do we have <u>anything</u> <u>to eat</u> in the refrigerator?

W I don't think so. Why? Are you <u>hungry</u>?

M Yes, I'm <u>starving</u> because I didn't have <u>breakfast</u>.

W Hmm… Let's go out to eat. What do you want to eat?

M I want some Italian food. How about some spaghetti?

W That sounds good.

- -

남 냉장고에 먹을 게 있어?

여 없는 거 같은데. 왜? 배고파?

남 어, 아침을 안 먹었더니 정말 배가 고파.

여 음…. 먹으러 나가자. 뭐가 먹고 싶어?

남 이태리 음식이 먹고 싶어. 스파게티 어때?

여 좋아.

refrigerator 냉장고 **starve** 굶주리다 **breakfast** 아침 식사 **Italian** 이태리의 **spaghetti** 스파게티

09

W Did you finish your homework, sweetie?

M No, not yet.

W Please stop playing computer games and do your homework now.

M If I finish it by eight o'clock, can I play computer games again?

W Yes, you can.

- -

여 숙제는 다했어, 얘야?

남 아니요, 아직이요.

여 컴퓨터 게임 좀 그만하고, 당장 숙제를 해야지.

남 8시까지 숙제 끝내면, 컴퓨터 게임을 다시 할 수 있어요?

여 그래, 그렇게 하렴.

sweetie 애정을 담아 남을 부르는 호칭 **yet** 아직 **finish** 끝내다 **do one's homework** 숙제를 하다

10

M Hi, Jessica. How was your spring break?

W It was great. I watched several movies, read some interesting books, and also exercised at the gym.

M Didn't you visit your grandmother?

W Yes, I did. I had fun with her. I will visit her again next month.

M I'm happy to hear that.

남 안녕, Jessica. 봄 방학은 어땠어?

여 정말 좋았어. 영화 몇 편을 봤고, 흥미로운 책들을 읽었고, 체육관에서 운동을 했어.

남 할머니 댁에는 안 갔었니?

여 아니, 갔지. 할머니하고 재미있게 지냈어. 다음 달에 다시 찾아뵐 거야.

남 그 말을 들으니 기쁘구나.

spring break 봄 방학 **several** 몇몇의 **exercise** 운동하다 **gym** 체육관 **visit** 방문하다 **have fun** 즐거운 시간을 보내다. 재미있다

11

W Sam, do you know how to download a song?

M Yes, that's easy.

W Then, can you show me how to do it?

M Sure. Which song do you want to download?

W I want *Heal the World* by Michael Jackson.

- -

여 Sam, 노래 내려받을 줄 아니?

남 응, 그거 쉬워.

여 그럼, 어떻게 하는지 나한테 보여 줄래?

남 그래. 어떤 노래 내려받고 싶니?

여 Michael Jackson의 〈Heal the World〉.

download 내려받다 **easy** 쉬운 **heal** 치료하다

12

W Did you pick a book?

M Not yet. I don't know which book to choose.

W It's not easy to select suitable books in English.

M I want to try *the Harry Potter* series.

W Okay then, read the first chapter without using a dictionary and see if it is okay.

M Good idea. Thanks for your advice.

- -

여 너 책 골랐니?

남 아직. 어떤 책을 골라야 할지 모르겠어.

여 영어로 된 적당한 책을 선택하는 게 쉽진 않지.

남 나 〈해리포터〉 시리즈를 시도해 보고 싶어.

여 좋아 그럼, 사전을 이용하지 않고 첫 장을 읽고 괜찮은지 봐.

남 좋은 생각이다. 조언 고마워.

pick 고르다 **choose** 고르다 **select** 고르다. 선택하다 **suitable** 적당

한 **series** 연속 간행물, 시리즈물 **chapter** 장, 챕터 **without** ~없이
dictionary 사전 **advice** 충고, 조언

13

M Do you want to <u>go shopping</u> with me?

W <u>Well</u>, what do you want to buy?

M <u>Nothing</u> special. I just want to look around.

W Then, <u>I'd better</u> go home and <u>get</u> some <u>sleep</u>.

M Why? Didn't you sleep well <u>last</u> <u>night</u>?

W No, I didn't. I stayed up <u>all</u> <u>night</u> playing online games.

- -

남 나랑 쇼핑 갈래?

여 글쎄. 뭘 사고 싶니?

남 특별한 건 없어. 그냥 둘러보고 싶어서.

여 그럼. 나는 집에 가서 잠을 좀 자는 게 낫겠어.

남 왜? 어젯밤 잠을 잘 못 잤니?

여 응. 온라인 게임 하느라 밤을 새웠거든.

••
go shopping 쇼핑하러 가다 **special** 특별한 **look around** 둘러보다
had better ~하는 게 낫다 **get sleep** 잠을 자다 **stay up all night**
밤을 꼬박 새우다

14

W Tom, I lost my <u>puppy</u>. What should I do?

M Oh, I'm sorry to hear that. How about making a <u>poster</u>? I'll help you.

M [Pause] What's its <u>name</u>?

W It's Ahji.

M <u>How old</u> is it?

W Just <u>three months</u> old.

M <u>What</u> does it <u>look like</u>?

W It has a <u>small</u>, <u>white body</u> and a big <u>black spot</u> on its left ear.

M Good. What's your <u>phone number</u>?

W My number is <u>010-5432-9867</u>.

- -

┌─────────────────────────────────────┐
│   개를 찾습니다   │
│   │
│   이름: ① 아지   │
│   나이: ② 3개월   │
│   외모: ③ 작고, 하얀색   │
│   ④ 왼쪽 귀에 크고 까만 점   │
│   연락처: ⑤ 010-5432-9876   │
└─────────────────────────────────────┘

여 Tom, 내 강아지를 잃어버렸어. 어떡하지?

남 오, 그거 유감이다. 포스터 만드는 게 어때? 내가 도와줄게.

남 이름이 뭐야?

여 이름은 아지야.

남 나이는?

여 딱 세 달 됐어.

남 어떻게 생겼니?

여 작고 하얀 몸에 왼쪽 귀에 커다란 검은 점 하나가 있어.

남 좋아. 네 전화번호는 뭐니?

여 내 번호는 010-5432-9867이야.

••
puppy 강아지 **poster** 포스터 **month** 달 **look like** ~처럼 생기다
spot 점 **left** 왼쪽; 왼쪽의 **lost** 잃어 버린

15

[Telephone rings.]

M Hi, Liz. It's me, Peter. I'm <u>at the park</u> near your house. Would you like to come out?

W Hi, Peter. Sure.

M Why don't you come here <u>with your puppy</u>? I'm here with mine.

W Oh, that's one of your <u>birthday presents</u>, right? I can't wait to see him.

M I think they could be <u>good friends</u> like us.

W They will. I'll be there <u>in five minutes</u>.

- -

[전화벨이 울린다.]

남 안녕, Liz. 나야. Peter. 나 너네 집 근처 공원에 있어. 너 나올래?

여 안녕, Peter. 물론이지.

남 네 강아지도 데려오지 그래? 나도 우리 강아지랑 함께 있어.

여 오, 네 생일 선물 중의 하나, 맞지? 보고 싶어 못 기다리겠어.

남 우리처럼 개들도 좋은 친구가 될 거라고 생각해.

여 그럴 거야. 5분 내로 갈게.

••
near ~ 근처에 **can't wait to-V** 빨리 ~하고 싶다

16

① M Pass me the salt, please.

W Here you are.

② M Can I take your coat?

W My pleasure.

③ M May I speak to Jennie?

W This is she.

④ M What's up?

W Not much.

⑤ M Whose bag is this?

W I guess it's Tom's.

....

① 남 소금 좀 건네주세요.

여 여기 있어요.

② 남 코트 받아 드릴까요?

여 도움이 되어 기뻐요.

③ 남 Jennie 좀 바꿔 주시겠어요?

여 전데요.

④ 남 무슨 일 있니?

여 별일 없어.

⑤ 남 이거 누구 가방이니?

여 Tom의 것 같은데.

•• **pass** 건네다 **take a coat** 코트를 받아 주다 **My pleasure.** 도움이 되어 기뻐요. **guess** 추측하다

17

W Good evening, shoppers! Thank you for shopping at CYJ Mart. For the next ten minutes, bananas are on sale at 50% off. A bunch of bananas is six dollars. For ten minutes, buy a bunch of bananas, and get another free. Hurry! Get your bananas now! Enjoy shopping.

....

여 좋은 저녁입니다. 손님 여러분! CYJ 마트에서 쇼핑해 주셔서 감사합니다. 지금부터 10분 동안 바나나를 50% 할인합니다. 바나나 한 송이에 6달러입니다. 10분간, 바나나 한 송이를 사시면 다른 한 송이를 무료로 얻으실 수 있습니다. 서두르세요! 바나나를 사세요! 즐거운 쇼핑되세요.

•• **shopper** 쇼핑객 **next** 다음의 **off** (할인, 공제) 공제하여, 감하여 **bunch** 다발, 송이 **free** 무료인, 공짜인 **hurry** 서두르다

18

W Sue is not very good at singing. She had a singing test today. She practiced a lot for the test. She was so nervous that she made a mistake. One of her classmates, Wendy made fun of her about the mistake. Sue felt very down. In this situation, what would you say to Sue?

....

여 Sue는 노래를 아주 잘 부르지 못합니다. 그녀는 오늘 노래 부르기 시험이 있었습니다. 그녀는 시험을 위해 많은 연습을 했습니다. 그녀는 너무 긴장해서 실수를 했습니다. 그녀의 학급 친구 중 한 명인 Wendy가 그 실수에 대해 그녀를 놀렸습니다. Sue는 매우 의기소침해졌습니다. 이 상황에서 당신은 Sue에게 뭐라고 말할까요?

① 내게 말하지 마.

② 나는 네가 너무 부러워.

③ 다시는 그러지 않을게.

④ 걱정하지 마. 그녀는 괜찮을 거야.

⑤ 힘 내! 다음에 잘하면 돼.

•• **be good at** ~을 잘하다 **practice** 연습하다 **nervous** 긴장한 **make a mistake** 실수하다 **make fun of** ~을 놀리다 **down** 의기소침한 **envious** 부러워하는

19

M My team lost the relay because of me.

W Why do you think so?

M I sprained my ankle yesterday, so I couldn't run fast enough.

W Don't worry. It's not because of you. I know you did your best.

M Do you really think so?

W Of course. It's okay.

....

남 나 때문에 우리 팀이 이어달리기에서 졌어.

여 왜 그렇게 생각하니?

남 어제 내가 발목을 삐어서 충분히 빨리 달릴 수 없었어.

여 걱정하지 마. 너 때문이 아니야. 나는 네가 최선을 다했다는 거 알아.

남 정말 그렇게 생각해?

여 물론이지. 괜찮아.

① 그거 참 안됐다.

② 너 화났겠구나.

③ 물론이지. 괜찮아.

④ 물론이지. 너는 그것을 할 수 있어.

⑤ 응, 그래. 나는 최선을 다했어.

lose 지다 **relay** 이어달리기 **because of** ~때문에 **sprain** 삐다, 삐끗하다 **ankle** 발목 **fast** 빨리, 빠르게 **enough** 충분히 **do one's best** 최선을 다하다

20

M Susan, <u>what</u> do you think of this <u>painting</u>?

W I think it is really <u>colorful</u>. <u>Who</u> painted it?

M Van Gogh <u>did</u> it.

W Oh, did he? I didn't know that.

M <u>What</u> do you think of Van Gogh?

W <u>I think he is one of the greatest artists ever.</u>

남 Susan, 이 그림에 대해 어떻게 생각해?

여 정말 다채롭다고 생각해. 누가 그것을 그렸니?

남 반 고흐가 그렸어.

여 오, 그가? 몰랐어.

남 반 고흐에 대해 어떻게 생각해?

여 <u>나는 그가 가장 위대한 화가 중의 한 명이라고 생각해.</u>

① 그거 좋은 생각이야.

② 우와, 멋지다!

③ 나는 네가 좋아할 거라 확신해.

④ 나는 내가 그림을 잘 그린다고 생각해.

⑤ 나는 그가 가장 위대한 예술가 중의 한 명이라고 생각해.

painting 그림 **colorful** 다채로운 **great** 위대한 **painter** 화가 **artist** 화가, 예술가

Further Study 정답   p. 54

1 He is going to <u>Seoul this afternoon</u>.

2 One of the boy's <u>classmates had it</u>.

3 The reason is that <u>he didn't have breakfast</u>.

4 He can play computer games again when <u>he finishes his homework</u>.

5 He thinks <u>(that) it is easy</u>.

6 She <u>stayed up all night playing online games</u>.

7 The man wants to meet her <u>at the park near her house</u>.

8 The reason is that <u>he sprained his ankle the day before the relay</u>.

On Your Own 모범답안   p. 55

A

I am going to talk about my favorite food. My favorite food is (1)<u>Korean</u> food. I especially like (2)<u>*bulgogi*</u>. I usually eat it at (3)<u>home</u>. I also eat it on (4)<u>special days like my birthday and holidays</u>. I like it because it is (5)<u>delicious</u>.

내가 좋아하는 음식				
(1) 국가	(2) 음식	(3) 장소	(4) 언제	(5) 왜
한국 일본 중국 이탈리아 미국	불고기 초밥/회 자장면 피자/스파게티 햄버거	집 식당	명절 내 생일 특별한 날 평상시	맛있음 건강에 좋음 가격이 저렴함 만들기 쉬움

제가 가장 좋아하는 음식에 대해 이야기하겠습니다. 제가 가장 좋아하는 음식은 한식입니다. 저는 특히 불고기를 좋아합니다. 저는 주로 그것을 집에서 먹습니다. 저는 또한 제 생일이나 명절 같은 특별한 날에 그것을 먹습니다. 저는 그것이 매우 맛있어서 좋아합니다.

B

My Pet	
(1) Kind	dog
(2) Name	Snoopy
(3) Age (month/year)	3 months old
(4) Appearance	has a small, white body and a black spot on his left ear
(5) What it likes to do	play with a ball
(6) What you do for your pet	feed him, take him for a walk every day

I am going to introduce my pet. I have a (1)<u>dog</u> named (2)<u>Snoopy</u>. He is (3)<u>three months</u> old. He (4)<u>has a small, white body and a black spot on his left ear</u>. He likes to (5)<u>play with a ball</u>. What I do for my pet is (6)<u>feed him and take him for a walk every day</u>. I love my pet very much. He is one of my best friends.

나의 애완동물	
(1) 종류	개
(2) 이름	Snoopy
(3) 나이(개월/년)	6개월
(4) 외모	몸이 작고 하얀색임. 왼쪽 귀에 까만 점이 있음
(5) 좋아하는 것	공놀이 하기
(6) 당신이 그것에게 해 주는 것	먹이 주기, 매일 산책 시키기

제 애완동물을 소개하겠습니다. 저는 Snoopy라는 이름을 가진 개 한 마리를 갖고 있습니다. 그는 6개월이 되었습니다. 그는 작고, 하얀색 몸에, 왼쪽 귀에 까만 점 하나가 있습니다. 그는 공놀이 하는 것을 좋아합니다. 제 애완동물을 위해 제가 하는 일은 그에게 먹이를 주고 매일 산책을 시키는 것입니다. 저는 제 애완동물을 매우 사랑합니다. 그는 나의 가장 좋은 친구 중의 한 명입니다.

06 Listening Test 정답   p. 60

01 ④	02 ④	03 ⑤	04 ①	05 ②
06 ③	07 ②	08 ①	09 ③	10 ③
11 ④	12 ②	13 ③	14 ④	15 ⑤
16 ④	17 ④	18 ⑤	19 ③	20 ④

01

①W A boy is playing a computer game.
②W A girl is jogging in the park.
③W A boy is doing his homework.
④W A girl is playing the cello.
⑤W A girl is listening to music wearing headphones.

- - - - - - - - - - - -

①여 한 소년이 컴퓨터 게임을 하고 있다.
②여 한 소녀가 공원에서 조깅을 하고 있다.
③여 한 소년이 숙제를 하고 있다.
④여 한 소녀가 첼로를 연주하고 있다.
⑤여 한 소녀가 헤드폰을 끼고 음악을 듣고 있다.

jog 조깅하다 **cello** 첼로 **listen to** ~을 듣다 **headphone** 헤드폰

02

W What are you doing?
M I'm looking at the puppies. I'd like to buy one.
W I see. Which one do you like, the white one or the brown one? Some of them are wearing a collar while others are wearing a ribbon.
M Well. I will take the brown one with the collar and the ribbon.
W Okay. Let's go in.

- - - - - - - - - - - -

여 뭐 하고 있어?
남 강아지들을 보고 있어. 한 마리 사고 싶어.
여 그래. 어느 것이 마음에 드니, 흰색 강아지 아니면 갈색 강아지? 어떤 것들은 목걸이를 하고 있고, 다른 것들은 리본을 하고 있네.
남 그러네. 나는 목걸이와 리본을 하고 있는 갈색 강아지를 살래.
여 그래. 들어가자.

look at ~을 보다 **puppy** 강아지 **collar** (개 등의 목에 거는) 목걸이 **while** 반면

03

[Beep]
M Hello, Mary. This is Mark. Do you remember that we arranged to meet tomorrow? We were supposed to meet at the public library but I'd like to change the meeting place. I think it is too far away for both of us. Why don't we meet at school? Please call me back as soon as possible.

- - - - - - - - - - - -

남 여보세요. Mary. 나 Mark야. 내일 만나기로 한 거 기억하지? 공공 도서관에서 보기로 했는데, 약속 장소를 바꾸고 싶어. 우리 모두한테 너무 멀다는 생각이 들어. 학교에서 만나면 어떨까? 최대한 빨리 답신 전화 줘.

arrange 정하다　**be supposed to-V** ～하기로 되어 있다　**public library** 공공 도서관　**place** 장소　**far away** 먼　**both** 둘 다　**as + 형용사 + as possible** 가능한 한 ～하게

04

W　Honey, I want to <u>talk</u> <u>about</u> our son, Jake.

M　Sure. Is there <u>anything</u> <u>wrong</u>?

W　As you know, he used to study very well and <u>exercised</u> <u>regularly</u>.

M　You <u>mean</u> he's changed?

W　Yes. <u>Nowadays</u> he plays <u>computer</u> <u>games</u> all the time. He doesn't do what he <u>has</u> <u>to</u> <u>do</u>.

M　I will talk to him.

여　여보, 우리 아들 Jake에 대해서 얘기하고 싶어요.

남　그래요. 무슨 문제가 있나요?

여　당신이 알다시피, 그는 공부도 매우 잘하고 운동도 규칙적으로 했어요.

남　그가 변했다는 뜻인가요?

여　네. 요즘에는 항상 컴퓨터 게임만 해요. 그가 해야 할 것들을 하지 않아요.

남　내가 그와 얘기해 볼게요.

① 걱정하는　　② 만족하는　　③ 지루한
④ 외로운　　⑤ 자랑스러운

talk about ～에 대해 말하다　**used to-V** ～하곤 했다　**exercise** 운동하다　**regularly** 규칙적으로　**mean** 의미하다　**nowadays** 요즘음　**all the time** 항상

05

M　Can I help you?

W　Yes, please. I'm <u>looking</u> <u>for</u> a present for my <u>dad's</u> <u>birthday</u>.

M　How about this <u>necktie</u>? Your dad might <u>like</u> it.

W　Well. I <u>prefer</u> this shirt. <u>How</u> <u>much</u> is it?

M　It's $5 <u>more</u> <u>expensive</u> <u>than</u> the tie.

W　Okay. I'll take it.

여　도와드릴까요?

남　네. 아빠 생신 선물을 찾고 있어요.

여　이 넥타이는 어떠세요? 아버지가 좋아하실 거예요.

남　글쎄요. 저는 이 셔츠가 마음에 들어요. 이것은 얼마예요?

여　그것은 넥타이보다 5달러 비쌉니다.

남　그래요. 이걸로 할게요.

① 은행　　　　② 백화점　　　　③ 장난감 가게
④ 도서관　　　⑤ 교회

present 선물　**necktie** 넥타이　**prefer** 선호하다　**How much ~?** ～은 얼마예요?　**expensive** 비싼

06

M　You look really good, Amy.

W　I started <u>working</u> <u>out</u> at the <u>health</u> <u>club</u>.

M　That sounds good.

W　Why don't you go with me? It will help you to <u>stay</u> <u>healthy</u>.

M　I will <u>think</u> <u>about</u> it. <u>How</u> <u>often</u> do you go?

W　I go only <u>on</u> <u>weekdays</u>. I mean every Monday, Wednesday, and <u>Friday</u>.

남　정말 좋아 보여, Amy.

여　헬스클럽에서 운동을 시작했어.

남　좋구나.

여　나랑 같이 가지 않을래? 건강을 유지하는 데 도움이 될 거야.

남　생각해 볼게. 얼마나 자주 가?

여　나는 주중에만 가. 그러니깐 월요일, 수요일, 금요일.

look good 좋아 보이다　**work out** 운동하다　**health club** 헬스 클럽　**stay healthy** 건강을 유지하다　**How often ~?** 얼마나 자주[종종] ～?　**on weekdays** 주중에

07

M　May I help you?

W　Yes. I'm <u>looking</u> <u>for</u> a skirt.

M　Would you <u>prefer</u> a <u>long</u>, a <u>knee</u> length or a <u>short</u> skirt?

W　I want a short skirt.

M　Then, how about this one with <u>white</u> and <u>black</u> <u>stripes</u>?

W　I like the solid one. Oh, the white one with the <u>red</u> <u>ribbon</u> is <u>pretty</u>. I will <u>take</u> it.

남 도와드릴까요?

여 네. 저는 치마를 찾고 있어요.

남 긴 치마, 무릎 길이, 또는 짧은 치마를 원하시나요?

여 짧은 치마가 좋아요.

남 그럼 흰색에 검정색 줄무늬가 있는 것은 어떠세요?

여 저는 단색이 좋아요. 오, 붉은색 리본이 달린 흰색 치마가 예쁘네요. 그것으로 할게요.

●●
knee 무릎 **length** 길이 **stripe** 줄무늬 **solid** (색 등이) 고른, 무늬 없는
take 사다

08

W How was your winter vacation?

M It was wonderful. I visited my aunt's house in the country.

W Wow! What did you do there?

M I went skiing. I also made a snowman and had a snowball fight.

W It sounds like you really had a great time.

- - - - - - - - - -

여 겨울 방학은 어땠어?

남 정말 좋았어. 시골에 있는 이모 댁에 갔어.

여 우와! 거기서 무엇을 했어?

남 스키를 타러 갔어. 눈사람도 만들고, 눈싸움도 했어.

여 정말 멋진 시간을 보낸 거 같구나.

●●
wonderful 훌륭한 **aunt** 이모, 고모, 숙모 **in the country** 시골에
make a snowman 눈사람을 만들다 **have a snowball fight** 눈싸움을 하다

09

W How may I help you?

M I heard you have a special offer every Wednesday.

W You mean our Wednesday Combo? We offer two pieces of fried chicken and a cola for 3 dollars.

M Great. I'll have one.

W Okay.

. . . .

여 어떻게 도와드릴까요?

남 매주 수요일에 특별 행사를 한다고 들었어요.

여 수요일 콤보를 말씀하시는 건가요? 튀김 닭 두 조각과 콜라를 3달러에 드립니다.

남 좋아요. 하나 주세요.

여 네.

●●
special 특별한 **offer** 제공 **a piece of** 한 조각의 ~

10

M How was your weekend?

W It was not bad. It was pretty good.

M What did you do?

W I went to the department store. I bought a bag and a dress. How about you?

M I stayed home and studied for our test.

W Poor you!

- - - - - - - - - -

여 주말은 어땠어?

남 나쁘지 않았어. 아주 좋았어.

여 무엇을 했어?

남 백화점에 가서 가방과 드레스를 샀어. 너는?

여 나는 집에서 시험 공부를 했어.

남 안됐다!

●●
pretty good 아주 좋은 **study for the test** 시험공부를 하다 **Poor you!** 안됐다!

11

W Tom, can you do me a favor?

M Sure. What can I do for you?

W Can I borrow your mobile phone, please? I need to call my mom right now.

M What's the matter with your mobile?

W Its battery is dead.

M Here you are.

. . . .

여 Tom, 내 부탁 좀 들어 줄래?

남 물론이지. 뭘 도와줄까?

여 네 휴대 전화 좀 빌릴 수 있을까? 지금 당장 엄마한테 전화해야 해.

남 네 휴대 전화기에 무슨 문제 있어?

여 배터리가 나갔어.

남 여기 있어.

●●
favor 부탁 **borrow** 빌리다 **mobile phone** 휴대 전화 **right now** 지금 당장 **matter** 문제 **battery** 배터리

12

w Hey, Tom. What's up?

M I can't find my e-book reader. I think I lost it.

w Oh, no. How did you lose it?

M I think I left it on the subway.

w Then, why don't you visit the Lost and Found at the subway station?

M Okay, I will.

여 이봐, Tom. 무슨 일 있니?

남 내 전자책 리더기를 못 찾겠어. 그것을 잃어버린 거 같아.

여 오, 이런. 어쩌다가 잃어버렸니?

남 지하철에 두고 온 것 같아.

여 그럼, 지하철 역 분실물 센터에 가 보는 게 어때?

남 알았어, 그렇게.

e-book reader 전자책 리더기 **lose** 잃어버리다 **leave** 남겨 두다 **Lost and Found** 분실물 센터

13

w ABC Mall customer service. How may I help you?

M I'm so upset that the item you sent me is not what I ordered.

w Let me check. You ordered a 32 gigabyte USB memory stick. What have you received?

M I got a 16 gigabyte USB memory stick.

여 ABC 몰 고객 센터입니다. 어떻게 도와드릴까요?

남 보내 주신 물건이 제가 주문한 것이 아니라서 무척 화가 나네요.

여 확인해 보겠습니다. 32기가바이트 USB 하나를 주문하셨군요. 무엇을 받으셨나요?

남 16기가 USB를 받았습니다.

customer service 고객 센터 **upset** 화가 난 **item** 물건, 품목 **order** 주문하다 **gigabyte** 기가바이트(10억바이트) **receive** 받다

14

① M 6 more students like winter more than fall.

② M Students' most favorite season is summer.

③ M The number of students who like spring and winter is the same.

④ M More students like fall more than spring.

⑤ M There are 3 students who like fall.

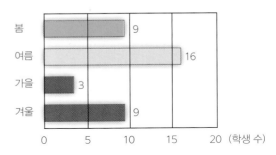

좋아하는 계절

① 남 가을보다 겨울을 좋아하는 학생이 6명 더 많다.

② 남 학생들이 가장 좋아하는 계절은 여름이다.

③ 남 봄과 겨울을 좋아하는 학생 수는 같다.

④ 남 더 많은 학생들이 봄보다 가을을 더 좋아한다.

⑤ 남 가을을 좋아하는 학생은 3명이다.

fall 가을 **favorite** 가장 좋아하는 **the number of** ~의 수 **same** 같은

15

M Mom, what's for lunch today?

w Well, do you have anything special in mind?

M I'd like to have chili spaghetti with meat balls.

w Okay. I'll make it for you. Let me check what we have first.

M [Pause] What do we need to buy? I'll go to the grocery store to get it.

w We need chili sauce and mushrooms.

남 엄마, 오늘 점심 뭐예요?

여 글쎄, 뭔가 특별히 생각한 게 있니?

남 미트볼이 든 매운 스파게티를 먹고 싶어요.

여 그래. 만들어 줄게. 우선 뭐가 있나 확인해 볼게.

남 우리 뭐 사야 할까요? 제가 식료품점에 가서 사올게요.

여 칠리소스와 버섯이 필요하구나.

in mind 염두에 둔 **chili** 칠리고추의, 매운 **grocery** 식료품점 **mushroom** 버섯

16

① M I have a toothache, Dr. Smith.

　W Let me see.

② M Shall we play basketball after school?

　W Sounds great.

③ M Where is the hospital?

　W It's over there.

④ M Can you make it by six?

　W Yes, I can make boxes very well.

⑤ M Will you go to the piano concert with me?

　W Sure, I'd love to.

---

① 남 치통이 있어요. Smith 선생님.

　여 어디 보자.

② 남 방과 후에 농구할까?

　여 좋아.

③ 남 병원이 어디에 있나요?

　여 저쪽에 있어요.

④ 남 6시까지 올 수 있니?

　여 응. 나는 상자를 아주 잘 만들 수 있어.

⑤ 남 나랑 피아노 연주회 갈래?

　여 물론이지. 그러고 싶어.

●●
toothache 치통 **hospital** 병원 **by** ~까지

17

W This is the final boarding call for passengers Tom and Jennie Smith booked on flight OZ821 to London. Please proceed to gate 7 immediately. The final checks are being completed and the captain will order the doors of the aircraft to be closed in about five minutes. I repeat. This is the final boarding call for Tom and Jennie Smith. Thank you.

여 이것은 런던행 OZ821편을 예약하신 Tom Smith와 Jennie Smith 씨에 대한 마지막 탑승 요청입니다. 속히 7번 게이트로 이동해 주십시오. 마지막 점검이 마무리 중이며 5분 내로 기장이 항공기 문을 닫으라는 지시를 할 겁니다. 반복합니다. 이것은 Tom Smith와 Jennie Smith 씨에 대한 마지막 탑승 요청입니다. 감사합니다.

●●
final boarding call 마지막 탑승 요청 **passenger** 승객 **book** 예약하다 **flight** 항공 편 **proceed** 이동하다. 나아가다 **immediately** 속

히. 즉시 **complete** 마치다. 완료하다 **captain** 기장 **order** 지시하다 **aircraft** 비행기 **repeat** 반복하다

18

M Mid-term exams will start next week. Jane is worried about her math grade because she is not good at math. She asks Tom to give her some advice. Tom was in the same situation as her last year but he is not worried about his grade anymore. He tells her to solve 10 questions every day. However, she is not sure about his advice. In this situation, what would Tom say to Jane?

남 중간고사가 다음 주에 시작됩니다. Jane은 수학을 잘 못해서 수학 성적이 걱정됩니다. 그녀는 Tom에게 조언을 좀 해 달라고 부탁합니다. Tom은 작년에 그녀와 같은 상황에 처해 있었지만 그는 이제 더 이상 수학 성적은 걱정하지 않습니다. 그는 그녀에게 매일 10문제를 풀라고 말합니다. 하지만, 그녀는 그의 충고에 확신이 서지 않습니다. 이 상황에서 Tom은 Jane에게 뭐라고 할까요?

① 내게 그만 물어봐.

② 천만에.

③ 나는 할 수 있을 것 같지 않아.

④ 나는 좀 더 연습해야 해.

⑤ 기억해. 연습이 완벽하게 만들어.

●●
mid-term exam 중간고사 **be worried about** ~에 대해 걱정하다 **grade** 성적 **advice** 조언 **situation** 상황 **not ~ anymore** 더 이상 ~아니다 **solve** 풀다 **sure** 확신하는

19

M What are you going to do after school this Friday?

W I'm going to the library. Why?

M I have two tickets for the movies. I'd like to go with you.

W Sounds great.

M What time shall we meet?

W How about at 3:30 p.m.?

남 이번 금요일 방과 후에 뭐 할 거니?

여 도서관에 갈 건데. 왜?

남 영화 표가 2장이 있어. 너랑 함께 가고 싶어서.

여 좋아.

남 몇 시에 만날까?
여 오후 3시 30분 어때?

① 늦지 마.
② 아주 좋아.
③ 3시 30분 어때?
④ 학교 앞에서 만나자.
⑤ 어디서 만나고 싶어?

••
after school 방과 후에   **movie** 영화

20

M Jennie, I'm really worried about my puppy, Snoopy.
W What's the matter with him?
M I don't know. He's not eating or drinking.
W From when?
M I don't think he's had anything since last night.
W Let's take him to the animal doctor.

··

남 Jennie, 내 강아지 Snoopy가 정말 걱정이야.
여 Snoopy한테 무슨 일이니?
남 나도 모르겠어. 먹거나 마시지도 않아.
여 언제부터?
남 어젯밤부터 아무것도 먹지 않은 것 같아.
여 수의사에게 데려가자.

① 나는 강아지를 좋아하지 않아.
② 그는 공 잡기를 좋아해.
③ 무서워하지 마. 너를 물지 않을 거야.
④ 수의사에게 데려가자.
⑤ 나는 오늘 아침 공원에서 개를 산책시켰어.

••
puppy 강아지   **since** ～이래로   **afraid** 무서워하는   **bite** 물다   **take A to B** A를 B에 데려가다   **animal doctor** 수의사   **walk one's dog** 개를 산책시키다

Further Study 정답   p. 64

1 He is looking at the puppies.
2 He plays computer games all the time.
3 She goes there every Monday, Wednesday, and Friday.
4 He went to his aunt's house in the country.

5 The reason is that the battery of her mobile phone is flat.
6 He thought he left it on the subway.
7 He will buy chili sauce and mushrooms.
8 The reason is that Snoopy hasn't eaten or drunk anything since last night.

On Your Own 모범답안   p. 65

A

I am going to talk about what I did over the weekend. On (1)Saturday, I (2)watched a movie (3)with my friends (4)at a movie theater. It was very (5)enjoyable. On (1)Sunday, I (2)took a rest (3)with my family (4)at home. It was very (5)relaxing. Overall, I had a (5)great weekend.

··

(1) 언제	(2) 무엇	(3) 누구와	(4) 어디에서	(5) 느낌
토요일 일요일	영화를 보았다 책을 읽었다 자전거를 탔다 휴식을 취했다 (～을) 공부했다 숙제를 했다 쇼핑을 했다	친구(들)와 부모님/가족과 형[남동생]/언니[여동생]와 혼자	영화관에서 집에서 친구 집에서 쇼핑몰에서 공원에서 도서관에서	좋은 재미있는 즐거운 신나는 피곤한 지루한 편안한

저는 제가 주말에 한 일에 대해 이야기하겠습니다. 토요일에 저는 친구들과 극장에서 영화를 보았습니다. 매우 즐거운 하루였습니다. 일요일에는 가족들과 집에서 휴식을 취했습니다. 매우 편안한 하루였습니다. 전반적으로, 저는 좋은 주말을 보냈습니다.

B

(1) My favorite season	(2) Reasons
summer	① like hot and sunny weather ② like swimming in the sea

My favorite season is (1)summer. The main reason I like (1)summer is that I ①like hot and sunny weather. Another reason is that I ②like swimming in the sea. Every other season, I hope (1)summer comes again soon.

(1)가장 좋아하는 계절	(2)이유
여름	① 뜨겁고 화창한 날씨를 좋아함 ② 바다에서 수영하는 것을 좋아함

제가 가장 좋아하는 계절은 여름입니다. 제가 여름을 좋아하는 주된
이유는 제가 덥고 맑은 날씨를 좋아하기 때문입니다. 또 다른 이유는 제가
바다에서 수영하는 것을 좋아하기 때문입니다. 다른 계절마다. 저는 여름이
곧 다시 오기를 바랍니다.

07 Listening Test 정답

p. 70

01 ①	02 ⑤	03 ②	04 ①	05 ④
06 ⑤	07 ③	08 ⑤	09 ④	10 ④
11 ①	12 ⑤	13 ⑤	14 ②	15 ⑤
16 ①	17 ④	18 ⑤	19 ④	20 ①

01

① W A girl is lining up in front of a ticket booth to buy a ticket.
② W The man inside the ticket booth is wearing glasses.
③ W People are standing in two lines.
④ W The woman with a purse has long curly hair.
⑤ W A man and a woman are holding hands.

....

① 여 한 소녀가 표를 사기 위해 매표소 앞에 줄 서 있다.
② 여 매표소 안의 남자는 안경을 쓰고 있다.
③ 여 사람들이 두 줄로 서 있다.
④ 여 핸드백을 들고 있는 여성은 긴 곱슬머리이다.
⑤ 여 남자와 여자가 손을 잡고 있다.

in front of ～앞에 **ticket booth** 매표소 **inside** 안에 **glasses** 안경
line 줄 **purse** (여성용) 지갑, 핸드백 **curly** 곱슬거리는

02

M Are you okay?
W Yes, I am.
M You have to be more careful when it rains or snows. The roads become slippery and dangerous.
W You're right. That's why there is a sign warning of the danger.
M Let's keep going.

....

남 너 괜찮니?
여 그래, 괜찮아.
남 비나 눈이 올 때는 더 조심해야 해. 길이 미끄럽고 위험해져.
여 맞아. 그래서 저기에 위험에 대해 경고하는 표지판이 있잖아.
남 계속 가자.

careful 조심스러운. 신중한 **slippery** 미끄러운 **dangerous** 위험한
warn 경고하다 **danger** 위험 **keep -ing** 계속 ～하다

03

W Do you remember our meeting planned for tomorrow?
M Of course. We are going to see a play.
W Right. The play starts at 4:30 p.m. When shall we meet?
M How about thirty minutes before the play starts?
W That sounds good. See you tomorrow.

....

여 내일 약속 기억하지?
남 그럼. 우리 연극을 보기로 했잖아.
여 맞아. 연극이 4시 30분에 시작해. 우리 언제 만날까?
남 연극 시작하기 30분 전에 만나면 어떨까?
여 좋아. 내일 보자.

remember 기억하다 **play** 연극

04

W The movie is starting soon. Shall we go inside?
M Sure. Let's check our seats.
W They are C1 and C2.
M Good! I can't wait to see the movie.
W Me too. I heard this movie is ranked number 1 in

ticket sales.

여 영화가 곧 시작해. 안으로 들어갈까?
남 그래. 우리 좌석을 확인해 보자.
여 C1과 C2 좌석이야.
남 좋아! 영화를 빨리 보고 싶어.
여 나도 그래. 이 영화가 박스 오피스 1위라고 하던데.

① 흥분된　　　② 겁 먹은　　　③ 자랑스러워하는
④ 걱정스러운　　⑤ 실망한

•• **soon** 곧　**go inside** 안으로 들어가다　**check** 확인하다　**seat** 좌석
rank (지위를) 차지하다　**sale** 판매　**scared** 겁 먹은　**disappointed** 실
망한

05

W You are late again. What's wrong with you?
M I had a terrible headache, so I went to a drugstore
　before coming to class.
W Why didn't you call me?
M I thought I would be able to arrive on time. I'm so
　sorry.
W Okay. Go and have a seat.

여 너 다시 지각이구나. 무슨 일이니?
남 두통이 심해서, 수업에 오기 전에 약국에 갔어요.
여 왜 나한테 전화하지 않았니?
남 저는 제시간에 도착할 수 있을 줄 알았어요. 정말 죄송해요.
여 괜찮아. 가서 자리에 앉아라.

① 약국　　　② 병원　　　③ 도서관
④ 학교　　　⑤ 은행

•• **terrible** 심한, 끔찍한　**headache** 두통　**drugstore** 약국　**be able
to-V** ~할 수 있다　**on time** 제시간에, 정각에

06

W Can you tell me how I can get to the bookstore?
M Sure. Go straight for one block. It is in the middle
　of the next block.
W You mean just go straight?
M Yes. It's on your right, across from the bakery.
W Thank you very much.

여 서점에 어떻게 가는지 알려 주시겠습니까?
남 그럼요. 한 블록 직진하세요. 다음 블록 중간에 있습니다.
여 직진하라는 말씀인가요?
남 네. 빵집 건너, 오른편에 있습니다.
여 정말 감사합니다.

•• **bookstore** 서점　**go straight** 직진하다　**in the middle of** ~의 중간
에　**across from** ~ 건너편에　**bakery** 빵집

07

[Beep]
M Hey, Kate. This is Michael. Tomorrow is Peter's
　birthday, so we are planning to have a birthday
　party for him. If you want to join us, please let
　me know. You can come to Peter's house at eight
　o'clock. It's a surprise party, so don't tell him. Bye.

남 여보세요, Kate. 나 Michael이야. 내일은 Peter의 생일이야. 그래서
　생일 파티를 열 계획이야. 우리와 함께 하고 싶으면, 알려 줘. Peter의
　집으로 8시까지 와. 깜짝 파티니깐 절대 말하면 안 돼. 안녕.

•• **plan** ~을 계획하다　**join** 함께 하다, 합류하다　**surprise party** 깜짝 파티

08

M What are you going to do this weekend?
W I'm planning to visit my grandparents.
M Where do they live?
W They live in New Jersey.
M I see. Have a great time with them.

남 이번 주말에 뭐 할 거야?
여 조부모님 댁에 갈 계획이야.
남 그분들은 어디 사셔?
여 뉴저지에서 사셔.
남 그렇구나. 그분들과 좋은 시간 가져.

•• **weekend** 주말　**visit** 방문하다　**grandparents** 조부모　**live in** ~에 살
다

09

M I'm home. Where's Rosa?
W She's in her room doing her homework.

M I'm hungry. Is <u>dinner</u> <u>ready</u>?

W Yes. It's on the <u>table</u>.

M I will call Rosa. Let's have dinner all <u>together</u>.

남 나 집에 왔어요. Rosa는 어디 있죠?

여 그녀는 방에서 숙제를 하고 있어요.

남 배고프네. 저녁은 준비됐어요?

여 그럼요. 식탁 위에 있어요.

남 Rosa를 부를게요. 다 함께 저녁 식사해요.

●●
I'm home. 다녀왔습니다. **hungry** 배고픈 **ready** 준비된 **call** 부르다
dinner 저녁 식사에 **all together** 다 함께

10

M I'm going to <u>see</u> a <u>concert</u> on Saturday. <u>Would you</u>
   <u>like</u> <u>to</u> come with me?

W Wow! I'd love to, but I don't have a ticket.

M <u>Don't</u> <u>worry</u>. I think tickets are <u>still</u> <u>available</u>. We
   can buy one <u>online</u>.

W Then, <u>let's</u> <u>do</u> <u>it</u> right now. I will <u>turn</u> <u>on</u> my
   computer.

M Good.

남 토요일에 콘서트를 볼 거야. 나랑 같이 갈래?

여 우와! 가고는 싶은데, 표가 없어.

남 걱정하지 마. 표가 아직도 판매 중일 거야. 온라인으로 살 수 있어.

여 그럼. 지금 바로 하자. 컴퓨터를 켤게.

남 좋아.

●●
worry 걱정하다 **still** 여전히, 아직도 **available** 이용 가능한 **online** 온
라인으로 **turn on** ～을 켜다

11

M Mom, I need to ask you to do me a <u>favor</u>.

W Sure, what is it?

M Would you mind <u>waking</u> me <u>up</u> at 5 a.m.
   tomorrow?

W No problem. Why do you want to <u>get</u> <u>up</u> so early?
   It's <u>Sunday</u> tomorrow.

M I have to go to the <u>airport</u> to <u>see</u> my friend <u>off</u>.

W Oh, I see.

남 엄마, 부탁을 좀 드려야 하는데요.

여 그래, 뭐니?

남 내일 아침 5시에 저 좀 깨워 주실 수 있을까요?

여 문제없어. 왜 그렇게 일찍 일어나려는 거니? 내일은 일요일인데.

남 친구 배웅하러 공항에 가야 해요.

여 아, 알았다.

●●
need ～할 필요가 있다 **do ~ a favor** 부탁하다 **wake up** ～을 깨우다
have to-V ～해야 한다 **airport** 공항 **see off** 배웅하다

12

M What's it <u>like</u> <u>out</u>?

W It's <u>raining</u> pretty hard and it's <u>windy</u> today.

M I think <u>rain</u> makes me <u>blue</u>. Oh, I should leave now.

W Why don't you stay <u>home</u> today?

M Sorry, Mom. I don't want to miss my <u>volunteer</u>
   <u>work</u>.

W Then, you'd better wear your <u>raincoat</u> and <u>rain</u>
   <u>boots</u>.

남 바깥 날씨 어때요?

여 오늘 비가 상당히 오고 있고 바람도 심하네.

남 비는 절 우울하게 만드는 것 같아요. 오, 저 지금 출발해야 해요.

여 오늘은 집에 있는 게 어떻겠니?

남 죄송해요, 엄마. 자원봉사 활동에 빠지고 싶지 않아요.

여 그렇다면, 우비와 장화를 착용하도록 해.

●●
hard 심하게 **widny** 바람이 부는 **blue** 우울한 **miss** 놓치다, 빠지다
volunteer 자원봉사 **raincoat** 우비 **rain boots** 레인부츠, 장화

13

M I need a new <u>travel</u> <u>bag</u>.

W Why?

M The <u>zipper</u> on my old one is <u>broken</u>.

W Oh, there are a lot of <u>bags</u> over there.

M [Pause] I like this one. It's <u>light</u> and it looks <u>strong</u>.

W I think the price is <u>reasonable</u>, too.

남 나 새 여행 가방이 필요해.

여 왜?

남 지퍼가 고장 났어.

여 오, 저기 가방이 많이 있어.

남 나 이게 마음에 들어. 가볍고 튼튼해 보여.

여 가격도 적당한 것 같아.

●●
travel bag 여행 가방 **zipper** 지퍼 **broken** 고장 난, 깨진 **light** 가벼운
strong 튼튼한 **price** 가격 **reasonable** 적당한, 합리적인

14

① M Tom doesn't do any activities on Sunday.

② M Tom only plays basketball on Saturday.

③ M Tom plays baseball once a week.

④ M Tom plays basketball twice a week.

⑤ M Tom plays soccer three times a week.

- -

Tom의 주간 활동 계획						
일요일	월요일	화요일	수요일	목요일	금요일	토요일
−	축구	축구	농구	축구	농구	야구

① 남 Tom은 일요일에는 아무 활동도 하지 않는다.

② 남 Tom은 오직 토요일에만 농구를 한다.

③ 남 Tom은 일주일에 한 번 야구를 한다.

④ 남 Tom은 일주일에 두 번 농구를 한다.

⑤ 남 Tom은 일주일에 세 번 축구를 한다.

●●
activity 활동 **play basketball** 농구를 하다 **play baseball** 야구를 하
다 **play soccer** 축구를 하다 **once a week** 일주일에 한 번 **twice** 두
번 **weekly** 주 단위의

15

M Oh, it was a nice dinner, wasn't it?

W Yes, it was. I overate because all the dishes were
so yummy.

M So did I.

W Let's watch a movie.

M Did you forget? We are supposed to go to see
fireworks at Yeouido tonight.

W Oh, I forgot. We'd better hurry up. Shall we take
the subway?

- -

남 오, 정말 근사한 저녁이었어, 그렇지 않니?

여 응, 그래. 모든 요리가 너무 맛있어서 나 과식했어.

남 나도 그랬어.

여 우리 영화 보자.

남 너 잊었니? 우리 오늘 밤 여의도에 불꽃놀이 보러 가기로 했잖아.

여 오, 깜빡했다. 서두르는 게 좋겠다. 우리 지하철 탈까?

●●
overeat 과식하다 **dish** 요리, 접시 **yummy** 맛있는 **forget** 잊다 **be
supposed to-V** ~하기로 되어 있다 **fireworks** 불꽃놀이 **hurry up** 서
두르다

16

① M Do you mind opening the window?

 W Yes, of course. Go ahead.

② M How often do you meet her?

 W Two times a week.

③ M What do you call that express train?

 W We call it the KTX.

④ M I'm really upset.

 W What's about?

⑤ M Do you want some more to drink?

 W Yes, please.

- -

① 남 창문을 열면 안 될까요?

 여 네, 여세요.

② 남 얼마나 자주 그녀를 만나니?

 여 일주일에 두 번.

③ 남 저 고속 열차를 뭐라고 부르니?

 여 우리는 그것을 KTX라고 불러.

④ 남 나 정말 화가 나.

 여 무엇 때문이니?

⑤ 남 음료수 더 마실래?

 여 네, 주세요.

●●
mind ~를 꺼려하다 **go ahead** ~하시오 **express train** 고속 열차
upset 화가 난

17

W I'd like to show you how to make a blueberry-
banana smoothie. First, cut a banana into pieces.
Then, freeze the pieces and 3 tablespoons of
blueberries for about 2 hours. After that put
the frozen banana pieces and blueberries into a
blender and add a small pack of cold milk. Blend
until smooth. That's really easy, isn't it? It's enough
for a meal.

- -

여 저는 블루베리 바나나 스무디 만드는 법을 보여 드릴게요. 우선, 바나나 하나를 여러 조각으로 자르세요. 그런 다음 바나나 조각들과 3 큰 술의 블루베리를 2시간 정도 얼리세요. 그 후 얼린 바나나 조각과 블루베리를 믹서기에 넣고 작은 팩의 차가운 우유를 첨가하세요. 부드러워질 때까지 섞어 주세요. 정말 쉽죠, 그렇지 않나요? 한끼 식사로도 충분합니다.

cut A into B A를 B로 자르다 **piece** 조각 **freeze** 얼리다 **frozen** 얼린 **blender** 믹서기, 분쇄기 **add** 첨가하다 **a pack of** 한 팩의 ~ **blend** 섞다, 혼합하다 **smooth** 부드러운 **enough** 충분한 **meal** 식사

18

M Parents' Day is coming. Tom wants to buy presents for his mom and dad. He goes to a department store. He looks around for an hour but he has no idea. A clerk is coming towards him. In this situation, what would Tom say to the clerk?

남 어버이날이 다가오고 있습니다. Tom은 엄마 아빠께 드릴 선물을 사고 싶습니다. 그는 백화점에 갑니다. 그는 한 시간 가량 둘러보지만 좋은 생각이 떠오르지 않습니다. 한 점원이 그에게 다가옵니다. 이 상황에서 Tom은 그 점원에게 뭐라고 말할까요?

① 무슨 일인가요?
② 이것은 너를 위한 거야.
③ 도와드릴까요?
④ 제게 무슨 짓을 하신 거예요?
⑤ 제게 추천해 주시겠어요?

Parents' Day 어버이날 **present** 선물 **look around** 둘러보다 **clerk** 점원 **towards** ~쪽으로

19

M You know what? I had an amazing day yesterday!
W What happened?
M Do you know the singer, PSY?
W Of course, I know him. He is a world-famous star now.
M Last night, he was sitting at the next table at a cafe. I took a picture with him. He gave me his autograph. Look!
W I can't believe it. I envy you.

남 너 그거 아니? 나 어제 놀라운 날이었어!
여 무슨 일 있었어?
남 너 가수, 싸이 알지?
여 물론. 그를 알지. 그는 이제 세계 유명 스타잖아.
남 어젯밤. 그가 카페에서 내 옆 테이블에 앉아 있었어. 그와 함께 사진 찍었어. 그가 사인도 해 줬어. 봐!
여 믿을 수가 없다. 네가 부러워.

① 우리와 같이 할래?
② 같이 가서 찾아보자.
③ 우와. 참 좋은 생각이구나.
④ 믿을 수가 없다. 네가 부러워.
⑤ 걱정하지 마. 내가 좋아서 하는 거야.

amazing 놀라운 **world-famous** 세계적으로 유명한 **next** 옆의 **take a picture** 사진을 찍다 **autograph** 사인, 서명 **believe** 믿다 **envy** 부러워하다

20

M What are you planning to do during the holidays?
W I am planning to go abroad.
M Where are you going?
W I haven't decided yet. What do you think of Hawaii?
M I heard that Hawaii is very beautiful.
W Okay. I'll give it a try.

남 휴가 기간 동안 뭘 할 계획이니?
여 해외로 가려고 계획하고 있어.
남 어디로 갈 거니?
여 아직 결정하지 못했어. 하와이 어떻게 생각해?
남 나는 하와이가 매우 아름답다고 들었어.
여 좋아. 한번 시도해 볼게.

① 좋아. 한번 시도해 볼게.
② 나는 3일 후 하와이를 떠날 거야.
③ 거기에 얼마나 머물렀니?
④ 여권을 가져오셔야 합니다.
⑤ 네 사진을 내게 좀 보내 줘.

during ~ 동안 **holiday** 휴가 **go abroad** 해외로 가다 **decide** 결정하다 **yet** 아직 **What do you think of ~?** ~에 대해 어떻게 생각하니? **give ~ a try** 시도해 보다 **passport** 여권

Further **S**tudy 정답

1 They become slippery and dangerous.
2 He went to a drugstore.
3 It will start at 8 o'clock.
4 She is doing her homework (in her room).
5 The reason is that he has to go to the airport to see his friend off.
6 The reason is that he doesn't want to miss his volunteer work.
7 The reason is that he thinks it's light and looks strong.
8 They are supposed to go to see fireworks at Yeouido tonight.

On **Y**our **O**wn 모범답안

A

My favorite kind of movie is (1)action. The reason why I like (1)action movies is that they are (2)fun and exciting. I usually watch them (3)once or twice a month. On the other hand, I don't like (1)horror movies. I don't like (1)horror movies because they are (2)very scary. I (3)almost never watch them. I like to watch movies (4)at the movie theater (4)with my friends. I hope I can watch one soon.

(1) 무엇을	(2) 왜	(3) 얼마나 자주	(4) 어디서 / 누구와
로맨스 / 공포 / 액션 / 만화 / 공상 과학 / 판타지 / 코미디	재미있는 / 흥미진진한 / 스릴 있는 / 감동적인 / 무서운 / 지루한 / 잔인한 / 폭력적인	매주 한 달에 한 번/ 두 번/세 번 거의 (거의) 전혀	극장에서 집에서 친구(들)와 가족과 혼자

제가 가장 좋아하는 영화 종류는 액션입니다. 제가 액션 영화를 좋아하는 이유는 그것들이 재미있고 흥미진진하기 때문입니다. 저는 한 달에 한두 번 정도 그것들을 봅니다. 반면에, 저는 공포 영화를 싫어합니다. 저는 공포 영화가 너무 무섭기 때문에 싫어합니다. 공포 영화는 거의 전혀 보지 않습니다. 저는 극장에서 친구들과 함께 영화 보는 것을 좋아합니다. 곧 한 편을 볼 수 있기를 희망합니다.

B

How to Make *Tteokbokki*	
(1) Name of the food	*tteokbokki*
(2) Ingredients	rice cakes, vegetables, red pepper paste, crushed garlic, and sugar
(3) How to make it	① add red pepper paste, crushed garlic, and sugar to a bowl and mix well. ② chop some vegetables you like. ③ put some water and the sauce into a pan and heat it. ④ add the rest of the ingredients and boil everything until the rice cakes are soft.

I'd like to tell you how to make (1)*tteokbokki*. To make (1)*tteokbokki*, you need (2)rice cakes, vegetables, red pepper paste, crushed garlic, and sugar. First, ①add red pepper paste, crushed garlic, and sugar to a bowl and mix well. Next, ②chop some vegetables you like. Then, ③put some water and the sauce into a pan and heat it. Finally, ④add the rest of the ingredients and boil everything until the rice cakes are soft. Enjoy it! It is easy to make but very tasty.

떡볶이 만드는 법	
(1) 음식 명	떡볶이
(2) 재료	떡, 야채, 고추장, 다진 마늘, 설탕
(3) 만드는 법	① 고추장, 다진 마늘, 설탕을 오목한 그릇에 넣고 잘 섞는다. ② 좋아하는 야채들을 썬다. ③ 팬에 약간의 물과 소스를 넣고 끓인다. ④ 나머지 재료들을 넣고, 떡이 부드러워질 때까지 끓인다.

저는 떡볶이 만드는 법을 알려 드리고 싶습니다. 떡볶이를 만들기 위해서는 떡, 야채, 고추장, 다진 마늘, 설탕이 필요합니다. 우선, 고추장, 다진 마늘, 설탕을 오목한 그릇에 넣고 잘 섞습니다. 그리고 좋아하는 야채를 썰어 줍니다. 그다음, 팬에 약간의 물과 소스를 넣고 끓입니다. 마지막으로, 나머지 재료들을 넣고 떡이 부드러워질 때까지 끓입니다. 드셔 보세요! 간단하지만 맛있습니다.

01 ①	02 ③	03 ②	04 ③	05 ②
06 ⑤	07 ②	08 ②	09 ②	10 ④
11 ①	12 ①	13 ②	14 ⑤	15 ③
16 ③	17 ④	18 ⑤	19 ④	20 ②

01

W　Which is your son?

M　My son is wearing a hat and mittens.

W　Is he wearing blue jeans with a green jacket?

M　No, he is wearing blue jeans with a red jacket.

W　Oh, I see. He is cute.

....

여　누가 당신 아들인가요?

남　제 아들은 모자와 벙어리 장갑을 끼고 있어요.

여　청바지와 초록색 재킷을 입고 있어요?

남　아니요. 청바지와 빨간색 재킷을 입고 있어요.

여　오, 알겠어요. 정말 귀엽네요.

•• **mittens** 벙어리 장갑　**jeans** 청바지　**cute** 귀여운

02

M　How may I help you?

W　I'm looking for my bag. I left it on the subway this morning.

M　I see. We've had several lost bags today, so please describe yours.

W　It is a shoulder bag with a long strap.

M　What color is it? We have green, white, and black bags.

W　Mine is black with a gold key chain.

....

남　어떻게 도와드릴까요?

여　제 가방을 찾고 있어요. 오늘 아침에 지하철에 두고 왔어요.

남　알겠습니다. 저희는 분실 가방 여러 개가 있어서, 당신의 것을 설명해 주세요.

여　긴 줄이 달린 숄더백입니다.

남　무슨 색깔인가요? 저희한테 녹색, 흰색, 검정색 가방이 있습니다.

여　제 것은 검정색이고, 금색 열쇠고리가 있습니다.

•• **subway** 지하철　**several** 여러 개의　**lost** 잃어버린　**describe** 묘사하다
shoulder bag 숄더백　**strap** 끈　**key chain** 열쇠고리

03

W　Do you need any help?

M　Yes, I want to pay my parking fee, but I don't know how to use this parking machine.

W　First, press this button. Then, insert the parking ticket into the parking machine.

M　Okay. It says $5.50.

W　Then, insert five dollars and fifty cents into the machine.

M　Okay. But I only have a $10 bill.

....

여　도움이 필요하세요?

남　네. 주차료를 지불하고 싶은데, 이 주차 기계를 어떻게 사용하는지 모르겠습니다.

여　먼저, 이 버튼을 누르세요. 다음에 주차 기계에 주차권을 넣으세요.

남　네. 5달러 50센트라고 나오네요.

여　그럼 5달러 50센트를 기계에 넣으세요.

남　네. 그런데 저는 10달러 지폐만 있습니다.

•• **pay** 지불하다　**fee** 요금　**machine** 기계　**press** 누르다　**insert** 집어넣다　**bill** 지폐

04

W　What's up?

M　I had a bad day today.

W　Why? What happened to you?

M　I lost my cell phone while I was taking a walk in the park.

W　That's too bad. Why don't you call your phone?

M　I will.

....

여　무슨 일이야?

남　오늘은 안 좋은 날이야.

여　왜? 무슨 일이 있었어?

남　공원에서 산책하다가 내 휴대 전화를 잃어버렸어.

여　안됐다. 네 전화기로 전화를 걸어 보는 게 어때?

남　그럴게.

cell phone 휴대 전화   **while** ~하는 동안   **take a walk** 산책하다
Why don't you ~? ~하는 게 어때?

05

M May I help you?

W Yes. I'd like to open an account.

M You mean a savings account?

W Yes. What should I do?

M Please give me your identification card and fill out
   this form.

W Okay.

남 도와드릴까요?

여 네. 계좌를 개설하고 싶습니다.

남 저축 예금 계좌 말씀이신가요?

여 네. 제가 무엇을 해야 하나요?

남 신분증을 주시고, 이 양식을 채워 주세요.

여 네.

① 병원   ② 은행   ③ 교실
④ 경찰서   ⑤ 체육관

open an account 계좌를 개설하다   **savings account** 예금 계좌
identification card 신분증   **fill out** ~을 채우다   **form** 양식

06

W What are you going to do after school?

M I have no plans. Why?

W Would you like to join me in doing volunteer work?

M Are you going to a nursing home?

W No, we are going to an orphanage this time.

M Okay. I will join you.

여 방과 후에 무엇을 할 거야?

남 계획이 없어. 왜?

여 나와 같이 자원봉사 활동에 참여하는 게 어때?

남 양로원에 갈 거야?

여 아니, 이번에는 고아원에 갈 거야.

남 그래. 나도 참여할게.

plan 계획   **volunteer work** 자원봉사 활동   **nursing home** 양로원
orphanage 고아원

07

[Telephone rings.]

M Susan's Restaurant. How may I help you?

W I'd like to make a reservation for dinner at 6:30 p.m.

M For how many people?

W Three adults and a 7-year-old child.

M I see. What's your family name, please?

W My family name is Kim.

[전화벨이 울린다.]

남 Susan 식당입니다. 어떻게 도와드릴까요?

여 오후 6시 30분에 저녁 식사를 예약하고 싶습니다.

남 몇 명이신가요?

여 어른 3명과 7살짜리 아이 한 명입니다.

남 네. 성이 어떻게 되시나요?

여 제 성은 김입니다.

make a reservation 예약하다   **adult** 성인   **family name** 성

08

M Did you buy a birthday gift for Billy?

W Yes, I did. Did you buy one, too?

M Not yet. I'm on my way to get one now. Can you
   come with me?

W Sure.

M Let's go to the store, then.

남 너 Billy의 생일 선물 샀어?

여 그럼. 샀지. 너도 샀어?

남 아직. 지금 사러 가는 길이야. 나랑 같이 갈 수 있어?

여 좋아.

남 그럼 가게에 가자.

gift 선물   **on one's way to** ~로 가는 길에   **come with** ~와 함께 가다

09

M Excuse me.

W Yes? Is there anything wrong?

M I believe you are sitting in my seat.

W Oh, really? Let me check my seat number on my
   boarding pass.

M Okay. Go ahead.

W Oh, I'm sorry. I'm in the <u>wrong</u> place.

- -

남 실례합니다.

여 네? 무슨 문제가 있나요?

남 지금 제 자리에 앉아 계십니다.

여 오, 정말이요? 제 탑승권의 좌석 번호를 확인해 볼게요.

남 네. 그러세요.

여 죄송합니다. 제가 다른 자리에 있었네요.

●●
believe 믿다 **seat** 좌석 **seat number** 좌석 번호 **boarding pass** 탑승권 **place** 장소

10

M Hello, <u>everyone</u>. It's very <u>nice</u> <u>to</u> <u>meet</u> <u>you</u> <u>all</u>. My name is Brian Johnson and I'm 16 years old. <u>I'm</u> <u>from</u> Seattle and I want to be a <u>teacher</u> when I <u>grow</u> <u>up</u>. I like this school and I want to make many <u>new</u> <u>friends</u> here.

- -

남 모두들 안녕하세요. 여러분을 만나서 정말 기쁩니다. 제 이름은 Brian Johnson이고, 16살입니다. 저는 시애틀에서 왔고 저는 커서 선생님이 되고 싶습니다. 저는 이 학교가 좋으며 많은 새로운 친구들을 사귀고 싶습니다.

●●
everyone 모두 **be from** ~출신이다 **grow up** 자라다

11

W Tom, could you <u>save</u> my <u>seat</u>, please? I'll be back soon.

M Sure. Oh, can I ask you a <u>favor</u>?

W What is it?

M When you come back, could you <u>get</u> some <u>snacks</u> for me?

W Okay. What do you want to have?

M <u>Popcorn</u> and <u>lemonade</u>, please. Here's some <u>money</u>.

- -

여 Tom, 내 자리 좀 맡아 줄래? 금방 올게.

남 그래. 오, 부탁하나 해도 될까?

여 뭐니?

남 올 때, 날 위해 간식 좀 사다 줄 수 있니?

여 그래. 뭐 먹고 싶니?

남 팝콘이랑 레모네이드. 여기 돈 있어.

●●
save a seat 자리를 맡다 **be back** 되돌아오다 **snack** 간식 **popcorn** 팝콘 **lemonade** 레모네이드

12

W Hey, Eddie. What's wrong?

M Hi, Sue. I'm so <u>tired</u>. I <u>can't</u> <u>sleep</u> very well these days.

W What do you usually do before going to bed?

M I <u>write</u> on my <u>blog</u> and my friends' blogs <u>as</u> <u>well</u>.

W If you want to <u>sleep</u> well, you should not use electronic devices <u>for</u> <u>at</u> <u>least</u> one hour before going to bed.

M Oh, I see. I'll try that.

- -

여 야, Eddie. 무슨 일이야?

남 안녕, Sue. 나 너무 피곤해. 요즘 잠을 잘 못 자.

여 잠자기 전에 주로 뭘 하니?

남 내 블로그와 내 친구들 블로그에 글을 남겨.

여 네가 잠을 잘 자고 싶다면, 적어도 잠자기 한 시간 전에는 전자 기기를 이용해서는 안 돼.

남 오, 알았어. 그렇게 해 볼게.

●●
tired 피곤한 **these days** 요즘 **usually** 주로, 대개 **write on the blog** 블로그에 글을 쓰다 **as well** 또한 **electronic device** 전자 기기 **at least** 적어도

13

M What can I do for you?

W I'd like to have these <u>groceries</u> <u>delivered</u>.

M Could you <u>fill</u> <u>out</u> this form, please?

W No problem. <u>How</u> much is it?

M It <u>depends</u> on their <u>weight</u>. Let me check.

- -

남 무엇을 도와드릴까요?

여 이 식료품들을 배달하고 싶습니다.

남 이 양식을 작성해 주시겠어요?

여 그럼요. 얼마예요?

남 무게에 따라 다릅니다. 어디 볼까요.

●●
grocery 식료품 **deliver** 배달하다 **depend on** ~에 달려 있다 **weight** 무게

14

① W Jennie will <u>visit</u> <u>her</u> <u>aunt</u> on Jeju Island.

② W Jennie will take an <u>airplane</u> to Jeju Island this <u>Friday</u>.

③ W Jennie wants to have a <u>pajama</u> <u>party</u> with her cousins.

④ W Jennie also wants to ride a <u>horse</u>.

⑤ W Jennie will be back on <u>Wednesday</u>.

Jennie의 여행 계획	
언제	이번 주 금요일
어디로	제주도
어떻게(교통수단)	비행기로
왜	고모 집을 방문하기 위해
기간	2박 3일
할 일	사촌들과 파자마 파티 하기, 말 타기

① 여 Jennie는 제주도의 고모 집을 방문할 것이다.
② 여 Jennie는 이번 주 금요일에 제주도 가는 비행기를 탈 것이다.
③ 여 Jennie는 사촌들과 파자마 파티를 하기를 원한다.
④ 여 Jennie는 또한 말을 타고 싶어 한다.
⑤ 여 Jennie는 수요일에 돌아올 것이다.

••
have a pajama party 파자마 파티를 하다 **cousin** 사촌 **ride a horse** 말을 타다 **2 nights and 3 days** 2박 3일

15

M Mom, can I <u>go out</u> and <u>play</u> <u>basketball</u> with Jake?

W Did you do your <u>homework</u>?

M Not yet. I will do it <u>after</u> playing <u>basketball</u>. I'll be back in <u>an hour</u>.

W Sorry, Tom. Why don't you do your <u>homework</u> with Jake first and then go out?

M Okay, I will.

남 엄마, Jake하고 나가서 농구 해도 되나요?
여 숙제는 했니?
남 아직이요. 농구 하고 나서 할게요. 한 시간 내로 돌아올게요.
여 미안하구나, Tom. Jake와 숙제 먼저 한 다음 나가는 게 어떻겠니?
남 네, 그렇게 할게요.

••
go out 외출하다

16

① M Why don't we <u>watch</u> <u>a movie</u>?
   W Sounds great.

② M I wish you <u>good</u> <u>luck</u>.
   W Thank you very much.

③ M Where are you from?
   W <u>I am going to</u> Sydney, Australia.

④ M What do you <u>think</u> of *bulgogi*?
   W I think it's <u>very</u> <u>tasty</u>.

⑤ M I think she's beautiful.
   W I don't <u>agree</u>.

① 남 우리 영화 볼까?
   여 좋아.
② 남 행운을 빌어.
   여 정말 고마워.
③ 남 너는 어디 출신이니?
   여 나는 호주, 시드니에 가는 중이야.
④ 남 불고기 어때요?
   여 아주 맛있는 것 같아요.
⑤ 남 그녀는 아름다운 것 같아.
   여 나는 동의하지 않아.

••
luck 운 **tasty** 맛있는 **agree** 동의하다

17

[Beep]

M Hi, Jennie. This is Tom. I'm just <u>calling</u> to <u>remind</u> you that we're going to <u>see</u> the <u>musical</u>, *Mamma Mia* tonight. The musical <u>starts</u> at 6 p.m. at the Lyric Theater in Darling Harbor. Why don't we <u>meet</u> <u>at</u> 4 p.m. and have an <u>early</u> <u>dinner</u> nearby? Please <u>call</u> <u>me</u> <u>back</u> as soon as you get this <u>message</u>.

남 안녕, Jennie. 나 Tom이야. 우리 오늘 밤 뮤지컬 〈맘마미아〉 보기로 한 거 상기시켜 주려고 전화했어. 뮤지컬은 Darling Harbor에 있는 Lyric 극장에서 오후 6시에 시작해. 오후 4시에 만나서 근처에서 이른 저녁 먹는 거 어때? 이 메시지 확인하는 대로 내게 전화해 줘.

••
remind ~을 상기시키다 **early** 이른, 빠른 **nearby** 근처에 **call back** 답신 전화하다 **as soon as** ~하자마자

18

M At the stationery store, Gloria meets her classmate, Sam. They both need a clear file folder for their project. They have to collect news articles in the file folder. Sam picks one up and pays for it. But Gloria picks up a file folder and several fancy items such as a diary, a pencil case, and a mug. They look expensive. Sam is worried about how much money she has. In this situation, what would Sam say to Gloria?

남 문방구에서 Gloria는 그녀의 학급 친구인 Sam을 만난다. 그들은 둘 다 그들의 프로젝트를 위해 투명 서류철이 필요하다. 그들은 서류철에 뉴스 기사를 모아야 한다. Sam은 하나를 골라 그것에 대해 지불한다. 하지만 Gloria는 서류철 하나와 일기장, 필통, 머그 같은 몇 가지 팬시 상품을 고른다. 그것들은 비싸 보인다. Sam은 그녀가 돈을 얼마나 갖고 있는지 걱정이 된다. 이 상황에서 Sam은 Gloria에게 뭐라 말하겠는가?

① 그건 그렇게 나쁘지 않네.
② 30분 정도 걸려.
③ 그녀는 몇 개나 가지고 있니?
④ 돈 좀 빌려 줄래?
⑤ 너는 그것을 모두 살 돈이 충분하니?

•• **stationery store** 문구점 **project** 프로젝트 **collect** 모으다 **article** 기사 **pay** 지불하다 **several** 여러 개의 **fancy item** (선물·장식용) 팬시 상품 **diary** 일기장 **mug** 손잡이 컵, 머그 **expensive** 비싼 **be worried about** ~에 대해 걱정하다

19

M Hi, Jennie. Come on in.
W Hi, Tom. What were you doing?
M I was making tomato pasta sauce.
W I didn't know that you could make pasta sauce. It smells great. May I taste it?
M Of course. Go ahead. How is it?
W It tastes fantastic. You're a really good cook.

남 안녕, Jennie. 어서 들어와.
여 안녕, Tom. 너 뭐 하고 있었니?
남 토마토 파스타 소스를 만들고 있었어.

여 네가 파스타 소스를 만들 수 있는지 몰랐네. 냄새가 아주 좋네. 맛을 봐도 되니?
남 물론이지. 어서 먹어 봐. 어때?
여 환상적인 맛이야. 너 정말 요리를 잘하는구나.

① 나 여전히 배고파.
② 나를 슬프게 하지 마.
③ 걱정하지 마. 모든 것이 괜찮아.
④ 환상적인 맛이야. 너 정말 요리를 잘하는구나.
⑤ 멋지게 들리는데. 너는 훌륭한 요리사가 될 거야.

•• **pasta** 파스타, 스파게티 **smell** ~한 냄새가 나다 **taste** ~의 맛을 보다 **fantastic** 환상적인 **cook** 요리사

20

M Hi, Jennie. You have had a haircut. I like your new hair style.
W Thank you.
M Where did you get your haircut?
W I go to the Barbie Shop in The Rocks.
M I feel like changing my hair style, too.
W What do you have in mind?

남 안녕, Jennie. 너 머리 잘랐구나. 너의 새 머리 스타일이 마음에 들어.
여 고마워.
남 어디서 머리 잘랐니?
여 나는 Rocks에 있는 Barbie Shop에 가.
남 나도 머리 스타일 바꾸고 싶다.
여 마음에 둔 스타일이 있니?

① 그거 안됐다.
② 마음에 둔 스타일이 있니?
③ 그녀의 머리는 길고 예뻐.
④ 그냥 머리만 감겨 주세요.
⑤ 그녀는 아주 짧은 금발머리야.

•• **haircut** 이발, 머리 깎기 **feel like -ing** ~하고 싶다 **have ~ in mind** ~을 염두에 두다 **shampoo** (머리를 샴푸로) 감다 **blond hair** 금발머리

Further Study 정답   p. 84

1 He is wearing a hat, mittens, jeans, and a red jacket.

2 Her bag is <u>a black shoulder bag</u> with <u>a long strap</u> <u>that has a gold key chain</u>.

3 The second step is <u>inserting[to insert] the parking</u> <u>ticket into the parking machine</u>.

4 She is <u>making a reservation for dinner</u>.

5 He wants her to <u>get some snacks for him when</u> <u>she comes back</u>.

6 He wanted to <u>go out and play basketball with Jake</u>.

7 They <u>are going to see the musical, *Mama Mia*</u> <u>tonight</u>.

8 The reason is that <u>they have to collect news</u> <u>articles for their project</u>.

On Your Own 모범답안

p. 85

A

Things to Do after School	
(1) Where are you going to go?	home
(2) What are you going to do there?	help my mom with the housework
(3) Why are you going to do that?	want to make my mom happy
(4) Who are you going to do that with?	my sister
(5) How long will it take you to do that?	about 1 hour

I am going to talk about what I am going to do after school today. After school, I am going to go (1)<u>home</u> and (2)<u>help my mom with the housework</u>. The reason why I am going to do it is that (3)<u>I want to make my mom happy</u>. I am going to do that with (4)<u>my sister</u>. I think it will take me (5)<u>about one hour</u> to do that.

방과 후 할 일	
(1) 어디에 갈 것입니까?	집
(2) 그곳에서 무엇을 할 것입니까?	엄마를 도와 집안일 하기
(3) 그것을 하는 이유는 무엇입니까?	엄마를 기쁘게 해드리고 싶어서
(4) 누구와 함께 그것을 할 것입니까?	내 여동생

(5) 그것을 하는 데는 얼마나 오래 걸립니까?	1시간 정도

저는 오늘 방과 후 제가 할 일에 대해 이야기하겠습니다. 저는 방과 후에 집에 가서 엄마를 도와 집안일을 할 것입니다. 제가 그것을 하려는 이유는 엄마를 기쁘게 해드리고 싶기 때문입니다. 저는 제 여동생과 그것을 할 것입니다. 제가 그것을 하는 데는 1시간 정도 걸릴 것 같습니다.

B

Planning a Trip	
(1) Where are you going to go?	Jeju Island
(2) Who are you going there with?	my family
(3) When are you leaving?	this Friday
(4) How are you going to get there?	by plane
(5) What are you going to do there?	① visit my aunt ② visit the teddy bear museum ③ go hiking on Mt. Halla
(6) How long are you going to stay?	2 nights and 3 days

I am going on a trip to (1)<u>Jeju Island</u> with (2)<u>my family</u> (3)<u>this Friday</u>. I am going there (4)<u>by plane</u>. I am going to ①<u>visit my aunt</u> there. I am also going to ②<u>visit the teddy bear museum</u> and ③<u>go hiking on Mt. Halla</u>. I am going to stay there for (5)<u>2 nights and 3 days</u>. I hope to have a great time there.

여행 계획	
(1) 어디로 갈 예정입니까?	제주도
(2) 누구와 그곳에 갈 예정입니까?	가족
(3) 언제 떠납니까?	이번 주 금요일
(4) 그곳에 어떻게 갈 예정입니까?	비행기로
(5) 그곳에서 무엇을 할 예정입니까?	① 숙모 방문하기 ② 테디베어 박물관 방문하기 ③ 한라산 등반하기
(6) 얼마나 오래 머물 예정입니까?	2박 3일

저는 이번 주 금요일에 가족과 제주도에 여행을 갈 예정입니다. 저는 그곳에 비행기로 갈 것입니다. 그곳에서 저는 숙모를 방문할 것입니다. 저는 또한 테디베어 박물관을 가 보고 한라산 등반을 할 것입니다. 저는 그곳에 2박 3일 동안 머물 예정입니다. 그곳에서 즐거운 시간을 보내길 기대합니다.

01 ④	02 ④	03 ①	04 ④	05 ②
06 ④	07 ⑤	08 ⑤	09 ②	10 ②
11 ②	12 ②	13 ④	14 ②	15 ⑤
16 ①	17 ④	18 ④	19 ③	20 ⑤

01

M　Congratulations on your gold medal.

W　Thank you very much.

M　How do you feel?

W　I still can't believe I won it. I'm very happy.

M　I hope you will do as well in your next competition.

W　I'll try my best.

––––––––––––––––––––––––––––––

남　금메달 딴 거 축하해요.

여　정말 고마워요.

남　기분이 어때요?

여　메달을 땄다는 게 아직 믿기지 않아요. 정말 행복해요.

남　다음 경기에서도 잘하기를 바랄게요.

여　최선을 다할게요.

• •
congratulations on ~을 축하하다　**gold medal** 금메달
competition 경기, 시합　**try one's best** 최선을 다하다

02

W　It's very hot today. I'm thirsty.

M　Would you like to drink something?

W　Yes. I'd like to drink orange juice. No. I will have a carton of chocolate milk.

M　Okay. I will grab it for you. I will have a cola, I think.

W　Actually, I'll just drink water. That would be better.

M　Alright.

––––––––––––––––––––––––––––––

여　오늘 너무 덥다. 갈증이 나네.

남　마실 것을 좀 줄까?

여　그래. 오렌지 주스를 마시고 싶어. 아니. 초콜릿 우유 마실게.

남　그래. 가져다 줄게. 나는 콜라 마실 거야.

여　실은, 나는 그냥 물을 마실래. 그게 나을 거야.

남　알았어.

• •
thirsty 목마른　**a carton of** 한 팩의 ～　**grab** 재빨리 손에 넣다
actually 실은

03

W　Excuse me. Are you Tony?

M　YES! Do I look that different?

W　Yes! I almost didn't recognize you.

M　Nice to hear that. I really tried hard to lose weight during the vacation. My weight was 85kg, and now I weigh 79kg.

W　Wow! You look like you've lost more than 10kg.

M　Thanks.

––––––––––––––––––––––––––––––

여　실례합니다. 당신 Tony인가요?

남　맞아! 나 그렇게 달라 보여?

여　응! 나는 너를 거의 못 알아볼 뻔했어.

남　듣기 좋은데. 방학 동안에 살을 빼기 위해 정말 열심히 노력했어. 몸무게가 85kg이었는데, 지금은 79kg이야.

여　우와! 10kg는 더 감량한 거 같아.

남　고마워.

• •
recognize 알아보다, 인식하다　**lose weight** 살을 빼다　**vacation** 방학
weight 무게　**weigh** 무게가 나가다

04

W　What's wrong? Why are you crying?

M　I'm moved by this movie. The last scene is very touching.

W　Oh, come on. It's just a movie.

M　I know. But I can't stop tears falling from my eyes.

W　I didn't know that you're such a sensitive man.

––––––––––––––––––––––––––––––

여　왜 그래? 너 왜 울고 있어?

남　이 영화에 감동 받았어. 마지막 장면이 너무 감동적이야.

여　왜 이래. 그건 그냥 영화야.

남　나도 알아. 하지만 눈에서 눈물이 멈추지 않아.

여　나는 네가 이렇게 감성적인 남자인지 몰랐어.

• •
move 감동시키다　**scene** 장면　**touching** 감동시키는　**tear** 눈물　**fall**
(눈물이) 흐르다　**sensitive** 감성적인, 예민한

05

W How can I go through this ticket gate?

M You can buy a ticket at the ticket booth or you can scan your transportation card here.

W I see. By the way, this station is on both line number two and line number seven. Which way should I go if I'd like to take line number two?

M Follow the signs. Line number two is green.

W Thank you.

여 이 개찰구를 어떻게 통과할 수 있나요?

남 매표소에서 티켓을 사거나 교통 카드를 이곳에 스캔하시면 됩니다.

여 알겠습니다. 그런데, 이 역은 2호선과 7호선이 있네요. 2호선을 타려면 어느 쪽으로 가야 하나요?

남 표지판을 따라가세요. 2호선은 녹색입니다.

여 감사합니다.

① 공항　　　　② 지하철 역　　　　③ 버스 정류장
④ 영화관　　　　⑤ 택시 정류장

go through ~을 통과하다　**ticket gate** 개찰구　**ticket booth** 매표소
scan ~을 스캔하다　**transportation card** 교통 카드　**follow** 따라가다

06

M Congratulations!

W Thank you very much. Without your support, I wouldn't be able to have been elected as a school president.

M You're welcome. How do you feel?

W I feel like I'm walking on air. I can't stop smiling.

M I can tell. Anyway, you deserve it.

남 축하해!

여 정말 고마워. 너의 지지가 없었으면, 전교 회장으로 선출되지 못했을 거야.

남 천만에. 기분이 어때?

여 구름 위를 걷는 기분이야. 웃음이 멈추지를 않아.

남 그렇게 보여. 그나저나 너는 그럴 자격이 있어.

Congratulations! 축하해!　**support** 지지　**be able to-V** ~할 수 있다
elect 선출하다　**school president** 전교 회장　**deserve** ~을 받을 만하다

07

M Oops! I'm sorry. Are you okay?

W Yes. Thank you for helping me to pick up my books.

M It was my fault. By the way, do you know where the library is?

W Yeah. I'm on the way there now to return these books.

M Good. I'll go with you. I'm a transfer student from Miami, so everything is strange.

W Welcome to our school.

남 이런! 미안해. 괜찮니?

여 응. 책 줍는 것을 도와줘서 고마워.

남 내 잘못이야. 그런데 도서관이 어디에 있는지 아니?

여 응. 이 책들을 반납하러 그곳에 가는 길이야.

남 잘됐다. 너랑 같이 갈게. 나는 마이애미에서 온 전학생이야. 그래서 모든 게 낯설어.

여 우리 학교에 온 걸 환영해.

pick up ~을 집다　**fault** 잘못　**on the way** ~로 가는 길에, 도중에
return 반납하다, 되돌아가다　**transfer student** 전학생　**strange** 낯선

08

W Where are you going?

M I'm going to play soccer with my friends.

W Did you finish your homework?

M I'll finish it when I get home.

W Oh, boy. You have to finish your homework first, if not you can't go out. You should rank the things you have to do according to importance, and finish them in that order.

M Okay, Mom.

여 어디 가니?

남 친구들과 축구 하러 가요.

여 숙제는 다 끝냈어?

남 집에 와서 끝낼 거예요.

여 오 이런. 숙제를 먼저 끝내지 않으면 나갈 수 없어. 중요도에 따라 네가 해야 할 일들의 순위를 매기고 그 순서에 따라 그것들을 끝내야 해.

남 네, 엄마.

rank 순위를 매기다 **according to** ~에 따라 **importance** 중요성
order 순서

09

M Welcome to Korea! Do you have jet lag?

W I think I'm fine.

M Good. Let me tell you today's schedule. We will go to your hotel now to check in. After that I will take you to a tourist spot. Then, we will have Korean food for dinner. Lastly, we will come back to the hotel.

W Sounds interesting.

M Shall we go now?

W Sure.

··········

남 한국에 오신 걸 환영합니다! 시차증은 없요?
여 괜찮은 거 같습니다.
남 좋습니다. 오늘 일정을 알려 드릴게요. 지금 호텔에 가서 체크인을 할 거예요. 그다음 관광지로 모셔다 드릴 거예요. 그런 다음, 저녁으로 한국 음식을 드실 거예요. 마지막으로 호텔로 돌아올 겁니다.
여 흥미롭게 들리네요.
남 이제 출발할까요?
여 네.
① 항공기 승무원   ② 여행 가이드   ③ 교사
④ 요리사   ⑤ 호텔 접수원

jet lag 시차증, 시차로 인한 피로 **schedule** 일정 **check in** 체크인하다
tourist spot 관광 명소 **lastly** 마지막으로

10

W Are these on sale?

M Yes. There's 50% off on sandals, 35% off on flats, 25% off on sneakers, and 10% off on heels.

W I see. Can I try these sandals in size 8?

M Sure. Here you are.

W [Pause] Thank you. They are very comfortable and fashionable. I will take them.

··········

여 이것들은 할인 중인가요?
남 네. 샌들은 50%, 플랫슈즈는 35%, 스니커즈는 25%, 힐은 10% 할인입니다.
여 알겠습니다. 이 샌들 8사이즈로 신어 볼 수 있을까요?

남 그럼요. 여기 있습니다.
여 감사합니다. 굉장히 편하고 유행하는 거네요. 그것들로 할게요.

on sale 할인 중인 **sandals** 샌들 **flats** 굽이 낮거나 없는 여성용 구두, 플랫슈즈 **sneakers** (천으로 된) 운동화 **comfortable** 편안한
fashionable 유행하는

11

W Excuse me, but can I ask you a favor?

M Sure. What can I do for you?

W After I check out, could you keep my luggage here in the hotel? I'd like to look around the city before I go to the airport.

M Sure. When are you coming back to pick it up?

W In about 3 hour's time. Thank you.

M My pleasure.

··········

여 실례합니다만, 부탁 좀 드려도 될까요?
남 물론입니다. 뭘 도와드릴까요?
여 제가 체크아웃한 후에, 제 짐을 여기 호텔에서 보관해 주실 수 있나요? 공항에 가기 전에 도시를 좀 둘러보고 싶어서요.
남 물론입니다. 언제 가지러 오실 건가요?
여 3시간쯤 후에요. 감사합니다.
남 천만에요.

check out (호텔에서) 체크아웃하다 **luggage** (여행용) 짐 **look around** 둘러보다 **pick up** ~을 가지러 오다, 데리러 오다

12

W It's a good day, isn't it?

M Yeah, it is.

W Let's go bike riding in the Han Riverside Park!

M Sorry, I can't. It's too difficult for me to learn to ride a bike. I think I don't have any sense of balance.

W Oh, I didn't know that. Why don't you ride on a bike with training wheels for about a month, and then give it a try without them?

M Okay, I'll try.

··········

여 날씨 좋다, 그렇지 않니?
남 응, 그래.
여 한강 고수부지에 자전거 타러 가자!
남 미안, 못 가. 자전거 타는 것을 배우는 것은 나에게 너무 어려워. 나는

균형 감각이 전혀 없는 것 같아.

여 오, 몰랐어. 한 달 정도 연습용 보조 바퀴를 단 자전거로 연습하고, 그다음에 보조 바퀴 없이 타 보는 것은 어때?

남 좋아, 해볼게.

too... to-V 너무 ⋯해서 ~할 수 없다 **difficult** 어려운 **sense of balance** 균형 감각 **training wheels** 훈련용 보조 바퀴 **give ~ a try** ~을 시도해 보다 **without** ~없이

13

W Excuse me. One of my bags hasn't arrived.

M Can I see your ticket, please? [Pause] Okay, so you were on flight ZY123 from London?

W Yes, that's right.

M Can you give me a description of your bag?

W Yes, it is a medium sized black bag with a red ribbon tied to the handle.

여 실례합니다. 제 가방 중 하나가 도착하지 않았어요.

남 티켓 좀 보여 주시겠어요? 네, 런던에서 온 ZY123편을 탑승하셨네요?

여 네, 맞습니다.

남 가방을 설명해 주시겠어요?

여 네, 손잡이에 빨간 리본이 묶여 있는 중간 크기의 검정색 가방이에요.

arrive 도착하다 **flight** 항공편, 항공기 **description** 묘사, 설명 **medium sized** 중간 크기의 **ribbon** 리본, 매듭 끈 **handle** 손잡이

14

① M The party will be at 5 p.m. on Friday, October 31st.

② M The party will be held for two hours.

③ M The party will be held at the community center.

④ M There will be a Halloween costume contest.

⑤ M People can make jack-o'-lanterns.

핼로윈 파티 초대장	
일시	10월 31일, 금요일
시간	오후 5시 – 8시
장소	지역 문화회관
활동	1. 핼로윈 의상 경연 대회
	2. 호박등 만들기
	3. 과자를 안 주면 장난을 칠 거야 하러 가기

① 남 파티는 10월 30일, 금요일 5시에 열릴 것이다.

② 남 파티는 2시간 동안 열릴 것이다.

③ 남 파티는 지역 문화회관에서 열릴 것이다.

④ 남 핼로윈 의상 경연 대회가 있을 것이다.

⑤ 남 사람들은 호박등을 만들 수 있다.

be held 열리다, 개최되다 **Community Center** 지역 문화회관 **costume** 의상 **jack-o'-lantern** 호박등 **invitation** 초대장

15

W Tom, are you free now?

M Yes. Why?

W Why don't we watch a 4D movie in the CYJ Theater?

M What's a 4D movie?

W I heard that the chairs you sit on move and you can even smell the food in the scene.

M Wow! That's amazing. Let's go right now.

여 Tom, 너 지금 한가하니?

남 응. 왜?

여 CYJ 극장에서 4D 영화 보는 거 어때?

남 4D 영화가 뭐니?

여 네가 앉는 의자가 움직이고 심지어 화면 속의 음식 냄새도 맡을 수 있다고 들었어.

남 우왜! 그거 놀랍다. 지금 당장 가자.

free 한가한 **4D movie** 4차원 영화 **even** 심지어 **smell** 냄새를 맡다 **scene** 장면 **amazing** 놀라운

16

① M What happened?

 W I'll have a party tonight.

② M Can you help me with my homework?

 W Sorry, but I can't.

③ M Give me a call again.

 W Okay, I will.

④ M What time shall we make it?

 W How about 2 p.m.?

⑤ M What are you going to do this winter?

 W I plan to learn to snowboard.

① 남 무슨 일 있었니?

여 나는 오늘 밤 파티를 열 거야.

② 남 내 숙제를 도와줄 수 있니?

여 미안하지만, 안 돼.

③ 남 나한테 다시 전화해.

여 그래, 그럴게.

④ 남 몇 시에 우리 만날까?

여 오후 2시 어때?

⑤ 남 이번 겨울에 무엇을 할 예정이니?

여 스노보드 타는 법을 배울 계획이야.

•• **give ~ a call** ~에게 전화하다 **plan** 계획하다 **snowboard** 스노보드를 타다

17

w Have you ever <u>heard</u> <u>about</u> koalas? The koala is one of Australia's <u>best-known</u> animals. They have small bodies with <u>gray</u> <u>fur</u>. Sometimes people call them '<u>koala bears</u>' but they are not <u>bears</u>. They live in <u>trees</u>. They only eat eucalyptus <u>leaves</u>. They spend about <u>18 hours</u> a day <u>sleeping</u> in trees. They usually live about 10 <u>years</u>.

여 코알라에 대해 들어 본 적이 있나요? 코알라는 호주의 가장 잘 알려진 동물들 중 하나입니다. 그들은 작은 몸집에 회색 털이 있습니다. 가끔씩 사람들은 그들을 '코알라 곰'이라고 부르지만 그들은 곰이 아닙니다. 그들은 나무에서 삽니다. 그들은 오직 유칼립투스 잎만 먹습니다. 그들은 나무에서 하루에 18시간 정도를 잠자며 보냅니다. 그들은 대개 10년 정도 삽니다.

•• **koala** 코알라 **best-known** 가장 잘 알려진 **gray** 회색의 **fur** 털 **sometimes** 가끔씩, 종종 **call** ~라고 부르다 **eucalyptus** 유칼립투스 나무 **spend + 시간 + -ing** ~하면서 시간을 보내다 **usually** 대개, 보통

18

M Bill and Susan like to visit <u>famous</u> restaurants to <u>try</u> their food. Today they went to a Thai restaurant which was <u>recommended</u> by many reviewers. Susan said the food was great. However, Bill <u>didn't agree</u> with her because all the <u>food</u> he tried was too <u>salty</u>, too <u>sweet</u> or too <u>spicy</u>. In this situation, what would Bill say to Susan?

남 Bill과 Susan은 음식을 맛보기 위해 유명한 식당들을 방문하는 것을 좋아합니다. 오늘 그들은 많은 비평가들이 추천한 태국 식당에 갔습니다. Susan은 음식들이 훌륭하다고 말했습니다. 하지만 Bill은 그가 먹어 본 모든 음식들이 모두 너무 짜거나, 너무 달거나 아니면 너무 매웠기 때문에 그녀의 의견에 동의하지 않았습니다. 이 상황에서 Bill은 Susan에게 뭐라고 말할까요?

① 네 의견에 동의해.

② 그 말을 들으니 기뻐.

③ 나는 단것을 먹는 것을 좋아해.

④ 나는 음식이 마음에 들지 않아.

⑤ 모든 음식들을 정말 맛있게 즐겼어.

•• **Thai** 태국; 태국의 **recommend** 추천하다 **reviewer** 비평가, 평론가 **agree with** ~에 동의하다 **salty** 짠 **sweet** 단 **spicy** 매운

19

w Excuse me. Are you <u>from</u> <u>around here</u>?

M Yes, I am. Do you need <u>any help</u>?

w Yes, please. Would you <u>mind</u> showing me <u>the way to</u> the Opera House?

M No, <u>not at all</u>. It's about <u>three blocks</u> that way.

w <u>It's very kind of you.</u>

여 실례합니다. 이 근처 사세요?

남 네. 도움이 필요하신가요?

여 네. 부탁 드려요. 오페라하우스 가는 길 좀 알려 주시겠어요?

남 물론이죠. 저쪽으로 세 블록 정도 가시면 됩니다.

여 정말 친절하시군요.

① 길을 잃은 것 같아요.

② 찾기 쉬울 겁니다.

③ 정말 친절하시군요.

④ 여기에서부터 10마일 정도 떨어져 있습니다.

⑤ 15분 정도 걸립니다.

•• **be from** ~출신이다 **mind** ~을 꺼려하다 **show ~ the way to** ~에게 ···로 가는 길을 알려 주다 **lost** 길을 잃은 **kind** 친절한

20

M I feel so <u>tired</u> these days. To be <u>healthy</u>, what should I do?

w Do you <u>exercise</u> regularly?

M No. But I'm trying not to use elevators and walk to school.

W Good job! Just don't give up.

M Aren't you hungry? I'd like to have hamburgers.

W Don't eat too much junk food.

- -

남 나 요즘 너무 피곤해. 건강해지려면 뭘 해야 할까?

여 너 규칙적으로 운동하니?

남 아니. 하지만 나는 엘리베이터를 타지 않으려 하고, 학교까지 걸어가려고 노력하고 있어.

여 잘했어! 포기하지만 마.

남 배고프지 않니? 햄버거가 먹고 싶다.

여 정크푸드는 너무 많이 먹지 마.

① 너 피곤하니?
② 아니야, 오늘은 내가 낼게.
③ 그것은 건강에 좋아.
④ 그녀는 뭘 먹고 싶어 하니?
⑤ 정크푸드는 너무 많이 먹지 마.

•• **tired** 피곤한 **healthy** 건강한 **exercise** 운동하다 **regularly** 규칙적으로 **elevator** 엘리베이터 **give up** 포기하다 **junk food** 정크푸드(인스턴트 음식 혹은 패스트푸드)

Further **S**tudy 정답   p. 94

1 The reason is that she won a gold medal.

2 He weighed 85kg.

3 The reason is that the boy is a transfer student from Miami.

4 She said they are very comfortable and fashionable.

5 The reason is that he wants to look around the city before he goes to the airport.

6 He thinks learning to ride a bike is too difficult for him.

7 The reason is that many reviewers recommended it.

8 To be healthy, he is trying not to use elevators and walk to school.

On **Y**our **O**wn 모범답안   p. 95

A

My Most Memorable Vacation	
(1) When was it?	last summer
(2) Where did you go?	my grandparents' house in Sokcho
(3) Who did you go there with?	my family
(4) What did you do?	swam in the sea, went to a fish market, and had a nice dinner at a seafood restaurant
(5) How was it?	fun and enjoyable

My most memorable vacation happened (1)last summer. I went to (2)my grandparents' house in Sokcho with (3)my family. While I was there, I (4)swam in the sea, went to a fish market, and had a nice dinner at a seafood restaurant. It was very (5)fun and enjoyable. I hope vacation comes soon so that I can go there again.

- -

가장 기억에 남는 방학	
(1) 그것은 언제였습니까?	작년 여름
(2) 어디에 갔습니까?	속초 조부모님 댁
(3) 누구와 그곳에 갔습니까?	가족
(4) 무엇을 했습니까?	수영하기, 수산시장 가기, 해산물 식당에서 근사한 저녁 식사 하기
(5) 기분이 어땠습니까?	재미있고 즐거웠음

저의 가장 기억에 남는 방학은 작년 여름이었습니다. 저는 그때 가족과 함께 속초에 있는 조부모님 댁에 갔습니다. 그곳에 있는 동안, 저는 바다에서 수영을 하고, 수산시장에 가고, 해산물 식당에서 근사한 저녁 식사를 했습니다. 정말 재미있고 즐거웠습니다. 저는 빨리 방학이 와서 그곳에 다시 가고 싶습니다.

B

Join Us for a Halloween Party!	
(1) Date:	Friday, October 31st
(2) Time:	6:00 p.m.
(3) Place:	the community center
(4) Activities:	A Halloween costume contest, making jack-o'-lanterns, going trick or treating

We are going to have a Halloween party. It will be on
(1)Friday, October 31st at (2)6:00 p.m. The party will
be at (3)the community center. There will be fun
activities like (4)a Halloween costume contest, making
jack-o'-lanterns, and going trick or treating. It will be a
great party. Don't miss it!

핼로윈 파티에 참석하세요!	
(1) 날짜:	10월 30일 금요일
(2) 시간:	저녁 6시
(3) 장소:	지역 주민센터
(4) 활동:	의상 경연대회, 호박등 만들기, 과자를 안 주면 장난을 칠 거야 하러 가기

우리는 핼로윈 파티를 열 예정입니다. 파티 시간은 10월 31일, 금요일,
오후 6시입니다. 파티는 지역 문화센터에서 열릴 것입니다. 핼로윈 의상
경연대회, 호박등 만들기, 과자를 안 주면 장난을 칠 거야 하러 가기 같은
재미있는 활동들이 있을 예정입니다. 멋진 파티가 될 것입니다. 놓치지
마세요!

10 Listening Test 정답   p. 100

01 ⑤	02 ④	03 ⑤	04 ②	05 ①
06 ③	07 ①	08 ③	09 ④	10 ⑤
11 ④	12 ④	13 ①	14 ④	15 ⑤
16 ②	17 ②	18 ③	19 ④	20 ④

01

W   It's freezing. I don't like winter.

M   I love winter, especially when it snows.

W   Oh, I heard on the news that it's going to snow
tomorrow.

M   Really? I hope it snows a lot so that I can make a
snowman.

W   Sounds exciting. I'll join you.

여   정말 춥다. 나는 겨울이 싫어.

남   나는 겨울이 좋아. 특히 눈이 올 때.

여   아, 뉴스에서 들었는데 내일 눈이 온대.

남   정말? 눈이 많이 내렸으면 좋겠어. 그래야 눈사람을 만들 수 있잖아.

여   재미있겠다. 나도 같이 할게.

••
freezing 몹시 추운   **especially** 특히   **make a snowman** 눈사람을 만
들다

02

M   Are you okay?

W   Yes. I went to the hospital yesterday, so I'm okay
now.

M   Good. I'm on the way to the library to return this
book.

W   Didn't you say you are planning to go to a
department store today?

M   I will go right after returning this book.

W   I see. I'll go home and take a rest.

남   너 괜찮아?

여   응. 어제 병원에 갔다 와서 지금은 괜찮아.

남   다행이다. 나는 도서관에 이 책을 반납하러 가는 길이야.

여   너 오늘 백화점에 갈 계획이라고 하지 않았어?

남   책을 반납하고 바로 갈 거야.

여   그래. 나는 집에 가서 휴식을 취할 거야.

••
return 반납하다   **plan to-V** ~하려고 계획하다   **department store** 백
화점   **right after** 곧 바로   **take a rest** 휴식을 취하다

03

W   Oh, look at this dress. It's so nice.

M   Why don't you try it on?

W   Let me check the price first. [Pause] Hmm... I don't
think I can buy it.

M   Why?

W   It is $57 but I only have $45. Moreover, I didn't
bring my credit card.

M   I can lend you some money if you want.

여 오, 저 드레스를 봐. 정말 멋지다.

남 한번 입어 보는 게 어때?

여 가격을 먼저 확인해 보고. 그것은 살 수가 없어.

남 왜?

여 가격이 57달러인데 나는 45달러 밖에 없어. 게다가 신용 카드도 안 가지고 왔어.

남 원한다면, 내가 돈을 좀 빌려 줄 수 있어.

••
try on 입어 보다. 신어 보다　**price** 가격　**moreover** 게다가　**credit card** 신용 카드　**lend** 빌려 주다

04

W Have you finished your packing?

M Almost. But I am wondering whether I have to pack an umbrella or not.

W Why? Is it going to rain?

M According to the forecaster, yes. I hope it won't rain during the trip. If it rains, there won't be many things to enjoy.

W You're right. I hope the weather stays fine.

여 짐은 다 쌌어?

남 거의. 그런데 우산을 가져가야 할지 고민이야.

여 왜? 비온데?

남 기상캐스터에 따르면 그래. 여행 중에는 비가 안 오면 좋겠다. 비가 오면, 즐길 수 있는 것이 많지 않을 거야.

여 맞아. 날씨가 좋기를 바랄게.

① 기쁜　　　② 걱정스러운　　　③ 놀란
④ 질투하는　　⑤ 신난

••
pack 짐을 싸다　**almost** 거의　**whether** ~인지 아닌지　(**weather**) **forecaster** 기상캐스터　**during** ~동안

05

W [Urgency in voice] Please help me.

M What's up?

W A man snatched my bag. Please help me find my bag. There are many important things inside it.

M Okay. Calm down. Did you see the thief? Do you remember anything about him?

W Well. He is about 175cm tall, and slim.

여 제발 도와주세요.

남 무슨 일입니까?

여 어떤 남자가 제 가방을 강탈했어요. 제 가방을 찾는 걸 도와주세요. 그 안에 중요한 물건들이 많아요.

남 네. 진정하세요. 도둑을 보셨어요? 그에 대해 기억나는 게 있어요?

여 글쎄요. 키는 한 175cm되고, 말랐어요.

① 경찰서　　　② 은행　　　③ 소방서
④ 우체국　　　⑤ 분실물 센터

••
snatch 강탈하다. 잡아 뺏다　**calm down** 진정하다　**thief** 도둑
remember 기억하다　**slim** 날씬한

06

M Did you hear where we are going for the field trip?

W No, not yet. Where are we going?

M It's a secret. Guess where?

W A park? A museum? A zoo?

M None of them. It's a place where we can ride a roller coaster.

W Really? Hooray! I will ride a bumper car there.

여 우리 현장 학습 어디로 가는지 들었어?

남 아니, 아직. 우리 어디로 가는데?

여 비밀이야. 어디일 거 같아?

남 공원? 박물관? 동물원?

여 모두 아니야. 롤러코스터를 탈 수 있는 곳이야.

남 정말? 최고! 나는 범퍼카를 탈 거야.

••
field trip 현장 학습　**secret** 비밀　**guess** 추측하다　**museum** 박물관
zoo 동물원　**place** 장소　**ride** ~을 타다

07

[Telephone rings.]

W Hello. Is this Junsu?

M Yes. Is this Jiseon?

W Yes. I'm calling to say sorry but I'm going to have to break our appointment for tonight. My parents can't come home early today, so I have to take care of my little brother.

M It's okay. I will just go to your home then. I'll play with your brother.

W Really? Thank you. He'll be <u>very</u> <u>happy</u> to see you.

....

[전화벨이 울린다.]

여 여보세요. 준수니?

남 그래. 지선이니?

여 응. 미안한데 오늘 밤 약속을 깨야 할 거 같아서 전화했어. 부모님께서 오늘 일찍 안 들어오셔서, 남동생을 돌봐야 해.

남 괜찮아. 그럼 내가 너희 집으로 갈게. 네 동생하고 놀게.

여 정말? 고마워. 너를 보면 동생도 정말 좋아할 거야.

••

appointment 약속 **tonight** 오늘 밤 **take care of** ~을 돌보다

08

W Are you done with your <u>project</u>?

M Not yet. I haven't even <u>decided</u> <u>the</u> <u>topic</u> yet.

W Oh, no. The project is <u>due</u> <u>Monday</u>. You only have <u>5 more</u> <u>days</u>.

M I know. If you have time now, could you help me with <u>choosing</u> a <u>topic</u> and <u>gathering</u> <u>information</u>?

W Sure. Why not?

....

여 너 과제는 다했어?

남 아직. 나는 주제도 정하지 못했어.

여 오, 이런. 과제는 월요일까지인데. 5일 밖에 남지 않았어.

남 알아. 지금 네가 시간이 되면. 내가 주제를 고르고 자료를 수집하는 것을 도와줄 수 있어?

여 물론이지. 왜 안되겠어?

••

project 과제. 연구 프로젝트 **decide** 결정하다 **topic** 주제 **due** 예정된 **choose** 선택하다 **gather** 모으다 **information** 정보

09

W <u>Congratulations</u>, Tim. <u>You've</u> <u>got</u> the <u>top</u> <u>score</u> <u>on</u> the final exam in my class.

M Really? I <u>can't</u> <u>believe</u> it. I'm so happy.

W I'm so <u>proud</u> <u>of</u> you. I hope you will <u>keep</u> <u>up</u> the good work.

M Thank you, ma'am. I made it <u>because</u> <u>of</u> <u>you</u>. I really appreciate <u>your</u> <u>help</u>.

W Thanks for saying so.

....

여 축하해. Tim. 우리 반 기말고사에서 제일 높은 점수를 받았어.

남 정말이요? 믿을 수가 없어요. 정말 행복해요.

여 네가 정말 자랑스럽구나. 계속 잘하기를 바란다.

남 고맙습니다. 선생님. 선생님 때문에 가능했어요. 정말 선생님의 도움에 감사드려요.

여 그렇게 말해 주어서 고맙다.

① 반 친구 – 반 친구 ② 엄마 – 아들 ③ 예술가 – 기자
④ 교사 – 학생 ⑤ 사장 – 직원

••

get the top score 최고 성적을 받다 **final exam** 기말고사 **be proud of** ~을 자랑스럽게 여기다 **keep up** 계속하다 **because of** ~때문에 **appreciate** 고마워하다. 감사하다

10

W May I help you?

M I'd like to buy some <u>fresh</u> <u>fruit</u>.

W All of my fruit is fresh. What would you like? <u>Apples</u>, <u>pears</u>, persimmons, oranges or <u>bananas</u>?

M Which fruits are <u>in</u> <u>season</u> now?

W Apples and persimmons are in season.

M Okay. Then I will <u>take</u> <u>some</u> persimmons. I like the <u>color</u> <u>orange</u>.

....

여 도와드릴까요?

남 신선한 과일을 사고 싶습니다.

여 제 과일들은 모두 신선합니다. 어떤 것을 좋아하세요? 사과, 배, 감. 오렌지. 아니면 바나나?

남 어느 과일이 제철인가요?

여 사과와 감이 제철입니다.

남 네. 그럼. 감 좀 주세요. 저는 주황색을 좋아하거든요.

••

fresh 신선한 **pear** 배 **persimmon** 감 **in season** 제철인

11

W Tom, I need your <u>help</u>.

M What is it?

W Would you mind <u>helping</u> me with my <u>science</u> <u>project</u>?

M Of course not. What is the <u>project</u> about?

W It's about <u>global</u> <u>warming</u>.

M Wow, that's an interesting topic. Let's go to the <u>library</u> to borrow <u>some</u> <u>books</u> related to it.

....

여 Tom. 네 도움이 필요해.

남 뭔데?

여 내 과학 과제를 도와줄 수 있니?

남 물론이지. 무엇에 관한 과제니?

여 지구 온난화에 관한 거야.

남 우와, 그거 흥미로운 주제다. 그것과 관련된 책 좀 빌리러 도서관에 가자.

•• **science** 과학 **global warming** 지구 온난화 **borrow** 빌리다
related to ~와 관련된

12

W What are you going to do this weekend?

M I'm going to make a photo book of my trip to Europe.

W You must have plenty of pictures, right?

M You're right. Actually a book is not enough.

W Why don't you buy an electronic album and put the pictures in it?

M That's a good idea. I might just do that.

····························

여 이번 주말에 뭐 할 예정이니?

남 유럽 여행 사진첩을 만들려고 해.

여 너 틀림없이 사진이 많을 텐데, 그렇지?

남 네 말이 맞아. 사실 한 권으로는 충분하지 않지.

여 전자 앨범을 하나 구입해서 사진들을 넣는 건 어때?

남 좋은 생각이다. 그렇게 해야겠다.

•• **photo book** 사진첩 **trip** 여행 **plenty of** 많은 ~ **enough** 충분한
electronic album 전자 앨범

13

[Telephone rings.]

W Hello. ABC Pizza. May I help you?

M Hi. I'd like to order a large BBQ chicken pizza.

W Would you like it delivered?

M No. I'll come and pick it up.

W Okay. It'll be ready in 15 minutes.

····························

[전화벨이 울린다.]

여 안녕하세요. ABC 피자입니다. 도와드릴까요?

남 안녕하세요. 치킨 BBQ 피자 큰 거 하나 주문하고 싶어요.

여 배달을 원하세요?

남 아뇨. 제가 가서 가져올 거예요.

여 네. 15분 내로 준비해 드리겠습니다.

•• **order** 주문하다 **large** 큰 **deliver** 배달하다 **pick up** 가져가다 **ready** 준비가 된

14

① W This graph shows how much money Jim spent every month.

② W Jim spent $30 allowance in March and July.

③ W Jim only spent half of his allowance in April.

④ W Jim spent the most money in May.

⑤ W Jim saved 23 dollars in June.

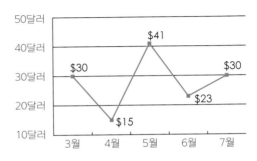

Jim은 매달 얼마를 썼는가

① 여 이 그래프는 Jim이 매달 얼마의 돈을 썼는지를 보여 준다.

② 여 Jim은 3월과 7월에 30달러의 용돈을 썼다

③ 여 Jim은 4월에 용돈의 반만 썼다.

④ 여 Jim은 5월에 가장 많은 돈을 썼다.

⑤ 여 Jim은 6월에 23달러를 저축했다.

•• **graph** 그래프 **spend** 쓰다 **allowance** 용돈 **save** 저축하다
expenditure 지출

15

W May I help you?

M I'd like to open an account.

W Which would you prefer, a checking account or a savings account?

M A checking account, please.

W Could you fill out this form and show me your ID, please?

M Oh, I left it on my office desk. I'll go grab it.

····························

여　도와드릴까요?

남　계좌를 개설하고 싶습니다.

여　당좌 예금 계좌와 저축 예금 계좌 중 어느 쪽을 더 선호하세요?

남　당좌 예금 계좌로 부탁 드립니다.

여　이 양식을 작성하시고 신분증을 보여 주시겠습니까?

남　오, 사무실 제 책상 위에 두고 왔네요. 가지러 다녀올게요.

•• **open an account** 계좌를 개설하다　**checking account** 당좌 예금
savings account 저축 예금　**fill out** ~을 작성하다　**form** 양식　**office**
사무실　**grab** 움켜쥐다

16

① M　How long does it take to get there?

W　It takes about 30 minutes.

② M　I can't believe it. I won the game.

W　Yes, I'm sure that you'll enjoy it.

③ M　Would you like to leave a message?

W　No, thank you. I'll call again.

④ M　Can you make it by 3 o'clock?

W　I'm afraid I can't. How about 4?

⑤ M　How about eating out tonight?

W　Why not? I know a nice place.

① 남　거기에 가는 데 얼마나 걸리니?

여　30분 정도 걸려.

② 남　믿을 수가 없어. 내가 그 경기에서 이겼어.

여　그래. 너는 분명히 즐기게 될 거야.

③ 남　용건을 남기시겠습니까?

여　아니요. 됐습니다. 다시 전화하겠습니다.

④ 남　3시까지 올 수 있니?

여　안 될 것 같아. 4시는 어때?

⑤ 남　오늘 밤 외식하는 거 어때요?

여　왜 안 돼요? 제가 좋은 곳을 알고 있어요.

•• **take** (시간이) 걸리다　**leave a message** 메시지를 남기다　**eat out** 외식
하다

17

M　What do you think of volunteer work? It's not hard.
Everyone, even 8-year-old kids, can do it. Most of
all, volunteering gives you and others happiness.
It could be a simple, small thing. For example,
you can talk with the elderly at a nursing home or

clean their rooms. Why don't you start volunteering
today, and give happiness to you and other people?

남　자원봉사 활동에 대해 어떻게 생각하세요? 그것은 어렵지 않습니다.
누구나, 심지어 8살 꼬마도 자원봉사를 할 수 있습니다. 무엇보다
자원봉사는 당신과 다른 사람에게 행복을 줍니다. 자원봉사는
간단하고 작은 것일 수도 있습니다. 예를 들면, 당신은 양로원을
방문해 어르신들과 얘기할 수도 있고 그분들의 방을 청소할 수도
있습니다. 오늘부터 자원봉사를 시작해서 당신과 다른 사람에게
행복을 전해 주는 것은 어떨까요?

•• **volunteer work** 자원봉사 활동　**kid** 아이　**happiness** 행복　**simple**
간단한　**the elderly** 어르신들, 노인들　**nursing home** 양로원
volunteer 자원봉사하다

18

W　Jenny has a headache. She has a fever and she
even has a runny nose. However, she goes to the
library with Peter to prepare for their final exam.
2 hours later, she tells Peter that she wants to go
home because her symptoms are getting worse.
In this situation, what would Peter say to Jenny?

여　Jenny는 머리가 아픕니다. 열이 나고 심지어 콧물도 납니다. 하지만
그녀는 기말고사를 준비하기 위해 Peter와 함께 도서관에 갑니다.
2시간 후, 그녀는 Peter에게 증세가 심해져서 집에 가고 싶다고
말합니다. 이 상황에서 Peter는 Jenny에게 뭐라고 말할까요?

① 아이스크림 먹자.

② 집에 가서 쉴 거야.

③ 너 병원에 가야 할 것 같아.

④ 이 책 빌리는 게 어때?

⑤ 열심히 공부하면 좋은 성적을 받게 될 거야.

•• **headache** 두통　**fever** 열　**runny nose** 콧물　**prepare for** ~을 준비
하다　**final exam** 기말고사　**symptom** 증상　**get worse** 점점 나빠지
다　**grade** 성적

19

M　What are you going to do this Sunday?

W　I'm going to an amusement park with my family.

M　Sounds like fun. What do you want to ride the
most?

W I want to ride the roller coaster the most. I can't wait.

M Sounds great. You look really excited!

W Yes, I'm looking forward to it.

남 이번 일요일에 무엇을 할 계획이니?

여 가족들과 놀이공원에 갈 예정이야.

남 재미있을 것 같은데. 무엇을 가장 타고 싶니?

여 나는 롤러코스터를 가장 타고 싶어. 빨리 가고 싶어.

남 좋겠다. 너 정말 들떠 보여!

여 응, 정말 기대하고 있어.

① 아니, 나는 할 수 없어.

② 응, 나는 정말 지쳤어.

③ 나는 사진을 잘 찍어.

④ 응, 정말 기대하고 있어.

⑤ 나는 타기 위해 오래 기다리는 것이 싫어.

•• **amusement park** 놀이공원 **ride** ~을 타다; 놀이 기구 **roller coaster** 롤러코스터 **excited** 신난, 들뜬 **exhausted** 지친 **look forward to** ~을 고대하다

20

M What are you doing, Jennie?

W I'm making invitations for my birthday party.

M They look good. Do you want to include one of these photos?

W Yes. Just pick one out of three. Which one do you like most?

M I like this one.

W Okay. This one goes on the card.

남 뭐 하고 있니, Jennie?

여 내 생일 파티 초대장을 만들고 있어.

남 근사해 보이는데. 이 사진들 중 하나를 붙이고 싶니?

여 응. 셋 중 하나만 골라 봐. 어느 것이 가장 마음에 드니?

남 나는 이게 좋아.

여 좋아. 이것을 카드에 넣을게.

① 그것은 7월 2일에 해.

② 그녀는 모자를 쓰고 있어.

③ 생일이 언제니?

④ 좋아, 이것을 카드에 넣을게.

⑤ 좋아, 여기에 우리 가족사진 두 장이 있어.

•• **invitation** 초대장 **include** 포함하다 **photo** 사진 **pick** 고르다 **one out of three** 셋 중 하나

Further Study 정답   p. 104

1 He is on the way to the library to return a book.

2 The reason is that a thief snatched her bag.

3 The reason is that she has to break their appointment for tonight.

4 It is due Monday.

5 They will go to the library to borrow some books related to it.

6 He is going to make a photo book of his trip to Europe this weekend.

7 The man ordered a large BBQ chicken pizza and it will take 15 minutes to be ready to pick up.

8 She wants to include one of three photos in the invitation.

On Your Own 모범답안   p. 105

A

Good morning. This is today's weather report. This morning, it is (1)warm and (1)sunny. The temperature is about (3)20 degrees. However, it will be (2)cold and (2)rainy this afternoon. The temperature will go down to (3)10 degrees. So (4)take an umbrella if you're going out. The (2)cold, (2)rainy weather will continue till tonight. This is Amy Han, and this has been your daily weather update. Thank you.

(1) 날씨 I	(2) 날씨 II	(3) 기온	(4) 조언
따뜻한 / 화창한 / 시원한 / 구름 낀 / 바람 부는 / 안개 낀	더운 / 습한 / 추운 / 쌀쌀한 / 비가 오는 / 눈이 오는	30 20 10 -5 -10	우산을 챙기세요 겉옷을 가져가세요 모자를 쓰세요 선글라스를 쓰세요 두꺼운 외투를 입으세요

안녕하십니까. 오늘의 일기 예보입니다. 오늘 아침은 날씨가 따뜻하고 맑습니다. 기온은 약 영상 20도입니다. 하지만 오늘 오후는 춥고 비가 오겠습니다. 기온은 10도까지 떨어지겠습니다. 그러므로 외출하시려면 우산을 챙기세요. 춥고, 비 오는 날씨는 오늘 밤까지 계속되겠습니다. 지금까지 Amy Han이었으며, 날씨 정보였습니다. 감사합니다.

B

How I Spend My Monthly Allowance

(1) How much allowance do you get every month?	40,000 won
(2) How do you usually spend it?	① 15,000 won: snacks ② 10,000 won: buses and subways ③ 10,000 won: shopping
(3) How much do you save every month?	5,000 won
(4) What do you want to do with the money you save?	buy a gift for my mom

Every month, I get (1)40,000 won for my allowance. I usually spend about ①15,000 won on snacks, and about ②10,000 won on buses and subways. I also spend ③10,000 won on shopping. I usually save (3)5,000 won of my allowance every month. I want to (4)buy a gift for my mom with the money.

어떻게 한 달 용돈을 쓰는가

(1) 매달 얼마의 용돈을 받습니까?	40,000원
(2) 주로 그것을 어떻게 씁니까?	15,000원: 간식 10,000원: 버스와 지하철 10,000원: 쇼핑
(3) 매달 얼마를 저축합니까?	5,000원
(4) 저축한 돈으로 무엇을 하고 싶습니까?	엄마께 드릴 선물을 삼

매달 저는 용돈으로 4만원을 받습니다. 저는 보통 15,000원 정도를 간식 사는 데 쓰고, 만원 정도를 버스와 지하철 타는 데 씁니다. 또한 저는 1만 원 정도를 쇼핑하는 데 씁니다. 저는 제 용돈에서 5천원을 매달 저축합니다. 저는 그 돈으로 엄마께 드릴 선물을 사고 싶습니다.

01 ④	02 ④	03 ②	04 ③	05 ②
06 ④	07 ⑤	08 ④	09 ⑤	10 ⑤
11 ⑤	12 ①	13 ④	14 ③	15 ①
16 ⑤	17 ②	18 ⑤	19 ⑤	20 ②

01

W   I love summer, it's too cold in winter. Which season do you like best?

M   I like winter a lot, because it snows.

W   Are you good at any winter sports?

M   I like snowboarding the most. But I enjoy skating, sledding, and skiing, too.

W   Wow! You're quite a sportsman.

여   나는 여름을 사랑해. 겨울은 너무 추워. 너는 어느 계절을 가장 좋아해?

남   눈이 오기 때문에 나는 겨울을 정말 좋아해.

여   너는 겨울 스포츠 잘해?

남   나는 스노보드 타는 것을 가장 좋아해. 하지만 스케이팅, 썰매 타기, 스키 타기도 즐겨.

여   우와! 너는 정말 스포츠맨이구나.

●●
be good at ~을 잘하다   snowboard 스노보드를 타다   sled 썰매를 타다   sportsman 스포츠맨

02

W   Get ready! Go!

M   Do you want to lose weight? Do you want to stay healthy? If so, come on to JJ Fitness Center.

W   Cut! You should say that with a big smile. Don't look so tired or exhausted.

M   Sorry. It's so hard to run and talk at the same time, though.

W   I know, but let's try that one more time.

여   준비하세요! 갑니다!

남 체중을 줄이고 싶으세요? 건강하고 싶으세요? 그렇다면 JJ 피트니스 센터로 오세요.

여 중지! 활짝 웃으면서 말해야 합니다. 피곤해 보이거나 지쳐 보이면 안 됩니다.

남 죄송합니다. 하지만 뛰면서 동시에 얘기하는 것은 너무 어렵네요.

여 알고 있습니다만, 한 번 더 해 보세요.

•• **get ready** 준비가 되다 **lose weight** 살을 빼다 **stay healthy** 건강을 유지하다 **fitness center** 피트니스 센터, 헬스 클럽 **tired** 피곤한 **exhausted** 지친 **at the same time** 동시에 **though** 하지만

03

w Did you buy game items again?

M Yes. Please don't tell Mom.

w Oh, come on. Why do you keep spending your money online?

M Because there was a promotion. If you pay 1,000 won, they give you 500 points for free.

w So, how much did you spend?

M I spent 2,000 won.

여 너 게임 아이템을 또 샀어?

남 응. 엄마한테는 얘기하지 말아 줘.

여 아, 진짜. 왜 온라인에서 계속 돈을 쓰는 거야?

남 왜냐하면 행사가 있었으니깐. 1,000원을 내면, 500점을 공짜로 준다고.

여 그래서, 얼마나 쓴 거야?

남 나는 2,000원을 썼어.

•• **item** 항목, 품목 **keep -ing** 계속 ~하다 **promotion** 행사 **point** 점, 점수 **for free** 무료로

04

w How was the science test? I don't think I did very well on it.

M Me either. I couldn't understand some of the questions. I think I'm going to fail.

w We studied really hard this time, though, didn't we?

M You're right. Let's forget about it and study for the test tomorrow.

w Okay. I will try.

여 과학 시험은 어땠어? 나는 잘 못 본 거 같아.

남 나도 그래. 나는 문제 몇 개를 이해할 수가 없었어. 낙제할 거 같아.

여 하지만 우리 이번에는 더 열심히 공부했는데, 그렇지 않니?

남 맞아. 잊어버리고, 내일 시험 준비를 하자.

여 그래. 해볼게.

① 자랑스러운　　② 지친　　③ 실망한
④ 긴장한　　⑤ 행복한

•• **Me either.** 나도 그래. **question** 질문 **fail** 낙제하다 **hard** 열심히 **forget about** ~에 대해 잊다 **disappointed** 낙담한 **nervous** 긴장한

05

w Look at the sign. No pets allowed.

M What? No way. [Pause] Oh, look at the sign more carefully. It says pets aren't allowed without a leash.

w I see. Our puppy will be fine, then.

M Right. Let's go in. Look at the children running on the grass. They look happy.

w The people lying on the grass look peaceful.

여 표지판을 봐. 애완동물은 출입 금지야.

남 뭐? 말도 안 돼. 표지판을 세심하게 봐. 줄을 하지 않은 애완동물은 출입 금지라고 쓰여 있어.

여 그러네. 우리 강아지는 괜찮네, 그럼.

남 맞아. 들어가자. 잔디 위에서 뛰어노는 아이들을 봐. 행복해 보인다.

여 잔디 위에 누워 있는 사람들은 평화로워 보여.

•• **allow** 허락하다 **carefully** 신중하게, 조심스럽게 **leash** 줄, 끈 **puppy** 강아지 **grass** 잔디 **lie** 눕다 **peaceful** 평화로운

06

w This store has many nice shoes.

M Why don't we go in and try some on?

w Let's do it. [Pause] The red sneakers are pretty. I think the ones with shoelaces are better.

M I prefer the brown sneakers with shoelaces.

w I like these boots. Winter is coming soon, I think I'll take the brown ones.

M Okay.

여 이 가게에는 멋진 신발들이 많아.

남 안으로 들어가서 신어 보는 건 어때?

여 그러자. 빨간색 스니커즈가 예쁘네. 신발 끈이 달린 것이 더 좋아 보여.

남 나는 신발 끈이 달린 갈색 스니커즈가 좋은데.

여 이 부츠도 마음에 들어. 겨울이 오고 있으니, 갈색으로 사야겠어.

남 좋아.

●●
sneakers 스니커즈 **shoelace** 신발 끈 **brown** 갈색의

07

M Do you <u>have time</u> this <u>afternoon</u>?

W Yes. Why?

M I have to <u>buy a gift</u> for my mom's birthday. I want you to help me <u>choose something for</u> her.

W Okay. What do you want to buy?

M I'm <u>thinking about</u> getting her a scarf because it's getting <u>cold</u>.

W <u>What a nice son</u>!

- - - - - - - - - - - - - - - - - - - -

남 오늘 오후에 시간 있어?

여 어. 왜?

남 엄마 생신 선물을 사야 해. 네가 선물 고르는 것을 도와주었으면 좋겠어.

여 그래. 무엇을 사고 싶은데?

남 날씨가 추워지니간, 스카프를 사 드릴까 해.

여 정말 좋은 아들이구나!

●●
gift 선물 **choose** 선택하다 **think about** ~에 대해 생각하다

08

W <u>Are you ready for</u> the test this <u>evening</u>?

M A test? Do we have a test today?

W <u>My goodness</u>. Did you <u>forget</u> we have a test in <u>English class</u>?

M Oh, no! What should I do?

W We have <u>three hours</u> to study. You can do it. <u>Don't worry</u>.

- - - - - - - - - - - - - - - - - - - -

여 오늘 저녁 시험 준비는 했어?

남 시험? 오늘 시험이 있어?

여 어머나. 오늘 영어 시간에 시험이 있는 것 잊었어?

남 오, 안 돼! 어떻게 하지?

여 공부할 수 있는 시간이 3시간 있어. 할 수 있어. 걱정하지 마.

●●
be ready for ~할 준비가 되다 **My goodness.** 어머나, 이런. **worry** 걱정하다

09

W Excuse me. Could you please <u>take a picture</u> for me and my boyfriend?

M Sure. <u>Stay still</u>. Ready! Three! Two! One!

W Thank you. <u>Do you want me</u> to take one, too?

M Okay, thanks.

W This place is <u>much more beautiful</u> than I thought.

M I think so too.

- - - - - - - - - - - - - - - - - - - -

여 실례합니다. 저와 제 남자 친구 사진을 찍어 주시겠어요?

남 그럼요. 가만히 계세요. 준비! 셋! 둘! 하나!

여 감사합니다. 저도 찍어 드릴까요?

남 네. 고맙습니다.

여 이곳은 제가 생각했던 것보다 훨씬 아름답네요.

남 저도 그렇게 생각합니다.

① 교수 – 학생   ② 여자 친구 – 남자 친구   ③ 친구 – 친구

④ 사진 작가 – 관광객   ⑤ 관광객 – 관광객

●●
take a picture 사진을 찍다 **still** 움직이지 않는

10

M Mom, please go to the <u>art supplies store</u> with me. I have to buy <u>materials for</u> my art class.

W Alright. What do you need?

M <u>Drawing paper</u>, watercolor paints, brushes, and crayons.

W You need <u>them all</u>?

M Yes. Those are the things that the <u>teacher</u> asked us to <u>bring</u>.

W Okay. Let's go.

- - - - - - - - - - - - - - - - - - - -

남 엄마, 미술용품 가게에 같이 가 주세요. 미술 수업에 필요한 것들을 사야 해요.

여 그래. 필요한 게 무엇들이니?

남 도화지, 물감, 붓, 그리고 크레용이요.

여 그것들이 전부 다 필요하니?

남 네. 선생님이 가져오라고 하신 것들이에요.

여 알았다. 가자.

art supplies store 미술용품 가게 **material** 재료 **drawing paper** 도화지 **watercolor paint** 물감 **brush** 붓 **crayon** 크레용

11

M What are you doing, Jennie?

W I'm looking for a map of Sydney.

M Why? Are you going to visit there?

W Yes. My dad is going to go there on business next week. I'm going with him.

M Sounds great. I'll tell you about many famous places to visit.

W Can you mark the places on my map, please?

....

남 뭐 하고 있니, Jennie?

여 시드니 지도를 찾고 있어.

남 왜? 거기 가려고?

여 응. 아빠가 다음 주에 거기로 출장을 가실 예정이야. 아빠와 함께 가려고.

남 멋지다. 방문할 여러 유명한 장소들에 대해 이야기해 줄게.

여 지도에 그 장소들 좀 표시해 줄래?

look for ~을 찾다 **map** 지도 **on business** 사업차 **famous** 유명한 **place** 장소 **mark** 표시하다

12

M I didn't do very well on my presentation today.

W Why? What happened? It was pairs work, wasn't it?

M Yes, that's right. I was responsible for making a PowerPoint presentation, but I forgot to bring it on my USB memory stick. My partner is still angry with me.

W Oh my god!

M What should I do?

W I think you should say sorry to your partner.

....

남 오늘 발표에서 잘하지 못했어.

여 왜? 무슨 일이니? 2인 1조로 하는 거 맞지, 그렇지 않니?

남 응. 맞아. 내가 책임지고 PPT를 제작하기로 했는데, USB에 담아 오는 걸 깜빡 했어. 내 짝은 여전히 나에게 화가 나 있어.

여 오 이런!

남 나 어떡해야 할까?

여 네 짝에게 사과해야 할 거 같은데.

do well on ~을 잘하다 **presentation** 발표 **pair work** 2인 1조 활동 **be responsible for** ~에 책임이 있다 **partner** 짝, 파트너

13

M Let's go out for dinner, Jennie.

W I'm not having dinner today.

M Why? What's wrong?

W I can't eat anything because I have a medical check-up tomorrow.

M Oh, that's too bad. I hope there's nothing wrong with your health.

....

남 저녁 식사하러 나가자, Jennie.

여 전 오늘 저녁 안 먹을래요.

남 왜? 무슨 일이야?

여 내일 건강 검진이 있어서 아무것도 먹을 수 없어요.

남 오, 안됐다. 건강에 이상이 없길 바랄게.

go out 외출하다 **medical check-up** 건강 검진 **health** 건강

14

① W On Sunday, Jennie did her volunteer work.

② W On Monday and Wednesday, Jennie played the piano.

③ W On Tuesday and Thursday, Jennie didn't do anything.

④ W On Friday, Jennie went shopping.

⑤ W On Saturday, Jennie went to the library.

....

Jennie가 지난주에 한 일						
일	월	화	수	목	금	토
자원봉사를 했다	피아노를 쳤다	농구를 했다	피아노를 쳤다	농구를 했다	쇼핑을 갔다	도서관에 갔다

① 여 일요일에 Jennie는 자원봉사 활동을 했다.

② 여 월요일과 수요일에 Jennie는 피아노를 쳤다.

③ 여 화요일과 목요일에 Jennie는 아무것도 하지 않았다.

④ 여 금요일에 Jennie는 쇼핑하러 갔다.

⑤ 여 토요일에 Jennie는 도서관에 갔다.

Tuesday 화요일 **Wednesday** 수요일 **Thursday** 목요일

15

M I'm so hungry.

W Me, too. We'd better finish this paperwork after we eat. What do you want to have for lunch?

M How about ribs at the VVIPs Buffet?

W Oh, sounds great. My mouth is watering.

M Have you tried their king prawn dish? It's fantastic.

W Let's hurry.

········

남 정말 배고파.

여 나도 그래. 식사를 한 후 이 서류 작업을 끝내는 게 좋겠어. 점심으로 뭘 먹고 싶니?

남 VVIPs 뷔페에서 갈비 요리 어때?

여 오, 좋은데. 입에 침이 고이네.

남 왕새우 요리 먹어 봤어? 환상적이야.

여 서두르자.

finish 끝내다 **paper work** 서류 작업, 문서 업무 **rib** 갈비 **buffet** 뷔페 **watering** 침이 고이는, 군침이 도는 **king prawn** 왕새우 **fantastic** 환상적인

16

① M I'm sure you'll do it better next time.

W It's nice of you to say so.

② M Do you have any classes today?

W No, I don't.

③ M Can I exchange this sweater, please?

W What's wrong with it?

④ M How do you like to study?

W I like to study in groups.

⑤ M Do you mind me opening the window?

W Yes, of course. It's too hot here.

········

① 남 다음번에는 분명히 더 잘할 거야.

여 그렇게 말씀해 주시니 감사합니다.

② 남 오늘 수업 있니?

여 아니, 없어.

③ 남 이 스웨터를 교환할 수 있을까요?

여 무슨 문제가 있나요?

④ 남 어떻게 공부하는 것을 좋아하니?

여 무리 지어서 공부하는 것을 좋아해.

⑤ 남 창문을 열면 안 될까요?

여 네, 물론이죠. 여기는 너무 더워요.

········

exchange 교환하다 **sweater** 스웨터 **in groups** 그룹으로 **hot** 더운

17

M Attention, students! We are going to have a project to research issues related to the Earth, for example, global warming, the greenhouse effect, etc. This will be done in groups. Therefore, make groups of five members and choose a topic. Please send me a list of group members and your topic by tomorrow. After you research it, you should write a 1,000-word report. Please hand it in by next Friday.

········

남 학생 여러분, 주목해 주세요! 지구 온난화, 온실 효과 등과 같이 지구와 관련된 쟁점들을 연구하는 프로젝트를 실시할 예정입니다. 이 프로젝트는 그룹으로 합니다. 그러므로 5명이 그룹을 만들고 주제를 선정하세요. 내일까지 그룹 멤버들의 명단과 주제를 보내 주세요. 주제를 연구한 뒤, 1,000 단어로 된 보고서를 작성해야 합니다. 보고서는 다음 주 금요일까지 제출해 주세요.

········

attention 주의, 집중 **research** 연구; 연구하다 **issue** 문제, 쟁점 **related to** ~와 관련된 **global warming** 지구 온난화 **greenhouse effect** 온실 효과 **choose** 고르다 **topic** 주제 **list** 명단 **report** 보고서 **hand in** 제출하다

18

W Sue goes to see a movie with Wendy. In the middle of the movie, Sue's mobile phone rings. She hurries to switch it to vibration mode. In this situation, what would Wendy say to Sue?

········

여 Sue는 Wendy와 영화를 보러 갑니다. 영화 중간에 Sue의 휴대 전화가 울립니다. 그녀는 서둘러 그것을 진동 모드로 바꿉니다. 이 상황에서 Wendy가 Sue에게 뭐라고 말할까요?

① 신경 쓰지 마.

② 그것은 정말 지루해.

③ 그렇게 말하지 마.

④ 제발 늦지 마라.

⑤ 휴대 전화를 꺼 줘.

in the middle of ~중간에 **ring** 울리다 **switch** 바꾸다 **vibration mode** 진동 모드 **boring** 지루한 **on time** 제시간에 **turn off** (전원을) 끄다

19

M Hi, how may I help you?

W I'm looking for a neck warmer. Can I have a look?

M Yes. We have several kinds. Come this way, please.

W [Pause] Oh, I like the black one. How much is it?

M The original price was $30 but we now have a 50% discount sale.

W Oh, I'm lucky. I'll take it.

남 안녕하세요. 어떻게 도와드릴까요?

여 넥 워머를 찾고 있어요. 볼 수 있을까요?

남 네. 여러 종류가 있습니다. 이쪽으로 오세요.

여 오, 이 검정색이 마음에 드네요. 얼마예요?

남 정상 가격은 30달러입니다만 지금은 50% 할인 판매하고 있습니다.

여 오, 제가 운이 좋네요. 그걸로 살게요.

① 다시 해 볼게요.

② 그거 안됐다.

③ 이상하게 생겼어.

④ 우리 어떻게 하지?

⑤ 오, 제가 운이 좋네요. 그걸로 살게요.

neck warmer 넥 워머 **several** 여러 개의 **kind** 종류 **original** 원래의 **price** 가격 **discount** 할인 **sale** 판매 **lucky** 운이 좋은

20

M Jennie, let's go see a movie this weekend.

W Okay. Do you have a special thing in mind?

M How about the *Hunger Games 2*?

W Sorry, I saw it last week.

M Oh, did you? What did you think of it?

W It was really exciting.

남 Jennie, 주말에 영화 보러 가자.

여 좋아. 특별히 마음에 둔 거 있니?

남 〈헝거게임2〉는 어때?

여 미안, 지난주에 봤어.

남 오, 그랬어? 어땠어?

여 정말 재미있었어.

① 기분이 안 좋아.

② 정말 재미있었어.

③ 재미있겠다.

④ 그것은 불가능할 것 같아.

⑤ 그게 더 좋은 생각인 것 같아.

awful 끔찍한, 지독한 **exciting** 재미있는 **impossible** 불가능한

Further **S**tudy 정답   p. 114

1 He likes winter best because it snows.

2 The reason is that he has to run and talk at the same time.

3 The reason is that the man forgot they have a test in their English class.

4 He is going to buy drawing paper, watercolor paints, brushes, and crayons.

5 She is going to visit Sydney.

6 He forgot to bring his PowerPoint presentation on his USB memory stick.

7 They will have ribs at the VVIPs Buffet for lunch.

8 She has to pay $15 for the neck warmer.

On **Y**our **O**wn 모범답안   p. 115

A

I'd like to get (1)a new smartphone for my birthday. The reason is that (2)mine is too old. If I get (1)a new smartphone, I will be able to (3)use the Internet anywhere. I hope my birthday comes soon.

(1) 무엇	(2) 이유 I	(3) 이유 II
책	책 읽기를 좋아함	지루할 때 읽을 수 있음
고양이/개	애완동물을 갖고 싶음	추운 날씨에 따뜻하게 해 줌
코트	추위를 못 견딤	외로울 때 함께 놀 수 있음
새 스마트폰	내 것이 너무 오래됨	어디서든지 인터넷을 사용함
새 자전거	내 것이 너무 작음	매일 자전거로 등교함

저는 생일 선물로 새 스마트폰을 받고 싶습니다. 왜냐하면 제 것은 너무 오래되었기 때문입니다. 새 스마트폰을 받으면, 저는 어디서든지 인터넷을 사용할 수 있을 것입니다. 저는 제 생일이 빨리 오기를 바랍니다.

B

Monday	Tuesday	Wednesday
cleaned my room	practiced the piano	watched a movie on TV
Thursday	**Friday**	**Weekend**
went shopping and bought some new clothes	went to my friend's birthday party	stayed home and studied for a test

I did a lot of things last week. On Monday, I cleaned my room. On Tuesday, I practiced the piano. On Wednesday, I watched a movie on TV. On Thursday, I went shopping and bought some new clothes. On Friday, I went to my friend's birthday party. On the weekend, I stayed home and studied for a test. It was a very busy week for me.

월요일	화요일	수요일
방 청소 하기	피아노 연습하기	TV로 영화보기
목요일	**금요일**	**주말**
쇼핑 가서 옷 사기	친구 생일 파티 가기	집에서 시험공부 하기

저는 지난 주에 많은 것을 했습니다. 월요일에, 저는 제 방 청소를 했습니다. 화요일에는 피아노 연습을 했습니다. 수요일에는 TV에서 영화를 봤습니다. 목요일에는 쇼핑을 가서 새 옷을 몇 벌 샀습니다. 금요일에는 친구의 생일 파티에 갔습니다. 주말에는 집에서 시험 공부를 했습니다. 매우 바쁜 한 주였습니다.

01 ②	02 ②	03 ⑤	04 ①	05 ③
06 ①	07 ④	08 ④	09 ⑤	10 ②
11 ⑤	12 ②	13 ①	14 ③	15 ④
16 ②	17 ④	18 ②	19 ⑤	20 ④

01

W The food in this restaurant is so good. I'm full now.

M I'm glad to hear you enjoyed our food.

W I took a bite of my boyfriend's sandwich, and it was good. I also enjoyed my steak and salad.

M Thank you for saying so.

W I will try spaghetti and pizza next time.

여 이 식당의 음식이 맛있어요. 정말 배불러요.

남 우리 음식을 좋아하셨다니 감사합니다.

여 남자 친구 샌드위치를 한 입 먹었는데, 좋았습니다. 제가 먹은 스테이크와 샐러드도 좋았습니다.

남 그렇게 말씀해 주셔서 감사합니다.

여 다음에는 스파게티와 피자를 먹어 볼게요.

full 배부른 **take a bite** 한 입 깨물다

02

M Hey, Violet. Stop! Look at the light. It's red.

W What does the red sign mean, Dad?

M Red means stop and green means go. So if you see the color red, you have to stop and wait for the green light.

W Okay. I will keep that in mind, Dad.

M Good girl.

남 이봐, Violet. 멈춰! 신호를 봐야지. 빨간불이잖아.

여 빨간색 신호는 무슨 뜻이에요, 아빠?

남 빨간색은 멈추고, 녹색은 가라는 뜻이야. 네가 빨간색을 보면, 멈춰서 녹색 불이 될 때까지 기다려야 해.

여 네. 명심할게요, 아빠.

남 착한 녀석.

mean 의미하다 **wait for** ~을 기다리다 **keep ~ in mind** ~을 명심하다

03

w Did you finish repairing my car?

m Yes, I did. I changed the tires, motor oil, and 2 windshield wipers.

w Thanks. How much is it in total?

m Changing the tires is $200, the motor oil is $25, and the windshield wipers cost $5 each.

w Okay. Here is my credit card.

여 제 차 수리를 끝내셨나요?

남 네, 끝냈습니다. 타이어, 자동차 오일, 그리고 창문 와이퍼 2개를 바꿨습니다.

여 고맙습니다. 전부 얼마인가요?

남 타이어 교체는 200달러, 모터 오일은 25달러, 창문 와이퍼는 각각 5달러입니다.

여 네. 신용 카드 여기 있습니다.

repair 고치다, 수리하다 **tire** 타이어 **motor oil** 모터 오일 **windshield wiper** (자동차 앞 유리의) 와이퍼 **in total** 전체, 합 **cost** 비용이 들다 **each** 각각의

04

w Oh, no. What should I do?

m Why? Why are you moving back and forth?

w I'll have an English Speech Contest tomorrow evening, but I keep forgetting the text.

m Relax. You'll be fine. Take a deep breath. You'll feel much better.

w Okay. Thanks.

여 오, 이런. 어떻게 하지?

남 왜? 왜 앞뒤로 왔다갔다하는 거야?

여 내일 저녁에 영어 말하기 대회가 있는데, 자꾸 말을 잊어버려.

남 긴장을 풀어. 괜찮을 거야. 숨을 깊게 쉬어 봐. 훨씬 나아질 거야.

여 그래. 고마워.

① 긴장한 ② 지루한 ③ 기쁜
④ 신난 ⑤ 지친

back and forth 앞뒤로 **English Speech Contest** 영어 말하기 대회

text 원문 **relax** 긴장을 풀다 **take a deep breath** 숨을 깊이 쉬다

05

[Telephone rings.]

w Hello. Front desk. How may I help you?

m Hello, this is Jack Adams in room 408. I'd like a wake-up call, please.

w Okay, sir. What time do you want it at?

m 6:30 in the morning. And I would like some more towels, please.

w Sure. They will be sent to your room right away.

m Thank you.

[전화벨이 울린다.]

여 여보세요. 안내 데스크입니다. 어떻게 도와드릴까요?

남 안녕하세요, 저는 408호의 Jack Adams입니다. 모닝콜을 부탁 드립니다.

여 네, 손님. 몇 시에 원하세요?

남 아침 6시 30분이요. 그리고 수건을 좀 더 가져다 주세요.

여 네. 방으로 바로 가져다 드리겠습니다.

남 감사합니다.

① 식당 ② 병원 ③ 호텔
④ 사무실 ⑤ 쇼핑몰

wake-up call 모닝콜 **right away** 즉시, 당장

06

w Please raise your left hand higher, and point to the sky.

m Like this?

w Right. You'd better smile more naturally.

m Okay. I'll try.

w That's good now. Stand still. [Pause] Nice shot! Please pose differently for the next picture now.

여 왼손을 좀 더 높게 들고, 하늘을 가리키세요.

남 이렇게요?

여 네. 좀 더 자연스럽게 웃으세요.

남 네. 해볼게요.

여 지금이 좋습니다. 가만히 계세요. 멋진 그림이네요! 다음 사진을 찍기 위해 자세를 바꿔 주세요.

배열하다 **furniture** 가구 **mop** 대걸레질하다 **exhausted** 지친

raise 들어 올리다 **point to** ~을 가리키다 **had better** ~하는 게 낫다
naturally 자연스럽게 **still** 움직이지 않는 **shot** 촬영, 숏, 사진 **pose** 포
즈를 취하다 **differently** 다르게

07

[Telephone rings.]

w Hello. Can I talk to Jake, please?

M Hello, this is Jake. Who's calling?

w It's me, Jessie. I'd like to know whether you can
help me to prepare for my party or not.

M Of course I can. What do you want me to do?

w Please blow up some balloons.

M No problem.

[전화벨이 울린다.]

여 여보세요. Jake와 통화할 수 있을까요?

남 여보세요. 제가 Jake입니다. 누구세요?

여 나야, Jessie. 파티를 준비하는 데 도와줄 수 있는지 궁금해서.

남 당연히 할 수 있지. 내가 무엇을 하면 될까?

여 풍선 좀 불어 줘.

남 문제없어.

Who's calling? 전화 거신 분은 누구세요? **whether** ~인지 아닌지
prepare for ~을 준비하다 **blow up** ~을 불다 **balloon** 풍선

08

w How was your weekend?

M I was busy doing a big cleanup. I dusted rooms,
rearranged furniture, and mopped the floor.

w Wow. You must be exhausted now.

M You're right. That's why I went to the sauna. I feel
much better now.

w Good.

여 주말은 어땠어.?

남 대청소 하느라고 바빴어. 방 먼지도 털고, 가구도 재배치하고, 바닥도
걸레질했어.

여 우와. 지금 정말 피곤하겠다.

남 맞아. 그래서 사우나에 갔어. 지금은 훨씬 좋아졌어.

여 다행이네.

busy 바쁜 **cleanup** 청소 **dust** 먼지를 털다 **rearrange** 재배치하다, 재

09

M Can I have my speech manuscript? I should look
through it again so that I won't make any mistakes
in front of people.

w Here you are. I think you're ready to deliver it.

M Thank you for saying so. What time is my meeting?

w It will be at 2 p.m., sir. Do you want some coffee or
tea?

M Coffee, please.

남 제 연설 원고를 볼 수 있을까요? 사람들 앞에서 실수를 안 하도록 다시
봐야겠어요.

여 여기 있습니다. 당신은 충분히 전달할 준비가 되어 있는 거 같아요.

남 그렇게 말해 주어서 고마워요. 회의가 몇 시인가요?

여 오후 2시입니다. 커피나 차를 드릴까요?

남 커피 부탁 드립니다.

manuscript 원고 **look through** ~을 검토하다 **make a mistake**
실수하다 **in front of** ~앞에 **deliver** 전달하다, 배달하다

10

w I'm looking for a present for my parents' 30th
wedding anniversary. Can you recommend me
something?

M These health bracelets and T-shirts are popular.
They have the same design but are available in
different colors.

w My parents already have the bracelets. The T-shirts
sound good.

M Come here and take a look.

w I like these red and blue ones. I'll take them.

여 저는 부모님의 결혼 30주년 선물을 고르고 있습니다. 추천해 주실 수
있나요?

남 이 건강 팔찌나 티셔츠가 인기 있습니다. 티셔츠는 같은 디자인에
색상이 다르게 나옵니다.

여 팔찌는 이미 가지고 계세요. 티셔츠가 좋아 보이네요.

남 이쪽으로 오셔서 구경해 보세요.

여 저는 이 빨간색과 파란색 것이 좋아요. 그것들로 주세요.

굉장한 **miss** 놓치다

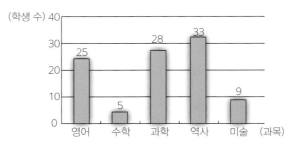

wedding anniversary 결혼 기념일 **recommend** 추천하다 **health**
건강 **bracelet** 팔찌 **popular** 인기 있는 **available** 구할 수 있는
different 다른 **take a look** 들여다보다

11

M How far do we have to go?

W Look, can you see the tower over there? That is the
Eiffel Tower.

M I can't wait to see it up close.

W I'd like to get a picture of us here.

M Why don't you ask that man?

W Okay. [Pause] Excuse me, sir. Would you mind
taking a picture of us?

남 우리 얼마나 더 가야 하지?

여 봐, 저기 탑 보이지? 저것이 에펠 탑이야.

남 가까이에서 빨리 보고 싶다.

여 여기에서 우리들 사진 찍고 싶은데.

남 저 남자에게 부탁해 보는 거 어때?

여 좋아. 실례합니다. 저희들 사진 좀 찍어 주시겠어요?

far 먼 **over there** 저기에 **can't wait to-V** 빨리 ∼하고 싶다 **close**
가까이 **picture** 사진

12

W Hi, Tom. You seem to be very busy these days.

M Yeah, I've been busy with my new project.

W You like Gustav Klimt, don't you? There's an
exhibition of his at the City Gallery now. Have you
already been there?

M No, not yet. How was it?

W It was awesome. Don't miss it.

여 안녕, Tom. 너 요즘 아주 바빠 보여.

남 응. 새 프로젝트로 바빠.

여 너 구스타프 클림프 좋아하지, 그렇지 않니? 시립 미술관에서 그의
전시회가 있어. 벌써 다녀왔니?

남 아니, 아직. 어땠어?

여 굉장했어. 놓치지 마.

seem ∼처럼 보이다 **exhibition** 전시회 **gallery** 미술관 **awesome**

13

W Do you remember the Ugg boots that I ordered a
week ago?

M Yes. Did you get them?

W No.

M Not yet? It's taking too long.

W They said there's no more stock in that size.

M That's too bad.

여 너 내가 일주일 전에 주문했던 어그 부츠 기억나?

남 응. 받았어?

여 아니.

남 아직이라고? 너무 오래 걸린다.

여 그 사이즈 재고가 더 이상 없대.

남 안됐다.

remember 기억하다 **order** 주문하다 **ago** ∼ 전에 **stock** 재고

14

① M This bar chart shows the survey result of favorite
teachers.

② M The most favorite teacher is the history teacher.

③ M Students prefer the English teacher to the
science teacher.

④ M Four more students like the art teacher better
than the math teacher.

⑤ M Only 5 students answered that their favorite
teacher teaches math.

가장 좋아하는 선생님

(학생 수) 40

30 — 25, 28, 33

20

10 — 5, 9

0

영어 수학 과학 역사 미술 (과목)

① 남 이 막대그래프는 가장 좋아하는 선생님에 대한 설문 조사 결과를 보

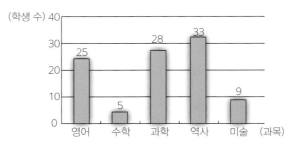

여 준다.

② 남 가장 인기 있는 선생님은 역사 선생님이다.

③ 남 학생들은 과학 선생님보다 영어 선생님을 더 좋아한다.

④ 남 수학 선생님보다 영어 선생님을 좋아하는 학생이 4명 더 많다.

⑤ 남 5명의 학생들만 그들이 가장 좋아하는 선생님이 수학을 가르친다고 대답했다.

bar chart 막대그래프　**survey** 설문 조사　**result** 결과　**history** 역사
prefer A to B B보다 A를 더 선호하다

15

W Why don't we have a <u>swimming race</u>?

M Okay. Let's wear <u>swimming caps</u> before we forget.

W That's a good idea. Here is mine. Wait a second. I think <u>something</u> is <u>missing</u>.

M What's wrong?

W Oh, I got it. We forgot to <u>warm up first</u>.

M Let's do it now.

여 수영 시합하는 거 어때?

남 좋아. 잊어버리기 전에 수영 모자 쓰자.

여 좋은 생각이다. 내 것 여기 있어. 잠깐만. 뭔가 빠진 것 같아.

남 뭐가 잘못된 거지?

여 오, 알겠어. 우리 먼저 준비 운동하는 것을 잊어버렸어.

남 이제 준비 운동을 하자.

race 경기, 경주　**wear** 입다, 쓰다　**swimming cap** 수영모, 수영 모자
missing 빠뜨린, 놓친　**warm up** 준비 운동하다

16

① M <u>Which one</u> is Jennie?

W She's <u>the one</u> talking with Sue.

② M Do you want <u>some more coke</u>?

W I think so, too.

③ W <u>How long</u> will you stay in New York?

M I'll stay there <u>for two weeks</u>.

④ M What do you think of your <u>new English teacher</u>?

W I think he's <u>nice</u>.

⑤ M Did you watch <u>the soccer game</u> last night?

W No, I didn't have <u>time to</u>.

① 남 어느 쪽이 Jennie니?

여 그녀는 Sue랑 이야기하고 있어.

② 남 너 콜라 더 마실래?

여 나도 그렇게 생각해.

③ 여 뉴욕에 얼마나 오래 머물 거니?

남 거기에 2주 머물 거야.

④ 남 새로 오신 영어 선생님 어떤 것 같아?

여 좋은 분인 것 같아.

⑤ 남 어젯밤 그 축구 경기 봤니?

여 아니. 그럴 시간이 없었어.

talk with ~와 이야기하다　**stay** 머물다

17

W Did you know? The Queen Mary 2 is the <u>biggest cruise ship</u> in the world. It can <u>carry around</u> 3,800 people. It is <u>345</u> meters long and it has <u>14</u> decks. It has a maximum speed of <u>56</u>km/h. It has restaurants, swimming pools, and <u>movie theaters</u>. Many people <u>take holidays</u> on this giant ship.

여 아셨나요? 퀸 메리 2호는 세계에서 가장 큰 유람선입니다. 그것은 3,800여 명의 사람들을 실어 나를 수 있습니다. 345미터 길이에 14개의 갑판을 갖고 있습니다. 최대 속도는 시간당 56km입니다. 그것은 식당, 수영장, 영화관들을 갖추고 있습니다. 많은 사람들이 이 거대한 배에서 휴가를 보냅니다.

cruise ship 유람선　**carry** 실어 나르다　**deck** 갑판　**maximum**
speed 최대 속도　**swimming pool** 수영장　**movie theater** 영화관
holiday 휴가　**giant** 거대한

18

W Jennie is Tom's sister. She always tries to be trendy. Her <u>birthday</u> is coming. Tom bought <u>a trendy T-shirt</u> for her. When she <u>wears</u> the T-shirt, she says she <u>likes</u> it <u>very much</u>. Tom is really <u>glad</u> about that. In this situation, what would Tom say to Jennie?

여 Jennie는 Tom의 여동생입니다. 그녀는 항상 유행에 따르려 노력합니다. 그녀의 생일이 다가옵니다. Tom은 그녀를 위해 유행하는 티셔츠를 샀습니다. 그녀는 그 티셔츠를 입는 정말 마음에 든다고 말합니다. Tom은 그 말을 듣고 무척 기쁩니다. 이 상황에서 Tom은 Jennie에게 뭐라고 말할까요?

① 그것은 내 스타일이 아니야.
② 네가 마음에 든다니 기뻐.
③ 나는 그녀가 정말 좋아할 거라 확신해.
④ 너는 이미 많은 티셔츠를 가지고 있잖아.
⑤ 나는 저것보다 이것이 마음에 들어.

●●
trendy 최신 유행의 **buy** 사다 **glad** 기쁜

19

M Jennie? Is that you? Jennie?

W Hi, Tom! How are you doing?

M Great. How about you?

W I'm fine. How's your mom?

M She's very busy with her volunteer work.

W Please say hello to your mom for me.

···

남 Jennie? 거기 너니? Jennie?

여 안녕, Tom! 어떻게 지내니?

남 아주 좋아. 너는 어때?

여 잘 지내. 어머니는 어떠셔?

남 자원봉사 활동으로 매우 바쁘셔.

여 어머니께 안부 인사 전해 줘.

① 나는 좀 긴장돼.
② 그 말을 들으니 유감이야.
③ 그녀를 다시 만나서 반가웠어.
④ 걱정하지 마. 너는 괜찮을 거야.
⑤ 어머니께 안부 인사 전해 줘.

●●
be busy with ~으로 바쁘다 **volunteer work** 자원봉사 활동 **say hello to** ~에게 안부를 전하다

20

W I heard that you are going to have a bazaar this Saturday. How's it going?

M I'm working on it. Can you come?

W I'd love to, but I can't.

M Oh, that's too bad. Why not?

W I have a dental appointment that day.

···

여 이번 토요일에 바자회를 연다고 들었어. 어떻게 되어가니?

남 열심히 준비 중이야. 너 올 수 있니?

여 그러고 싶은데 갈 수 없어.

남 오, 정말 유감인데. 왜 못 와?

여 그날 치과에 진료 예약이 되어 있어.

① 그거 좋겠다.
② 오전 10시면 좋겠어.
③ 너는 시간이 더 필요할지도 몰라.
④ 그날 치과에 진료 예약이 되어 있어.
⑤ 아마 다음번에 만날 수 있을 거야.

●●
bazaar 바자회 **work on** ~에 노력을 들이다. 착수하다 **dental** 치과의
appointment 약속 **get together** 만나다

Further Study 정답   p. 124

1 She has an English Speech Contest tomorrow, but she keeps forgetting the text.

2 She asked him to blow up some balloons.

3 He did a big cleanup.

4 It is for her parents' 30th wedding anniversary.

5 The reason is that he has been busy with his new project these days.

6 She ordered Ugg boots a week ago.

7 In the swimming pool, they have to wear swimming caps.

8 The reason is that his sister always tries to be trendy.

On Your Own 모범답안   p. 125

A

Restaurant Review	
(1) What kind of restaurant did you visit recently?	an Italian restaurant
(2) Who did you go with?	my sister
(3) What did you order?	a large pepperoni pizza, chicken salad, and drinks
(4) How did it taste?	very delicious
(5) Will you visit the restaurant again? Why?	Yes / the food was good and the service was excellent

Recently, I visited an (1)Italian restaurant with (2)my sister. We ordered (3)a large pepperoni pizza, spaghetti, and drinks. It was (4)very delicious. I think I will visit the restaurant again because (5)the food was good and the service was excellent.

음식점 후기	
(1) 최근 어떤 종류의 식당에 갔습니까?	이탈리안 식당
(2) 누구와 함께 갔습니까?	여동생
(3) 무엇을 주문했습니까?	라지 페퍼로니 피자, 스파게티, 음료
(4) 맛은 어땠습니까?	매우 맛있었음
(5) 그곳에 또 갈 것입니까? 왜 그렇습니까?	예 / 음식이 맛있고, 서비스가 훌륭함

최근에, 저는 여동생과 이태리 식당에 갔습니다. 우리는 라지 페퍼로니 피자, 스파게티, 그리고 음료를 시켰습니다. 매우 맛있었습니다. 저는 음식이 맛있고 서비스도 좋으므로 또 그 식당에 다시 갈 것 같습니다.

B

My Favorite Teacher	
(1) What subject does he/she teach?	history
(2) What does he/she look like?	① very tall, slim ② wears glasses
(3) Why do you like him/her?	③ kind to students ④ makes the lessons interesting ⑤ does not give us much homework

My favorite teacher is my (1)history teacher. He is ①very tall and slim. He also ③wears glasses. There are three reasons why he is my favorite teacher. First, he is ③kind to students. Second, he ④makes the lessons interesting. Lastly, he ④doesn't give us much homework. I am so glad that I have such a nice teacher.

내가 가장 좋아하는 선생님	
(1) 그/그녀는 무엇을 가르칩니까?	역사
(2) 그/그녀는 어떻게 생겼습니까?	① 키가 크고 날씬하심 ② 안경을 쓰심
(3) 왜 그/그녀를 좋아합니까?	③ 학생들에게 친절하심 ④ 수업을 재미있게 하심 ⑤ 숙제를 많이 안 내주심

제가 가장 좋아하는 선생님은 제 역사 선생님입니다. 선생님은 매우 키가 크고 날씬하십니다. 그리고 안경을 쓰셨습니다. 제가 선생님을 가장 좋아하는 데는 세 가지 이유가 있습니다. 첫째로, 그분은 학생들에게 친절하십니다. 또한, 그분은 수업을 재미있게 하십니다. 마지막으로 우리에게 숙제를 많이 내주시지 않습니다. 저는 그렇게 좋으신 선생님이 계셔서 매우 기쁩니다.

01 Actual Test 정답 p. 132

01 ③	02 ②	03 ①	04 ⑤	05 ③
06 ③	07 ④	08 ④	09 ③	10 ⑤
11 ③	12 ②	13 ④	14 ①	15 ②
16 ③	17 ①	18 ⑤	19 ④	20 ⑤

01

W It's 2 o'clock already.

M Do you have an appointment?

W Yes, I do. Since I am running late, I will not drive. I will use a public transportation.

M Are you thinking of taking the subway?

W No. If I take it, I would have to walk a lot. I'll take a bus.

M Okay.

여 벌써 2시네.

남 약속이 있어?

여 어. 늦어서 운전은 안 하려고. 대중교통을 이용할래.

남 지하철을 탈 생각이니?

여 아니. 그것을 타면, 너무 많이 걸어야 할 거야. 버스를 탈 거야.

남   그래.

have an appointment 약속이 있다   **drive** 운전하다   **public transportation** 대중교통   **take the subway** 지하철을 타다

02

W   Andrew, your birthday is coming soon. What present do you want?

M   Well. I haven't thought about it.

W   Last year I gave you an MP3 player, and your parents gave you a laptop computer.

M   Right. And my best friend gave me a novel. I wish I had a new smartphone.

W   I'm sorry but I can't afford that. I'll think about something else.

M   Don't take it seriously, anything is fine.

여   Andrew. 네 생일이 다가오고 있어. 무슨 선물을 원해?
남   글쎄. 생각을 안 해 봤어.
여   작년에 나는 MP3 플레이어를 줬고, 너희 부모님은 노트북을 주셨지.
남   맞아. 그리고 나의 제일 친한 친구는 소설책을 줬어. 새 스마트폰을 받으면 좋으련만.
여   미안하지만, 나는 그것을 사줄 만한 여유가 없네. 다른 것을 생각해 볼게.
남   심각하게 받아들이지 마. 아무거나 괜찮아.

laptop computer 노트북 컴퓨터   **novel** 소설   **afford** 여유[형편]가 되다   **seriously** 심각하게

03

W   Where do you live? Do you live far from here?

M   I live in Mokdong. It takes 10 minutes by bus to get there.

W   That's good. I live quite far away. If I leave now, I'll probably get home at 11:30.

M   That far? Does it take an hour and a half to get home?

W   That's right.

여   어디 사세요? 여기서 멀리 사시나요?
남   저는 목동에 삽니다. 거기 가는 데 버스로 10분 정도 걸립니다.
여   좋네요. 저는 상당히 멀리 삽니다. 지금 출발하면, 11시 30분에 집에

도착할 겁니다.
남   그렇게 멀어요? 집까지 가는 데 한 시간 반이나 걸려요?
여   맞습니다.

far from ~로부터 멀리   **quite** 꽤   **take** (시간이) 걸리다

04

W   Did you watch the new soap opera last night?

M   No. How was it?

W   It was very interesting. I think I've fallen in love with it.

M   Oh, come on. You're a high school senior. You should study harder than ever before. Don't watch TV. You can watch as much TV as you want after entering the college.

W   Okay. I'll stop watching it.

여   너 어젯밤 새 연속극 봤니?
남   아니. 어땠는데?
여   정말 흥미로웠어. 나는 그 드라마와 사랑에 빠진 것 같아.
남   오. 야. 너는 고3이잖아. 예전보다 더 열심히 공부해야지. TV를 보면 안 돼. 대학에 입학한 후에 네가 원하는 만큼 TV를 볼 수 있어.
여   알았어. 안 볼게.

① 놀란   ② 지친   ③ 무서운
④ 안도한   ⑤ 걱정스러운

soap opera 연속극   **fall in love with** ~와 사랑에 빠지다   **high school senior** 고3   **as ~ as** ~만큼   **enter the college** 대학에 입학하다   **scared** 겁 먹은   **relieved** 안도한

05

W   I'd like to send this package to England.

M   Okay. Please put it on the scale. How would you like to send it? By air or surface mail?

W   By air, please.

M   Alright. Would you like express delivery or standard shipping?

W   Standard, please.

여   이 소포를 영국으로 보내고 싶습니다.
남   네. 저울에 올려 주세요. 어떻게 보내고 싶으세요? 항공편 또는 일반

우편물?

여 항공편으로 보내 주세요.

남 알겠습니다. 특급 배송으로 하시겠습니까 아니면 일반 배송으로 하시겠습니까?

여 일반 배송으로 해 주세요.

package 소포　**scale** 저울　**surface mail** 일반 우편물　**express delivery** 긴급 배송　**standard shipping** 일반 배송

06

W I'm very excited at this baseball game. Which team do you root for, Noah?

M I go for the Tigers. What about you?

W I'm a big fan of the Lions.

M I see. Looks like some people are reading match programs while waiting for the game to start.

W Look at the cheer leaders. They are very beautiful.

여 나는 이 야구 경기가 정말 기대되는데. Noah, 너는 어느 팀 응원해?

남 나는 타이거즈를 응원해. 너는 어때?

여 나는 라이온스의 광팬이야.

남 그래. 어떤 사람들은 경기 시작 전에 경기 책자를 읽고 있어.

여 치어리더를 봐. 정말 아름답다.

excited 신이 난　**root for** ~을 응원하다　**match program** 경기 책자　**a big fan of** ~의 광팬　**cheer leader** 치어리더

07

W Are you ready to go to the museum with me?

M Yes, I am. But why are you going to the museum?

W Because I have to write a report about a piece of art.

M Does it mean that you have to see the original?

W Right. I have to submit my entrance ticket to prove I visited it.

여 나와 함께 박물관에 갈 준비가 됐어?

남 그럼. 그런데 박물관에는 왜 가는 거야?

여 미술 작품 하나에 대해서 보고서를 써야 해.

남 직접 가서 봐야만 하는 거야?

여 맞아. 방문했다는 것을 증명하기 위해 입장권을 제출해야 해.

report 보고서　**a piece of art** 미술 작품 (하나)　**submit** 제출하다　**entrance ticket** 입장권　**prove** 증명하다

08

W How was your weekend?

M I went to my uncle's house to celebrate my cousin's 1st birthday.

W Oh, really? Who does the baby resemble more, his mom or dad?

M I think he resembles his dad more. He's so cute.

W What did you buy for him?

M I gave him a T-shirt.

여 주말은 잘 보냈어?

남 내 사촌의 첫돌을 축하하기 위해 삼촌댁에 갔었어.

여 오, 정말? 아기는 누구를 더 닮았어. 엄마 아니면 아빠?

남 내 생각에는 그는 아빠를 더 많이 닮았어. 정말 귀여워.

여 그를 위해서 무엇을 샀니?

남 티셔츠를 사 주었어.

celebrate 축하하다　**cousin** 사촌　**resemble** 닮다　**cute** 귀여운

09

W Excuse me. Does this bus go to Gimpo Airport?

M No. You should take the number 651 bus. It will be here in 7 minutes.

W Thank you. By the way, how long does it usually take to get there?

M It will probably take 35 minutes from here.

W Thank you. Drive safely!

여 실례합니다. 이 버스는 김포공항에 갑니까?

남 아니요. 651번 버스를 타세요. 7분 안에 올 겁니다.

여 감사합니다. 그나저나, 거기에 가는 데 보통 얼마나 걸리나요?

남 여기서 35분 정도 걸릴 거예요.

여 감사합니다. 안전 운전하세요!

① 택시 기사　　② 조종사　　③ 버스 기사
④ 경찰관　　⑤ 승객

by the way 그런데　**probably** 아마도　**safely** 안전하게

10

M What do we have to buy?

W Let me check the grocery list. We have to buy eggs, milk, bacon, bread, and fruit.

M I think we have some milk in the refrigerator.

W Do we?

M Yes. I bought it yesterday on the way home.

W I see. Let's skip that then.

....

남 무엇을 사야 해?

여 구매 목록을 확인해 볼게. 계란, 우유, 베이컨, 빵, 과일을 사야 해.

남 냉장고에 우유가 좀 있는 거 같아.

여 그래?

남 응. 내가 어제 집에 오는 길에 샀어.

여 알았어. 그럼 그건 사지 말자.

••
grocery list 구매 목록 **refrigerator** 냉장고 **skip** 건너뛰다

11

M Hey, Jennie. What's up?

W Did you hear the news? Kate has a new boyfriend. Guess who it is?

M I have no idea.

W William Smith, the class president.

M Oh, I can't believe it.

W Can you keep it secret?

....

남 이봐, Jennie. 무슨 일이니?

여 너 소식 들었어? Kate에게 새 남자 친구가 생겼대. 누구게?

남 모르겠는데.

여 William Smith, 반장.

남 오, 믿을 수 없어.

여 그것을 비밀로 해 줄 거지?

••
guess 추측하다 **class president** 반장 **secret** 비밀

12

M What are you planning to do during the winter vacation, Jennie?

W I'm going to English Camp in Canada. What about you?

M I haven't decided yet. Mom wants me to go to an English Camp like you but I don't want to.

W Then, what do you want to do?

M I just want to read a lot of books at a book club.

W If I were you, I would do what I wanted to.

....

남 이번 겨울 방학 동안 무엇을 할 계획이니, Jennie?

여 나는 캐나다 영어 캠프 갈 예정이야. 너는?

남 아직 결정하지 못했어. 엄마는 너처럼 내가 영어 캠프에 참여하길 원하시지만 난 원치 않거든.

여 그럼, 너는 뭐 하고 싶니?

남 나는 그냥 북클럽에서 책을 좀 많이 읽고 싶어.

여 만약 내가 너라면, 나는 내가 하고 싶은 것을 할 거야.

••
plan 계획하다 **vacation** 방학 **decide** 결정하다

13

M Let's go to the jazz festival tomorrow night. I have two tickets for it.

W Sounds great. I like live jazz.

M It starts at 6 p.m. What time shall we meet?

W How about at 5 p.m.? Wait. Sorry, I can't go with you.

M Why?

W I have to go to a birthday party for my grandpa.

....

남 내일 밤 재즈 페스티벌에 가자. 티켓이 두 장 있어.

여 좋아. 나는 라이브 재즈를 좋아해.

남 저녁 6시에 시작해. 우리 몇 시에 만날까?

여 5시 어때? 잠깐만. 미안하지만, 나 너랑 같이 못 가.

남 왜?

여 할아버지 생신 잔치에 가야 해.

••
live 생방송의, 살아 있는 **start** 시작하다 **grandpa** 할아버지

14

① W Tom rarely walks his dog.

② W Tom never cleans his room.

③ W Tom always does his homework.

④ W Tom sometimes goes to the library.

⑤ W Tom only does voluntary work on Sundays.

....

Tom의 주간 활동	일	월	화	수	목	금	토
개 산책시키기	✓	✓	✓		✓		✓
방 청소하기							
숙제 하기	✓	✓	✓	✓	✓	✓	✓
도서관 가기				✓	✓		✓
자원봉사 활동 하기	✓						

① 여 Tom은 개를 거의 산책시키지 않습니다.
② 여 Tom은 절대 방 청소를 하지 않습니다.
③ 여 Tom은 항상 숙제를 합니다.
④ 여 Tom은 가끔씩 도서관에 갑니다.
⑤ 여 Tom은 일요일에만 자원봉사 활동을 합니다.

rarely 거의 ~ 않는 **walk one's dog** 개를 산책시키다 **voluntary work** 자원봉사 활동 **weekly** 주간의

15

M Jennie, have you read the books, *Who Moved My Cheese?* and *The Little Prince?*

W Yes, a long time ago. Why?

M I have to read and write a summary of them. Do you remember the storylines?

W Sorry. Unfortunately, I don't remember them well.

M Which do you think is more interesting? I'll read that first.

W I think *The Little Prince* is more interesting than *Who Moved My Cheese?*.

남 Jennie, 〈누가 내 치즈를 옮겼을까?〉와 〈어린 왕자〉 이 책들 읽어 봤니?
여 응, 오래 전에. 왜?
남 읽고서 요약문을 써야 해. 너 줄거리 기억나니?
여 미안, 불행히도, 그것들을 잘 기억 못 해.
남 네 생각에 어느 것이 더 재미있어? 그것을 먼저 읽을게.
여 〈어린 왕자〉가 〈누가 내 치즈를 옮겼을까?〉보다 더 재미있어.

prince 왕자 **long time ago** 오래 전에 **summary** 요약 **storyline** 줄거리 **unfortunately** 불행하게도 **interesting** 재미있는, 흥미진진한

16

① M What do you do in your free time?

W I play with my dog.

② M I don't like this song.

W Neither do I.

③ M I didn't do well on the final exam.

W Don't mention it.

④ M Why are you so happy?

W I came first in the race.

⑤ M Do you remember my friend, Joe?

W Yes, I remember him well.

① 남 여가 시간에는 뭘 하니?
여 개랑 놀아.
② 남 나는 이 노래를 안 좋아해.
여 나도 그래.
③ 남 이번 기말고사를 잘 보지 못했어.
여 천만에.
④ 남 왜 그렇게 기분이 그렇게 좋아?
여 경주에서 1등 했어.
⑤ 남 내 친구, Joe를 기억하니?
여 그래, 잘 기억해.

free time 여가 시간 **neither** (부정문) ~도 마찬가지이다 **do well on** ~을 잘하다 **final exam** 기말고사 **mention** 언급하다, 말하다 **come first** 일등으로 들어오다

17

W Hello, visitors to CYJ Art Gallery! We are providing free tickets for family programs at the reception desk. Ticket distribution starts at 10:00 a.m. on a first-come, first-served basis. Programs often fill up so we recommend arriving a little before 10:00 a.m.

여 안녕하세요. CYJ 미술관 방문객 여러분! 접수처에서 가족 프로그램들에 참여할 수 있는 무료 티켓을 제공하고 있습니다. 티켓 배부는 선착순으로 오전 10시에 시작됩니다. 종종 프로그램들의 정원이 차니 오전 10시 전에 도착하시기를 권해 드립니다.

provide 제공하다 **reception desk** 접수처, 안내처 **distribution** 배부 **on a first-come, first-served basis** 선착순으로 **fill up** (정원이) 차다, 가득 채우다 **recommend** 추천하다, 권유하다 **arrive** 도착하다

18

W Sam and Sally are drinking a cola <u>in the street</u>. After drinking her cola, Sally looks around to find <u>a trash can</u>. Unfortunately, there's no <u>trash can</u> nearby. There is only a <u>sign</u> saying 'NO TRASH' near a tree. Sally runs to the tree then puts her empty can <u>under</u> it. In this situation, what would Sam say to Sally?

······································

여 Sam과 Sally는 거리에서 콜라를 마시고 있습니다. 콜라를 마신 후 Sally는 쓰레기통을 찾습니다. 불행히도 근처에 쓰레기통이 없습니다. 나무 근처에 "쓰레기 금지"라는 표지판이 있습니다. Sally는 그 나무로 달려가서 그 아래에 캔을 놓습니다. 이 상황에서 Sam은 Sally에게 뭐라 말할까요?

① 마음껏 먹어.
② 나 배불러. 많이 먹었어.
③ 탄산음료를 너무 많이 먹지 마.
④ 간식 좀 더 먹을래?
⑤ 쓰레기는 쓰레기통에 버려야 해.

•••
street (길)거리 **find** 찾다 **trash can** 쓰레기통 **nearby** 근처에 **sign** 표지판 **trash** 쓰레기 **empty** 빈

19

M Mom, look at this! It's my <u>first</u> trophy.
W Congratulations, son!
M Thank you. I didn't <u>expect</u> to get this runner's up award.
W I thought your painting was <u>the best</u>.
M I didn't win, but I <u>did my best</u>.
W <u>I'm really proud of you.</u>

······································

남 엄마, 이것 좀 보세요! 저의 첫 트로피에요.
여 축하해, 아들!
남 감사해요. 2등상을 받으리라 기대하지 않았는데.
여 나는 네 그림이 최고라고 생각했어.
남 우승은 놓쳤지만, 최선을 다했어요.
여 <u>네가 정말 자랑스럽구나.</u>

① 쉬워 보이는데.
② 너 안 좋아 보인다.
③ 하지만 정말 슬프다.
④ 네가 정말 자랑스럽구나.
⑤ 그가 들으면 기뻐할 거야.

•••
trophy 트로피 **expect** 기대하다 **runner's up award** 2등상 **painting** 그림 **do one's best** 최선을 다하다 **terrible** 안 좋은, 심한, 형편없는 **be proud of** ~을 자랑스럽게 여기다

20

W Anne, Jake and I are going to do <u>volunteer work</u> at an orphanage tomorrow. Why don't you <u>join us</u>?
M It's up to Tom. We're supposed to do our <u>group homework</u>.
W Do you think he wants to join us?
M I'm sure he does. Anyway I'll ask him <u>right away</u>.
W <u>I hope both of you can join us.</u>

······································

여 Anne, Jake와 나는 내일 고아원에서 자원봉사를 할 예정이야. 너도 우리랑 함께 하지 않을래?
남 Tom에게 달렸어. 그룹 숙제를 하기로 했거든.
여 네 생각에 그가 우리와 함께 하고 싶어 할 거 같니?
남 그럴 거라 확신해. 어쨌든 지금 당장 그에게 물어볼게.
여 <u>너희 둘 다 우리와 함께 할 수 있기를 바라.</u>

① 모르겠어.
② 행운을 빌어 줘.
③ 그것은 불공평하다고 생각해.
④ 이제 내가 이걸 할 수 있다는 걸 알았어.
⑤ 너희 둘 다 우리와 함께 할 수 있기를 바라.

•••
orphanage 고아원 **join** 참여하다 **be up to** ~에 달려 있다 **be supposed to-V** ~하기로 되어 있다 **anyway** 어쨌든 **right away** 지금 당장 **both** 둘 다

02 Actual Test 정답

p. 140

01 ④	02 ④	03 ③	04 ⑤	05 ①
06 ②	07 ③	08 ④	09 ⑤	10 ③
11 ⑤	12 ⑤	13 ③	14 ③	15 ②
16 ⑤	17 ②	18 ③	19 ③	20 ⑤

01

W There are so many different cookie shapes. I can't pick one.

M How about this bear shaped one? It's our best-seller. This heart shaped one is popular, too.

W Are these ones chocolate chips?

M Yes. The pink heart in the round one is strawberry flavor, too.

W I see. Oh, tomorrow is November 11th. I will take these long sticks covered with chocolate.

M Okay.

· ·

여 여기에 굉장히 다양한 모양들의 쿠키가 있네요. 하나를 고를 수가 없어요.

남 이 곰 모양은 어떠세요? 제일 잘 팔립니다. 이 하트 모양도 인기 있습니다.

여 이것들은 초콜릿 칩인가요?

남 네. 둥근 것 안의 분홍색 하트는 딸기 맛입니다.

여 알겠습니다. 오, 내일은 11월 11일이네요. 저는 이 초콜릿으로 감싼 긴 막대 모양으로 살게요.

남 알겠습니다.

● ●
shape 모양 **pick** 고르다 **best-seller** 베스트 셀러 **popular** 인기 있는
heart 하트 모양, 심장 **round** 둥근 **flavor** 향 **stick** 막대

02

W Why is traffic suddenly moving so slowly?

M Look to the right. There is a school, so this is a school zone. You have to slow down.

W Oh, that's why.

M The speed limit is 30kph and you can see speed bumps on the ground.

W I see. I will drive more slowly and carefully.

· ·

여 왜 갑자기 차들이 천천히 움직이지?

남 오른쪽을 봐. 학교가 있어서 여기는 스쿨존이야. 너는 속도를 줄여야 해.

여 아, 그래서였구나.

남 제한 속도가 30킬로미터야. 그리고 바닥에 과속 방지 턱을 볼 수 있어.

여 알았어. 좀 더 천천히 조심해서 운전할게.

● ●
traffic 차량, 교통 **suddenly** 갑자기 **slowly** 천천히 **school zone**
학교 구역 **slow down** 속도를 줄이다 **speed limit** 제한 속도 **speed
bump** 과속 방지 턱 **ground** 바닥, 땅 **carefully** 조심스럽게

03

W Excuse me. I'm looking for the book *Chicken Soup for the Soul*.

M I'm sorry, but it is out of stock now.

W When will you get new stock in?

M If I order it now, it will probably take 3 days. It will be delivered to our bookstore on the 11th.

W Okay. I'll reserve a copy.

· ·

여 실례합니다. 〈영혼을 위한 닭고기 수프〉라는 책을 찾고 있습니다.

남 죄송합니다. 현재 재고가 없습니다.

여 언제 들어오나요?

남 지금 주문을 하면, 3일 정도 걸릴 겁니다. 저의 서점에 11일에 배송될 겁니다.

여 알겠습니다. 한 권 예약해 주세요.

● ●
out of stock 재고가 없는 **order** 주문하다 **probably** 아마도 **deliver**
배달하다 **reserve** 예약하다 **copy** (책·잡지 등의) 한 부, 한 권

04

W What are you thinking about?

M I'm thinking about tomorrow's party. I will have a Christmas party with my classmates.

W That sounds like fun. What are you going to do?

M We will have dinner, watch a movie, and exchange gifts. I can't wait for tomorrow.

W Have fun!

· ·

여 무슨 생각을 하고 있어?

남 내일 파티에 대해서 생각하고 있어. 학급 친구들과 크리스마스 파티를 열 거야.

여 재미있겠다. 무엇을 할 거야?

남 저녁을 먹고, 영화 보고, 선물 교환을 할 거야. 내일이 빨리 왔으면 좋겠어.

여 재미있게 놀아!

think about ~에 대해 생각하다　**classmate** 급우, 학급 친구
exchange 교환하다　**gift** 선물

05

M How may I help you?

W I need an ID picture for my passport.

M Okay, have a seat here in this chair and keep your back straight.

W Like this?

M Yes. Look into the lens and smile. One! Two! Three!

남 어떻게 도와드릴까요?

여 여권에 사용할 증명사진이 필요합니다.

남 네. 여기 이 의자에 앉으시고 등을 쪽 펴 주세요.

여 이렇게요?

남 네. 렌즈를 바라보시고 웃으세요. 하나! 둘! 셋!

ID picture 증명사진　**passport** 여권　**seat** 좌석: 자리에 앉히다　**back** 등　**straight** 곧게　**lens** 렌즈

06

M How would you like your hair done?

W My hair is quite long. I'd like it cut shoulder-length.

M Okay. Are you going to keep this straight hair style?

W I'm tired of it. I want to have my hair waved.

M Alright. What about your hair color?

W I prefer brown to black.

남 머리 모양을 어떻게 해 드릴까요?

여 제 머리가 너무 길어요. 어깨 길이로 자르고 싶어요.

남 네. 이 생머리 스타일을 계속 하실 건가요?

여 생머리가 지겨워요. 웨이브로 하고 싶습니다.

남 알겠습니다. 머리 색깔은 어떻게 하고 싶으세요?

여 저는 검정색보다 갈색이 좋아요.

shoulder-length 어깨 길이　**be tired of** ~에 질리다　**waved** 웨이브의
prefer A to B B보다 A를 선호하다

07

W What are you doing?

M I'm looking for the best bank to take advantage of exchange rates.

W Why are you exchanging money? Are you going abroad?

M Yes. I will go to Hong Kong for a business trip.

W I see. Have fun.

여 지금 뭐 하고 있어?

남 환율 우대를 받을 수 있는 은행을 찾고 있어.

여 돈은 왜 환전하려고 하는데? 외국에 나갈 거야?

남 그래. 출장으로 홍콩에 가.

여 알았어. 재미있게 다녀와.

take advantage of 우대 받다. ~을 이용하다. ~을 기회로 활용하다
exchange rate 환율　**exchange money** 돈을 환전하다　**go abroad**
해외에 가다　**business trip** 출장

08

W Oh! It's already 5 p.m.

M Why? Did you forget what you had to do?

W It's not that. I'll just prepare dinner for us.

M Honey. Why don't we have pizza delivered? I've wanted some for the past several days.

W Really? Okay. I'll get the phone book. Please think about what you'd like to order.

여 오! 벌써 5시네요.

남 왜요? 해야 할 일을 잊어버렸어요?

여 그게 아니고요. 저녁 준비를 하려고요.

남 여보. 그냥 피자 배달시키는 게 어때요? 지난 며칠간 먹고 싶었어요.

여 정말요? 좋아요. 전화번호부를 가져올게요. 주문하고 싶은 것에 대해 생각해 보세요.

already 이미, 벌써　**have to-V** ~해야 한다　**prepare** 준비하다
deliver 배달하다　**several** 몇몇의　**phone book** 전화번호부

09

M　Open your mouth wider. Say "Ah!"

W　"Ah!"

M　Good. You have a lot of cavities. Have you been eating a lot of sweets?

W　Yes. But I brush my teeth three times a day.

M　Brushing three times a day is important but you have to brush your teeth within three minutes of eating sweets. Okay?

W　I understand.

. . . .

남　입을 좀 더 크게 벌리세요. "아" 하세요.

여　"아!"

남　좋습니다. 충치가 많네요. 단것을 많이 드셨나요?

여　네. 하지만 하루에 3번 양치질을 합니다.

남　하루에 3번 양치하는 것이 중요하지만, 단것을 먹고 3분 안에 양치를 해야 합니다. 아시겠죠?

여　알겠습니다.

① 아빠 – 딸　　　② 교사 – 학생　　　③ 의사 – 간호사
④ 점원 – 손님　　　⑤ 치과 의사 – 환자

●●
wide 넓게　**cavity** 충치　**sweet** 단것　**brush one's teeth** 양치질하다
important 중요한

10

W　Let's prepare some medicine for emergencies. Our first-aid kit is empty.

M　That's a good idea. What do we have to buy?

W　Let's buy some pills for headaches, stomachaches, and toothaches.

M　What about rubbing alcohol and band-aids?

W　I bought band-aids yesterday when I got a paper cut.

M　I see.

. . . .

여　응급 의약품을 준비하자. 우리 구급약 상자가 비었어.

남　좋은 생각이야. 무엇을 사야 하지?

여　두통약, 복통 약, 치통 약을 사자.

남　소독용 알코올과 밴드는 어때?

여　어제 내가 종이에 베였을 때 밴드는 샀어.

남　알았어.

●●
medicine 약　**emergency** 응급 사태　**first-aid kit** 구급상자　**empty** 텅 빈　**pill** 알약　**headache** 두통　**stomachache** 복통　**toothache** 치통　**rubbing alcohol** 소독용 알코올　**band-aid** 밴드　**paper cut** 종이에 베인 상처

11

W　What are you doing with that needle, Tom?

M　I'm doing my homework. It's not easy.

W　What's your homework?

M　Making a bag from old jeans. It's a method of recycling.

W　Why don't you ask your mom for help?

M　She's out now. Could you give me a hand?

. . . .

여　바늘을 가지고 뭐 하고 있니, Tom?

남　숙제 하는 중이야. 쉽지 않네.

여　숙제가 뭔데?

남　낡은 청바지로 가방 만들기. 재활용 방법의 하나야.

여　엄마한테 도와 달라고 하지 그래?

남　지금 외출하셨어. 너 나 좀 도와줄래?

●●
needle 바늘　**method** 방법　**recycling** 재활용　**give ~ a hand** ~을 도와주다

12

W　You look really tired. What's up?

M　I can't seem to get much sleep at the moment.

W　Do you have a lot of stress?

M　No. I think I am drinking too much coffee because of my new coffee machine.

W　Try not to drink too much coffee. Why don't you drink herb tea instead of coffee?

M　Okay, I will try to.

. . . .

여　너 진짜 피곤해 보여. 무슨 일 있니?

남　요즘 잠을 잘 잘 수 없어.

여　스트레스가 많니?

남　아니. 새 커피 머신 때문에 커피를 너무 많이 마시나 봐.

여　커피를 많이 마시지 않도록 해 봐. 커피 대신 허브 차를 마시는 게 어때?

남　그래, 그렇게 해 볼게.

tired 피곤한 **at the moment** 지금 **machine** 기계 **herb tea** 허브
차 **instead of** ~대신에

13

w Hello, 411 customer service. How may I help you?

m I'd like to set up the Internet in my house. Could
you let me know the number to call?

w Hold on, please. The number you have asked is
1537-8249. It's TNT Telecom.

m Thank you. Have a nice day.

w Same to you.

여 안녕하세요, 411 고객 센터입니다. 어떻게 도와드릴까요?

남 집에 인터넷을 설치하고 싶은데요. 전화할 전화번호를 알려
주시겠어요?

여 잠시만 기다려 주세요. 문의하신 번호는 1537-8249입니다. TNT
Telecom입니다.

남 감사합니다. 즐거운 하루 되세요.

여 당신도요.

customer service 고객 센터 **set up the Internet** 인터넷을 설치하다
hold on 전화를 끊지 않고 기다리다 **Same to you.** 당신도 그러시기를.

14

① w This is a boarding pass for Tom Smith.

② w The flight is OZ857 leaving on June 7th.

③ w Tom Smith will be seated in seat 39F traveling
from Seoul to Sydney.

④ w The flight has a boarding time of 3:10 p.m.

⑤ w Tom Smith has to board at Gate 6.

탑승권		
승객명	출발지	도착지
Tom Smith	시드니	서울
항공편	날짜	탑승 시간	탑승구	좌석 번호
OZ857	6월 7일	오후 3시 10분	6번 출구	39F

① 여 이것은 Tom Smith의 탑승권입니다.

② 여 비행기는 6월 7일에 떠나는 OZ857편입니다.

③ 여 Tom Smith는 서울에서 시드니까지 여행하는 동안 39F 좌석에 앉을
겁니다.

④ 여 이 항공기의 탑승 시간은 오후 3시10분입니다.

⑤ 여 Tom Smith는 6번 탑승구에서 탑승해야 합니다.

boarding pass 탑승권 **flight** 항공권 **seat** 좌석; 자리에 앉다 **from
A to B** A에서부터 B까지 **boarding time** 탑승 시간 **board** 타다, 탑승
하다

15

m Mom, let's eat out this Christmas Eve.

w That's a good idea, but every restaurant will be
really crowded that day.

m We can make a reservation in advance.

w What do you want to have?

m I have no idea. Oh, how about Mexican food?
There's a famous Mexican restaurant that's just a
15 minute walk from our house.

w First, let's book for a table for four on the Internet.
Then we can think about what we will eat later.

남 엄마, 크리스마스이브에 외식해요..

여 좋은 생각인데, 하지만 그날은 모든 음식점들이 아주 붐빌 거야.

남 미리 예약하면 돼요.

여 뭘 먹고 싶니?

남 모르겠어요. 아, 멕시코 음식 어때요? 우리 집에서 걸어서 15분 거리에
유명한 멕시코 음식점이 있어요.

여 우선, 인터넷으로 4인 좌석 테이블 하나를 예약하자. 그런 다음 무엇을
먹을지 나중에 생각할 수 있잖아.

eat out 외식하다 **Christmas Eve** 크리스마스이브 **crowded** 붐비는,
복잡한 **make a reservation** 예약하다 **in advance** 미리 **Mexican
food** 멕시코 음식 **book** 예약하다

16

① m Why are you so excited?

w I got the latest smartphone.

② m I like that singer very much.

w So do I.

③ m Can you tell me why you are late?

w I missed the bus.

④ m May I see your passport?

w Sure. Here it is.

⑤ m How's it going?

W I'll go by airplane.

- -

① 남 왜 이렇게 신났어?
　 여 최신 스마트폰을 샀어.
② 남 나는 저 가수가 정말 좋아.
　 여 나도 좋아.
③ 남 왜 늦었는지 말해 줄래?
　 여 버스를 놓쳤어요.
④ 남 여권을 보여 주시겠어요?
　 여 네. 여기 있습니다.
⑤ 남 어떻게 지내니?
　 여 비행기로 갈 거예요.

●●
excited 흥분한, 신난 **So do I.** 나도 그래. **late** 늦은 **miss** 놓치다
passport 여권 **by airplane** 비행기로

17

M Do you know how important it is to have 3 meals a day regularly? When you skip a meal, your metabolism begins to slow down. Then, the next time you eat something, your metabolism is not able to break the food down as quickly. As a result, the food is stored as fat. So please, don't skip meals. It is a small but important thing you can do to be healthy.

- -

남 당신은 규칙적으로 하루 세 끼 식사를 하는 것의 중요함을 아시나요? 식사를 거르면 당신의 신진대사가 느려지기 시작합니다. 그다음, 당신이 뭔가를 먹을 때, 당신의 신진대사는 빨리 그 음식을 분해할 수 없습니다. 그 결과, 그 음식은 지방으로 축적됩니다. 그러니, 부디 식사를 거르지 마세요. 그것은 당신이 건강할 수 있는 작지만 중요한 일입니다.

●●
important 중요한 **meal** 식사 **regularly** 규칙적으로 **skip** 건너뛰다
metabolism 신진대사 **slow down** 느려지다 **be able to-V** ~할 수
있다(= can) **break down** ~을 분해하다 **as a result** 그 결과로 **store**
저장하다 **fat** 지방 **healthy** 건강한

18

W Tom is going to take a trip to Europe this summer vacation. Today, his mom bought a backpack for him at the department store. He is very excited but he has to wait for a month. It feels like that he

can't wait until then. In this situation what would Tom say to his mom?

- -

여 Tom은 이번 여름 방학에 유럽으로 여행 갈 예정입니다. 오늘, 그의 엄마는 백화점에서 그에게 배낭을 사 줬습니다. 그는 너무 신났지만 한 달을 기다려야 합니다. 그는 그때까지 기다릴 수 없을 것 같습니다. 이 상황에서 Tom은 엄마에게 뭐라고 말할까요?

① 마음에 드세요?
② 제 가방 좀 찾아 주시겠어요?
③ 여행 빨리 가고 싶어요.
④ 여행 가고 싶지 않아요.
⑤ 색깔이 마음에 안 들어요.

●●
take a trip to ~로 여행 가다 **backpack** 배낭 **department store**
백화점 **until then** 그때까지

19

W I'd like to ride a bike. Can you lend me yours? Mine is broken.
M Okay. Let's go bike riding together. You can use mine and I'll use my brother's.
W When and where shall we meet?
M How about 2 p.m. tomorrow at my house?
W Okay, Peter. I'm glad to have a friend like you.
M What are friends for?

- -

여 자전거 타고 싶다. 네 것을 빌려 줄 수 있니? 내 것이 고장 났어.
남 좋아. 같이 자전거 타러 가자. 너는 내 것을 쓰고 나는 내 남동생 것을 쓰면 돼.
여 언제 어디서 만날까?
남 내일 2시 우리 집에서 어때?
여 좋아. Peter. 너 같은 친구가 있어서 기쁘다.
남 친구 좋다는 게 뭐니?

① 만나서 반가워.
② 나를 슬프게 하지 마.
③ 친구 좋다는 게 뭐니?
④ 그 얘기를 들으니 유감이야.
⑤ 큰 도움이 될 거야.

●●
ride a bike 자전거를 타다 **lend** 빌리다 **yours** 너의 것 **mine** 나의 것
broken 고장 난 **big help** 큰 도움

M Hey, Alice. You <u>look</u> quite <u>down</u>. What happened?

W My cat went to <u>heaven</u> last night.

M Oh, I'm <u>sorry</u> to hear that. Was it <u>sick</u>?

W Yes, he had a <u>heart</u> <u>problem</u>.

M <u>Look on the bright side. He won't feel pain any more.</u>

남 이봐, Alice. 너 굉장히 우울해 보인다. 무슨 일 있니?

여 내 고양이가 어젯밤에 천국으로 갔어.

남 오, 유감이다. 고양이가 아팠었니?

여 응, 심장에 문제가 있었어.

남 밝은 면을 봐. 그는 이제 더 이상 고통스럽지 않을 거야.

① 나는 아무 문제없어.

② 그가 곧 괜찮아지기를 바랄게.

③ 그것에 대해 너무 걱정하지 마.

④ 수의사에게 데려가지 그래?

⑤ 밝은 면을 봐. 그는 이제 더 이상 고통스럽지 않을 거야.

• •

down 우울한, 의기소침한 **heaven** 천국 **problem** 문제 **worry** 걱정하다 **vet** 수의사 **bright** 밝은 **pain** 고통, 통증

MEMO

MEMO

MEMO

MEMO

내신 및 시·도 교육청 영어듣기평가 완벽 대비

Listening 올리고
중학영어듣기 모의고사

① 최신 기출 유형의 철저한 분석 및 반영

최근 5년간 전국 16개 시·도 교육청 영어듣기능력평가 기출 문제를 철저히 분석하고, 문제 유형, 유형별 출제 비율, 빈출 표현, 소재까지 다각도로 반영하여 완벽한 실전 대비를 할 수 있습니다.

② 영어 교과서 표현들과 소재 반영으로 내신 영어 완벽 대비

영어 교과서의 주요 표현들과 소재를 반영하여 내신까지 효과적으로 대비할 수 있습니다.

③ 영어 말하기 수행평가, 서술형 평가 대비 문제 수록

5지 선다형에서 한층 더 심화된 서술형 문제를 수록하여 모의고사보다 높은 난이도로 듣기 실력을 강화할 수 있습니다. 또한 본문의 주제와 소재를 활용한 다양한 Activity를 통해 말하기 수행평가까지 함께 대비할 수 있습니다.

④ 전 지문 받아쓰기 제공

매회 모의고사마다 전 지문에 대한 받아쓰기를 수록하여 놓친 부분을 꼼꼼하게 점검할 수 있을 뿐만 아니라, 집중력과 듣기 실력을 강화할 수 있습니다.

⑤ 본문 주요 어휘 및 표현 정리

출제 빈도가 높은 본문의 주요 어휘, 표현을 한눈에 볼 수 있도록 정리하여 효율적인 어휘 학습으로 어휘 실력을 향상시킬 수 있습니다.